ONE LAST TRIP

My Life and Journey with the Most Ordinary, Extraordinary Man I Knew

SYDNEY L. RINARD

LORI RINARD GAMBILL

Copyright © 2021 Lori Rinard Gambill
All rights reserved
First Edition

PAGE PUBLISHING, INC.
Conneaut Lake, PA

First originally published by Page Publishing 2021

ISBN 978-1-6624-4187-5 (pbk)
ISBN 978-1-6624-4188-2 (digital)

Printed in the United States of America

Contents

Chapter 1: Who Is Sydney Rinard? 5
Chapter 2: Day 1: Sunday, August 5, 2018 7
Chapter 3: Where Did Sydney Rinard Come From? 13
Chapter 4: Day 2: Monday, August 6, 2018................................27
Chapter 5: Leroy and Mary..39
Chapter 6: Day 3: Tuesday, August 7, 2018 64
Chapter 7: Sydney Rinard..77
Chapter 8: Day 4: Wednesday, August 8, 2018 105
Chapter 9: College and Early Marriage 121
Chapter 10: Day 5, Part 1: Thursday, August 9, 2018................140
Chapter 11: Fatherhood...152
Chapter 12: Tincup, Colorado...174
Chapter 13: Day 5, Part 2: Thursday, August 9, 2018................187
Chapter 14: Retirement 201
Chapter 15: Studebakers, Chevys, and All Things Automobile...236
Chapter 16: Day 13: Friday, August 17, 2018 264
Chapter 17: Celebrations of Life 271
Chapter 18: Epilogue: July 2019...286

CHAPTER 1
Who Is Sydney Rinard?

An Introduction

God loves everyone. He does. But sometimes he sends someone to us who channels that love so well that their life revolves around sharing it. Not in fancy lights or productions. Just by being them.

This book is about one such person. My dad, Sydney Rinard.

He was an ordinary man.

But he was an extraordinary man.

Those who were lucky enough to know him already understand that. In his gentle, humble ways, he touched so many lives. He would help anyone in need. Anyone. He would fix things for them, give them rides, help them financially, or give them a place to stay. He adored his family, gave generously to his church, and made us laugh constantly.

I know there are a lot of guys like that out there. Other daughters could write this book about their own dads. But this book is about mine. I felt I must write it so you could get to know him too. I want the entire world to become friends with Sydney Rinard. I know in the following pages he will touch your heart as well. In fact, he even wrote many of the pages himself. If he were still alive, he would be too modest to allow me to write it. He's gone now, and God has put on my heart to tell his story. However, this story of his unique soul has been an easy book to write. He was, and still is, my Superman.

This book is really two separate books combined together. One is the biography of his life, and one chronicles the final trip Dad and I took together after his death. His ashes and I traveled the roads to visit some of his most favorite places, culminating with a special burial. I have intertwined the chapters of the two books to help you better understand and know this most amazing man.

Thank you for taking this journey with me through his life. I can't wait to introduce him to you! So let's get started!

Chapter 2

Day 1
Sunday, August 5, 2018

Missouri (St. Louis), Oklahoma (Oklahoma City)

Today begins my journey. Dad and I are taking one last trip. This is a trip that has been months in the making. Eight months, specifically. The day I picked up his ashes from the funeral home, I knew this was a necessary and unquestionable adventure.

I'm excited and emotional and ready to get going. I've packed up the clothes and necessities, booked all the hotels and inns, changed the oil in the car, and triple-checked my "trip book." My trip book is a three-ring binder with tabs for each day. Here, I placed maps, hotel confirmations, and activities for that day. I even built trip-tics for each drive between stopping spots. I will admit that I am a bit nerdy with my planning, but since I'll be traveling alone for the majority of this trip, I want to make sure there are no surprises. My grandma Mary (Dad's mom) was exactly the same way. She was extremely organized, in charge, took care of business. But she laughed a lot and loved her family like nobody else. Dad always said I was Mary but that I managed to only receive the good parts of her! I take that as a compliment, as I always looked up to her as how to be a "matriarch."

I have thirteen glorious days ahead of me. I'll be making many stops throughout. Most of them have a big significance to Dad, which is the purpose of this journey. I want to honor him and his life, cumulating with burying his ashes in his favorite and most peaceful place here on earth.

So I am off! Dad is sitting next to me in the car, ready for our trip together. I am really not crazy. I am a passionate Christian, so I know that Dad really isn't here in my car, but he is breathing easy and pain-free in heaven with Jesus. He is so excited to be there, as he taught me and anyone who would listen to him that our time on this earth is but a moment and heaven is for eternity. It will be filled with joy and love, and the issues of this life will be forever gone. I'm excited for it too, but I know I still have work to do on this planet, so it will have to wait.

A few weeks ago, I went to my local craft store and found a perfect wooden box to hold Dad's ashes. It had a hinged lid with a small hole on top. There is a piece of plastic covering the hole and a pop-out piece of wood that I could write on. So I took my pen and wrote "Love you Dad!" I decided not to put his name or dates of his birth or death, just the simple sentiment of my feelings. He was a very simple man, and this is the perfect message. I filled the box with his remains, nailed it shut, and painted it black. For some reason, I felt compelled to fill a small jar with some additional ashes and taped a photo of him on it. I will discover toward the end of my trip why God had me do this.

At the same time, I found a simple wire cross with a big base that I knew would be perfect to place by his ashes. It was about a foot tall and reddish brown, and once again, the simplicity and beauty of it reminded me of Dad. He was a woodworker and craftsman in his free time, building furniture and perfectly lathed wood creations. He would have designed this cross himself. Maybe he did. I have felt his approval every step of the way so far.

I have spent the better part of the last couple of weeks getting ready for this trip. Since I will be gone for thirteen days and I will be driving through desert and mountains and everything in between, choosing clothing to pack has been a bit challenging. I knew the temperatures would range from a hundred degrees as highs to lows in the forties at night. Plus, I'm a woman—we always overpack! But I am now prepared for anything, and my suitcase is finally in the car.

I have also decided that I will try to eat out as little as possible and bring along my own food for breakfasts, lunches, etc. Some food

ONE LAST TRIP

I've already packed, but I plan to stop at grocery stores along the way to pick up fresh food for sandwiches and the like. When I pick up my husband, Kevin, in Denver later in the week, we will be staying in a cabin at a resort, so we'll have a full kitchen and a grill to make suppers. I also have the all-important snacks, which I cannot survive road trips without. And no, they are not healthy!

Other preparations have included gathering camera gear (I'm a photography hobbyist) and computer stuff, including all the cords and chargers that go with it, and getting an oil change and tire rotation for the car. I also recently bought a dash camera for my car, knowing that I have some spectacular drives ahead of me that would be fun to capture on video. I sound like a tech person, but trust me, I am far from it. My son actually set it up for me.

Last but not least, I have my voice recorder. Over the years, I enjoy taking a few days to myself to travel somewhere to refresh, restore, and take a breather from the stresses of everyday life. My wonderful husband is good with it and encourages me to get away. Since I am a photographer, I call these my photography pilgrimages and come home with hundreds of photos and great memories of people I meet. I love to talk with people and hear their stories or simply share a particular part of that adventure. I use my voice recorder to journal my thoughts, feelings, and things that I see while I travel. It's fun to listen to later, but it's also a great way to remember the little things along the way that I will probably forget down the road. I am including most of my recordings in this book to help tell this story. They are italicized and in blue font. Please note that I have transcribed them exactly as I spoke them, so they may seem rambling or repetitive at times. I will also be including some of my Facebook posts that I shared each day.

As I pump gas at the station near my house, my excitement is building! I cannot wait to get on the road and get this journey started!

Hello, it is August 5, 2018, a little after 9:00, and I'm just starting my new and exciting journey. I'm heading out to Colorado to take my dad's ashes and to bury them out in Tincup Cemetery, which was

> *one of his favorite places when he was alive. We used to travel out there all of the time. And I'm very excited to be able to take a part of him and leave him there so he can forever be a part of this wonderful and beautiful place that we used to stay every summer.*
>
> *I'm really excited! I just got out of the St. Louis area heading west, and I will be spending the night tonight in Oklahoma City. And I get to see Alex, so I'm really excited to spend a few hours with him and take him to dinner. Just good to see him... I don't get to see him that much. But I'm glad I'm able to add this part to my journey.*

Tonight I'll be in Moore, Oklahoma, just outside of Oklahoma City. It's a good place to stop as it's a seven- to eight-hour drive, but most importantly, my son Alex lives and works there. I always look for reasons to see him. I love that kid! He's not really a kid; he's twenty-three. But he's *my* kid, and I cherish every moment we get to spend together! He and my dad had a special relationship. I will talk more about that a bit later, but this is a very important and special stop on this expedition with Dad.

> *It was really neat this morning, I was packing up the last of the bags, because there were a few that I kept inside the house overnight. I had everything else packed up last night before I went to bed. So this morning, I had a bag that I picked up to put in the car. It was my little picnic basket. Right on top of it, there was a ladybug just sitting there. First, I thought that's strange. I wonder why it's there. But then I looked online a little bit to see what ladybugs symbolize, and it's really cool. Ladybugs are the symbol for lady luck and that they bring luck and abundance wherever they go. So I guess to me it's very symbolic that there was a ladybug on my picnic*

basket for many reasons. And I also read another definition that said something about that it brings abundant joy and meaning in life. There's a lot of meanings for the symbolism of the ladybug, but they're all excellent. I know that my dad sent the ladybug, and he put it on the picnic basket because whenever we would travel to Colorado, which we did almost every summer, we always did picnics... always. (I laughed.) Almost every day. So it's very symbolic to me that there was a ladybug on my picnic basket. And I know Dad sent it to me, and I'm so happy that I have the honor to be able to take him with me and do this journey so Dad and I can have this one last trip together.

So now I'm on Interstate 44 heading west across Missouri. It's not a bad drive, at least there are hills and trees. We used to take this interstate a couple of times a year when the kids were young, when we would meet my mom coming from Kansas City and head to Branson. We also drove it quite a bit when Alex was living in Rolla, attending college at Missouri University of Science and Technology (formerly University of Missouri-Rolla). Here, he received his Bachelor of Science in Mechanical Engineering, summa cum laude. Dad was also a mechanical engineer, having received his bachelor's degree from Kansas State University.

Alex and Dad are practically one and the same. It's uncanny how much they are alike. They are both mechanical engineers, both love old cars and tinkering with them, and both have the same dry sense of humor, which must be in the Rinard DNA. They even look alike. When Alex could barely walk, Dad had him out in his workshop, teaching him. The workshop was attached to their garage and was specifically planned in the original house plans, which Dad designed. It was large, probably close to twenty feet by twenty feet. Dad had every tool imaginable for woodworking, car repair, home repairs. You name it, he probably had it! Together they played with tools and wood, built circuit boards that taught Alex about electricity, and got under the hoods of the cars to have lessons on the inner workings of the modern automobile. It was a wonderful haven for the both of them, and they both adored each other.

> *I just crossed over the state line, so I'm in Oklahoma. I cannot believe this traffic. It has just been insane! Interstate 44 across Missouri has always been bad, but today was really bad, especially once I got to Springfield. I don't know. Maybe people are coming home from the weekend or the lake or something. But hopefully, I'll get there soon. It keeps pushing my time back for seeing Alex, but I'll still get to see him, and I'm looking forward to it!*

    Oklahoma is an interesting state. It has the third largest number of Native American tribes in the US, only behind Alaska and California, with over thirty official tribes, including Shawnee, Apache, Cherokee, Cheyenne/Arapaho, Chickasaw, Choctaw, Kickapoo, Osage, and Seminole. Oklahoma was the forty-sixth state in the USA, becoming a state on November 16, 1907. The capital is Oklahoma City, and they have a population of around four million. The major industries for Oklahoma are farming (wheat and cattle), oil, and natural gas. The state animal is the buffalo, and the state flower is the Oklahoma Rose.

    The famous Route 66 travels through Oklahoma. Route 66 was one of the original highways within the US highway system, established in 1926. It originally ran from Chicago, Illinois, to Santa Monica, California (a total of over two thousand miles). Oklahoma is centrally located along the route, and it has the country's longest section. Route 66 in Oklahoma is now part of Interstate 40 and State Highway 66, and it passes through Oklahoma City. So this famous route is now a permanent part of my trip!

    I'm approaching Oklahoma City now. It's been a long day of driving, but that's ok. I've enjoyed the solitude, giving me time for reflection, prayer, and singing at the top of my lungs to the radio! Just a few more minutes and I'll be hanging out with Alex. Day #1 destination complete!

CHAPTER 3

Where Did Sydney Rinard Come From?

A Brief Ancestry

Meet Sydney Rinard's Ancestors

It's always best to start at the beginning. I'll begin with Dad's grandparents.

My grandma (Dad's mom) and my aunt (Dad's sister) became very interested in our family genealogy at least thirty years ago. This was before the internet made everything easier. It was also before ancestry websites and DNA analysis, which I have since done two different ones. They worked for years and years doing research, pulling records from family bibles and personal keepsakes and stories. They would actually go around the country to different towns and counties to find public records of births, weddings, and deaths of family members. They would visit cemeteries and photograph headstones. They were able to track down military records, immigration information, and the like. With all this information, they put together books and books of family history and stories, with very complete family trees. What they accomplished was absolutely amazing! My grandma died in 2003, and my aunt passed in 2014. Since I was the only grandchild and my aunt had no children and because I was so interested in it, I inherited all the many boxes of research. I haven't been able to go through it all yet, but I have seen most of it. I will be using a lot of this information to help you understand my family and why Dad was the man he was.

Dad's grandparents were Alonzo Leroy Rinard and Anna Lebert Rinard. His great-grandparents were Adam S. Rinard and Isabel Wilson Rinard. His great-great-grandparents were Shadrack Rinard and Nancy Porter Rinard. His great-great-great-grandparents were George Rinard and Catherine Ready Rinard. His great-great-great-great-grandparents were Adam Rhinehart (Rinard) and Catherin Stover Rinard. I know, that's a lot of Rinards. I won't go that far back. I will begin with Alonzo and Anna.

Alonzo (Lon) was born on March 3, 1875, in Blackford City, Indiana. Both of his parents died when he was about two years old. He was adopted and raised by relatives—Abraham and Mary "Polly" (Rinard) Stonebraker. Mary was actually his aunt—his father's sister. They moved to Lincoln County, Kansas, where they resided in Pawnee Rock. Abraham and his brothers had all moved to Kansas and were able to take advantage of an offer from the county for double the amount of free land by the Homestead Act available to settlers who were Civil War veterans. Alonzo attended school through eighth grade then set out on his own. He was fifteen. By 1898, Alonzo was working as a candy-maker for the Palace Candy Kitchen and Bakery in Salina.

Anna Lebert was born on October 9, 1881, in Brookville, Kansas. Her parents emigrated from Germany in 1880. She grew up on her family farm west of Glendale, Kansas. At an early age, her job on the farm was to herd a small herd of cattle to keep them from straying since they didn't have many fences. She, along with her sisters and brother, also had many household chores and tended the garden. When she was young, she was thrown from a horse and dragged until she was unconscious. This led to hearing loss, which deteriorated as she got older. She eventually had to use a hearing aid, but it affected her quality of living and ability to communicate with others freely.

When Anna became of age, she and her sister Lena moved to Salina, Kansas, and lived in a boarding house. They made a modest living sewing clothes. Lena got married and moved to California. Eventually, Anna joined her out west, and they started a dressmaking business together.

ONE LAST TRIP

After a couple of years, Anna decided to move back to Salina. Her other sister, Lizzie, had married a man named Will Stonebraker (Alonzo's brother). One day Alonzo visited the homestead and took a liking to his new sister-in-law. A meeting was arranged for Alonzo and Anna, and a romance began.

Ultimately, Alonzo went to work for the railroad in Western Kansas and met a man named Walter P. Chrysler (who would eventually go on to fame with Chrysler Corp.). Alonzo moved to Denver, Colorado, to find work with Mr. Chrysler so he could create financial support to get married and have a family. He worked in a candy store and did night watchman work for a brickyard. He was bit by a rattlesnake and almost died of smallpox. He decided to return home to Salina to Anna. He had written her letters, but they never reached her. The story told was that Anna's neighbor would steal their mail, including Alonzo's letters. Since she never heard from Alonzo, Anna assumed that the romance was over. She made extended visits to family, where she met another man. They had a nice romance and almost married, but there were too many differences in their lifestyles, so it ended. Anna returned to Salina, and once again, she and Alonzo crossed paths. This time, it took off for good!

Alonzo had been assisting his Uncle John with police work and eventually took a job of his own in 1908 as Salina's merchant policeman to guard downtown businesses. He walked eighteen miles nightly, seven days a week. One year later, Anna and Alonzo were married.

From the *Union* newspaper, Salina, Kansas:

A wedding of unusual beauty and of great interest to Saline county people took place Tuesday, 18 Nov 1908, at 11:30 a.m. at the home of the bride's parents, Mr. and Mrs. Martin Lebert of Glendale township in Saline county when their daughter Anna and Mr. Alonzo Rinard were united in marriage.

The ceremony took place in the parlor. A bower of flowers was erected in a corner, and here was where the bride and groom and the officiating clergyman, Rev. A. O. Swinehart, of the Lutheran church of Tescott, stood. The ring ceremony was used. Just before the bridal party entered, Miss Anna Sondegard sang "Love Me and the World Is Mine." As the bride and groom entered unattended, Miss Lavina Sondegard played Lohengrin's wedding march.

The bride, who is a handsome brunette, was attired in a light gray tailored suit with blouse ensuite. She carried a bouquet of bride's roses. The decorations throughout the room were white chrysanthemums and greenery. Great quantities of these flowers, together with Calla lilies, carnations, roses and orange blossoms were enjoyed in decorating the dining room. All the flowers used for decorative purposes were sent from California, where the bride lived for two years.

An elegant dinner was served to over 100 guests by Misses Minnie and Freda Lebert and Mrs. Lon Stonebraker. Following the ceremony, a reception was held, which was prettily appointed and carried out in an artistic manner.

ONE LAST TRIP

The bride is the daughter of Mr. and Mrs. Martin Lebert and one of the most charming and accomplished young women of Saline county. Her parents are numbered with the early pioneers of the county and the large number of beautiful and useful presents indicate the high esteem in which she is held by her many associates and friends. She is a cousin of W. H. Ringle of this city.

The groom lost his parents by death when he was a child and was reared in Lincoln county by Mrs. Mary [Rinard] Stonebraker. But he made his home here for several years. He is a night policeman hired by the business men. Rinard is a capable, whole-souled and generous young man, ambitious and industrious. He will take his bride to a beautiful furnished home on North Ninth Street.

Anna, Jeanette, Clarence, Alonzo, and Leroy Rinard

Alonzo and Anna eventually invested in a three-story boarding house in Salina, where Anna ran it completely by herself. They lived on the main floor with their three children—Clarence, Jeanette, and Leroy (Dad's father, my grandpa). In the first eleven months, they profited $7,000, and that was during the World War I Depression times. Dad wrote, "The Rinard kids lived in a 3-story boarding house across the street from Memorial Hall, a white frame house next to the 3-story brick apartment house on corner of Ash and 9th. Grandma took in roomers in the upper floor of her house with an outside stairway directly to the room and an extra bedroom on the front of the house. One roomer moved out and left a slot machine in the room. It had fancy scrollwork on it, and it was magnificent. Grandma let us play with it. It used pennies, and the back cover was missing so we could put a penny in the front, pull the lever, and spin the wheels. Then we could reach around the back and pick up the penny and play again. One wheel was broken and would just spin, so the machine never paid off. We had a lot of fun playing with it."

Anna also sold Larkin products door-to-door and did so well she was able to purchase some beautiful furniture for their house. She prided herself in being independent and was very good at making ends meet. She only had a sixth-grade education, but she was good at numbers.

Alonzo registered for the draft in World War I but never actually served in the military.

Anna and Alonzo's children grew up pretty much on their own. Alonzo worked all night and slept indoors during the day, so the kids were expected to play outdoors in quiet. Anna was busy cleaning and managing their rooming house, so the kids concocted a neighborhood gang that got into a lot of mischief. My grandpa Leroy once said, "I guess you would have called us delinquents, but that concept did not exist yet." Some of their stories that I have heard are legendary.

One time, Alonzo's oldest son, Clarence, created a magic show and made a tent from a bedsheet attached to the side of their house. He invited neighborhood kids to watch and, at one point, held up a lit match, which caught the sheet on fire and singed the side of the house before the fire department got there. This woke up Alonzo, who was not amused!

Their best adventure was to gain revenge upon the "elite" of their classmates at school. They, along with some friends, pooled their money together, snuck into one of the printing shop of their friend's dad, and made elegant invitations for the biggest costume Halloween party ever. They instructed everyone to meet at Memorial Hall, which was across the street from their home. That night, the "gang" hid across from the entrance to watch everyone arrive in fancy costumes, but the hall remained locked and dark. The gang was afraid of retaliation, so they never told anyone about their part of this trick, except to a few family members.

In 1925, Alonzo was laid up with multiple injuries from a car accident while he was patrolling the business district. For three weeks, Anna had to use her boarding house income and entrepreneurship abilities to raise money for them to live on as there were no work benefits in those days. If you didn't work, you didn't get paid.

*****

Article from the *Salina Journal*, Thursday, February 11, 1937:

Lon Rinard, Merchant Police, Circles Globe Now Completing Circle Eighth Time Having Walked Nights for 28 Years

Down the street, heads up, his pockets heavy with keys, comes Lon Rinard, Salina's merchant policeman, walking his way around the earth for the eighth time. While the rest of the city snoozes comfortably, Rinard goes about his lifetime business of figuratively "putting out the cat."

For more than twenty-eight years, Lon Rinard has been on the job guarding other people's property from nocturnal prowlers. During that time he has walked a distance estimated at 184,000 miles—or about seven and a half times around this terrestrial sphere.

He is a familiar figure in Salina's night life and, by the same token, the night life is a familiar sight to him. A night watchman gets a different slant on a city, one that is hard to convey to the humdrum fellow who goes to bed with the chickens.

Rinard carries a businesslike .38 caliber revolver but has had little occasion to use it. He is reluctant to use a gun in the business district. And only once in twenty-eight years has he been shot at. That occurred years ago in the alley between Seventh and Santa Fe, a half business block north of Iron Avenue. "The other fellow was too far away for me to see what he looked like," Rinard said. "His bullet was quite a bit closer. I heard it go past. Then he ran."

Another article of equipment is an assortment of keys weighing close to two pounds. To accommodate the keys and gun, Mrs. Rinard customarily lengthens the pockets of her husband's clothing and reinforces them.

Rinard averages eighteen miles of pavement every night, winter and summer. To get that kind of mileage, he has to take care of his feet and watch his weight. He buys special-made shoes and usually has five or six pairs at a time to provide "spares." Sometimes he changes shoes during the night to rest his feet. A pair of thick composition half-soles will last two weeks, but ordinary leather shoes will wear out in a week on the grueling rounds of the business district. At regular intervals Rinard goes to a foot specialist just to be sure his feet will not give him any trouble. His soft thick-soled, capless shoes are another insurance.

Born in Indiana, Rinard came to Pawnee Rock, Kansas, with his parents in 1878. And a year later the family moved to Lincoln

ONE LAST TRIP

County, where they homesteaded. As a young man Rinard took a fling at several kinds of work.

The year the Spanish-American War broke out (1898), he was employed as a candy maker by George and Pete Holtzmeister. They ran the old Palace candy kitchen and bakery where the Manhattan Restaurant is now located. Rinard was standing in the front door of the shop when the whistles blew, signaling that the war had been declared.

After that he tried railroading several times and then went to Denver. He worked there as candy maker and also found employment for a time in a brickyard. Finally he returned to this territory.

All in all, Rinard has had six different trades during his lifetime. He has been candy maker, railroader, brickyard worker, stationary engineer, fireman, and merchant policeman. When he tried the last, he found his right niche. He has a real liking for the work and takes pride in it.

Rinard was a night watchman before he became a merchant policeman. He worked at that for a year in Denver. The year following, he worked as a watchman for the Union Pacific Railroad at Salina and Plainville, and later for the Lee Hardware Company.

In October of 1908, Rinard became Salina's merchant policeman. George W. Thorns was city marshal then, and John R. Stonebraker (who was later killed) was assistant. Salina had no chief of police at that time.

During all these years, Rinard has watched over the city, helping protect the business district from night marauders. He works seven days a week and has never had a vacation in over twenty-eight years, except for two occasions when he was hurt.

Twelve years ago (1925), he was struck by a car and laid up three months with a fractured pelvic bone, broken shoulder, and fracture of the foot. During the recent sleet storm, he fell on the ice, breaking his arm. This time he was laid up only from Tuesday to the following Saturday. Members of the family said Rinard fretted to get back on the job and, with his arm in a cast, was soon patrolling the alley with his assistant (possible twenty-three-year-old son Leroy).

"When I first started out, the job was more simple," Rinard admits. "I just had to catch the back doors and observe. Later the white way (a brilliantly lighted street in a business district) was put in and I took care of that. Now my job is as much headwork as footwork." Rinard checks doors and windows. He checks lights. He even checks furnaces and hot water heaters. He does a multitude of things to make the business district run more smoothly in the daytime.

There are fourteen switches controlling what he terms the "flat rate lights." These he turns off at 11:20 each night. They control some of the windows and signs. Then there are a number of independent switches on store fronts which are turned off at different hours. The last light to go out is on a shoe store on North Santa Fe Avenue. Rinard flicks the switch there at 1 o'clock in the morning. He turns off the white way lights on the street at dawn.

About 1 o'clock in the morning Rinard starts lowering awnings on the west side of the streets so that those will all be down and the stores cool when the morning sun is up. In the winter he works thirteen and half hours up to 7:30 in the morning. In the summer he goes home at 4:30.

He is the custodian of keys to every principal place of business in his territory, running from the Iron Avenue bridge west to the *Salina Journal* office, and from Elm Street south to Walnut. His is the duty of guarding about ninety business houses.

Many and varied have been his experiences with prowlers, and numerous robberies have been prevented by him in the last twenty-eight years. Sometimes the dark figure coming down the alley is a businessman who has a right there. Sometimes it is a town kid, who is given some friendly advice about staying where the lights shine. Sometimes it is a suspicious character and Rinard takes him to the police station for investigation.

One of the cases in which the tall merchant policeman figured was an attempted robbery five years ago (1932) at the Watson Theater. That time Rinard's methodical call saved the theater company $1,500. "It was about 4 o'clock in the morning," Rinard said. "You see, I make the building regularly. I unlocked the door and went inside. I heard a noise upstairs and though it was Scotty, who worked in the studio. He sometimes worked late and stayed there. I yelled at him and there was no answer. I started to investigate and heard the alley door open. I went to the door and looked out. Then I saw two men running down Fifth Avenue. They turned east on Iron."

Here again Rinard found the city police a valuable ally in his work. He saw an officer coming down Fifth and signaled the policeman with his flashlight. The officer approached and, with Rinard, entered the theater to investigate. The two men found the safe had been moved out of the office and blasted open. When they turned it over, the door fell open revealing about $1,500 in receipts. The thieves were that close to success. The police got busy and picked up one suspect, but his partner escaped. The case on the suspect did not end with a conviction, but the theater's money was saved.

"I enjoy night work," Rinard said. "It is a business with me. I like my employers. They appreciate my work and I appreciate the confidence they have in me."

*****

When Alonzo was about to retire, he wrote this letter to his wife, Anna:

> *I think we have done very good during our married life all these years which we started out with nothing, we might say, but how we have worked and denied ourselves of everything for the sake of others, but I think we are well rewarded when we look backward and see our children so honored and successful. We can thank God for all of our Blessings and we still must ask God to help and guide us in the future. I give you, Anna, the credit for the managership I nor no other man could accomplish what I have. With your affection you have carried on. I think you are wonderful to bear up. You have been a wonderful wife and pal and pardner [sic] in all our married life. And now I believe we have accomplished our*

aim—that is, we will be in shape financially that we will get along the few more years of our life. I can quit this night work any time this summer. I want you to take it as easy as possible and don't worry too much. I would rather talk to you than to write, but this is the best way. So we will live for each other, sharing our trouble, be a pal and pardner [sic] in everything, hoping the future will be bright. With love to a wonderful wife and pal and pardner [sic].

After he retired, when his grandkids would come into town for a visit, Alonzo would sit with them on the front porch and tell stories about history. They feel they developed their fondness of history because of him. He liked to read Westerns and about the Wild West that was finishing its glory days in his childhood. Phil remembers that as they would all sit on the large porch of that rooming house, it seemed that everyone who walked past would wave and say "Hi, Lon!" Every holiday, there was a large American flag sticking out from the porch.

During the family visits, he would sneak away with his son-in-law to Oakdale Park to watch gentlemen play roque, which was similar to croquet, on a private court there. Away from Anna, they sipped wine and beer that was not allowed in the house. Alonzo never played much with the grandkids but always had comic books on top of the refrigerator and Royal Crown (RC) Cola in the fridge.

Eventually, Alonzo and Anna sold the rooming house on Ash Street and moved around the corner and down the same block to a smaller duplex, across from the county courthouse, to live out their lives in retirement. What they could not foresee was notification in the 1960s that the city planned to take over the land of that large block of residences and clear it for urban renewal expansion of government buildings. The amount of money offered by the city to purchase their older home was not enough to be able to afford to purchase another home elsewhere, and when they sought a retirement home, they found a long waiting list, but their time was running out to vacate the premises.

ONE LAST TRIP

It was at that time that Alonzo suffered a stroke and died on December 30, 1965. He had always aspired to live to be one hundred years old. Unfortunately, he was ten years shy of that.

>Obituary of Alonzo Leroy Rinard

>*Alonzo Leroy Rinard, 90, 240 N. 9th, died Thursday at Asbury Hospital. Born 4 Mar 1875 in Blackford county, Ind. He had lived in Salina 75 years. He was a merchant policeman in Salina for 37 years before retirement. He was a member of St. John's Lutheran Church.*

>*Survivors include the widow, Anna, of the home; two sons Clarence A., San Antonio TX and Leroy, Cedar Rapids, IA; a daughter Mrs. Walter Brandt, Kansas City, MO; nine grandchildren and a great grandchild.*

>*Burial will be in Gypsum Hill Cemetery.*

Rev. Norman Ullestad delivered the eulogy at his funeral on January 3, 1966: "As we think of the dear one who has just left our midst, we think of his faithfulness to God throughout these years. But we are also mindful of the fact, as Lon was mindful, that God had been faithful to him. That through these years of his life, God had been with him to strengthen him and to guide him. Just as God was with him and his wife to strengthen them as they faced the last few days together in quiet confidence, knowing that God was their dwelling place, that they were prepared to go to him and to meet each other there. What a tremendous word of hope in just these words: 'Lord, thou has been our dwelling place in all generations.'" Alonzo's favorite hymn was "Beautiful Savior."

Alonzo's daughter, Jeanette, said, "Lon was a good looking man—tall with blue eyes and brown hair with regular features. I remember my mother saying years later as he lay in his casket, 'Wasn't he a nice looking man?' And he was. Father was tall, taking long strides as he walked. He was a man with twinkling eyes when he would make some small joke. He always wore a mustache, except one time when he cut it off and we made him grow it back because he did not look like our father."

Alonzo's death left Anna alone with the predicament of having to move soon with nowhere to go, in addition to the grieving loss of her lifelong mate. She was lonely and worried for her future. The next-door neighbor, Mrs. Wood, checked in on Anna daily. She usually brought something to share for breakfast. Because of her hearing issues, when she woke up in the morning, Anna would usually unlatch the back door for Mrs. Woods to come in.

On March 16, 1966, Mrs. Woods discovered Anna dead in her bed, but the back door had been unlatched. Anna had died alone in her sleep, most likely from being worn out from worry and care or maybe just a broken heart. She never feared death, and after Alonzo died, she longed to join him.

Chapter 4

Day 2
Monday, August 6, 2018

Oklahoma, Texas, New Mexico (Los Alamos)

It's day 2, August 6, and I have just left Oklahoma City. I didn't get a chance to catch up last night with this recorder, but I will tell you what I did last night.

I arrived in Moore, Oklahoma, about 5:00. I checked into the hotel, then I went over to Alex's house. I was really excited to see him. When he answered the door, he came out and gave me a big bear hug, which made my heart melt! And I got to see his roommate, who also gave me a big hug! They were hungry, so we went out to eat to this little place called The Garage. It's a really fun place. They've got burgers and stuff like that. But the way it's decorated, it looks like a garage, gas station thing. Great place.

Alex and I

The boys had been out driving around that afternoon because they are trying to find a new house to rent. Alex's house is too small since his friend moved in from St. Louis to start his new job at the base. They are college buddies and are having so much fun now that his friend accepted a job at the same Air Force base as Alex. They were driving around earlier and were excited and wanted to show me some of the places they had looked at. We drove around and saw some of the different neighborhoods. We came back and dropped his roommate off, then Alex wanted to show me his office. We had seen the base back in April when we were here for his birthday, but we didn't go into his actual office, because of security and all that. But since he has been working here about a year and it was a Sunday evening, he felt it was fine for us to walk around a little bit. So we went to the base, and he actually took me into his office. Then we walked around through the hangars where they had the B-1 bombers and the B-52 bombers that had come in for maintenance, service work…that type of thing. It was really cool to be able to walk around these planes while they were in the hangars. I didn't get to go up and touch them. We were so close that we were actually walking under their wings, and you could really see in the planes. Very awesome.

So anyway, that was what we did last night. This morning, I am on Highway 40 heading west. I will end up in Los Alamos, New Mexico, tonight to stay with my Uncle Phil and Aunt Carole, and I'm excited to see them and catch up a little bit. I think it's going to be a pretty dull drive. There's really nothing to look at here in Western Oklahoma across Texas and Eastern New Mexico.

Dad would really have loved to tour the Air Force base where Alex works. He is a civilian mechanical engineer at the base, as an employee of the Department of Defense. It was a scholarship opportunity where they paid for his last two years of college, and in turn, he agreed to work there for two years. He has completed one year so far, and his duties and projects are finally starting to get more interesting. He has been given an expanded leadership position, which allows him to do more design work and even the opportunity to have a team that works under him. At one point, when we were walking around, Alex said he wished Papa could see all this, and I told him that Dad had been walking with us the whole time! Dad was so proud of Alex, and I have no doubt that he keeps a watchful and loving eye over Alex all the time!

I saw proof that Alex and Dad are related—he and his co-workers perform the same crazy office antics that Dad would absolutely find hilarious! When one of them is out of the office for the day, the others will copy or draw funny pictures of the poor absent employee then post them around. They have competitions in bowling, go-kart racing, and other fun activities, and they include awards with Olympic-type podiums for the necessary winners' photos. They also participate in mud runs (5Ks) together, which include costumes and experiments with facial hair. My visit with Alex was a very important stop on Dad's journey—he treasured his grandson!

Here we are again, Dad and I. We've hit the road and are continuing our western quest. His ashes box is right beside me in the passenger seat, where it's been since the beginning and will be until our final destination.

> *Observations about Western Oklahoma: I'm not really sure what God was intending for this area of the country, but I think he might have forgotten about this part. It's fairly flat and there's not much vegetation. I don't know, it looks like they're trying to farm, but I can't even imagine wanting to live here. And every now and then, you run across a little grove of trees, and you just wonder* Why is that there? *and* How did that get there? *What really makes me laugh is that there is this barren field and then there's one tree in the middle of it. How did that happen? Anyway, not a very exciting place.*

I have to say, it's a bit brutal driving across Western Oklahoma. Towns and people are few and far between. The farms look a bit sad. Of course, I grew up in Kansas, so I'm used to the beautiful big farms of wheat, corn, soybeans, milo, and hay. These are sparse. The roads are definitely getting flatter, and it's a pretty straight shot.

> *Another observation about Oklahoma is that their soil out here is almost bright red. I guess it's iron or some mineral in here. It's like clay red. So I have to wonder what kind of crops would grow in this type of soil. There are some farms, I'm just passing one now, and he's got some kind of crop growing. I'd be curious to see what is growing. It's a very strange thing.*

I did some research, and the red soil is called Port Silt Loam. It's the state soil of Oklahoma. Turns out it's reddish in color because of the weathering of red sandstones, siltstones, and shales. I was mistaken when I assumed it was from iron. I have to say, it really is an impressive color!

The most valuable crop that Oklahoma farmers grow is wheat. They also grow hay, cotton, and soybeans. Oklahoma is the fifth leading source of beef in the country, and that is the principal source of agricultural income in the state.

> *Now I see over the horizon they have a whole line of those wind turbines. I guess power stations. There's a whole line of big white ones. They look very cool. But I can see that there's a lot of wind out here. There's not much to stop it.*

More research showed me that because of its central location, the western half of Oklahoma is located in America's wind corridor (from Canada to Texas), where the majority of the country's best wind resources are located. Oklahoma's wind resources are the second best in the US. Their production of wind energy supplies a large part of the state's electricity. During a typical day, wind farms will produce enough electricity for over forty thousand homes. These are impressive facts! It explains why I had to keep both hands on the wheel most of the day!

> *I forgot to tell this funny story from last night. When I got to the hotel I was staying in, it was about five o'clock. This was in Moore, not very far from Alex's house. Kevin and I had stayed in this hotel two years ago when Alex was living here for his internship. It's in a nice area...a safe area. I pulled up to the hotel, and there were no cars there at all. It was five o'clock, and I thought that was kind of a bit odd. I pulled into the little circular part where you go in to check-in. I walked in, and there's nobody there. Behind the desk, there was this little room. I guess it's an office or something, and this older gentle-*

man, kind of a thin guy, pops his head out, sees me standing at the desk, and goes back into the room. (Laugh.) I thought, Well, that was kind of strange. Then just a minute later, he comes out, comes up to the desk, and says, "Hey! How are you doing? Are you checking in?"

And I said, "Yes." I did notice his name tag, which showed his name, and Front Desk, so I guess he was legit. He pulls up my registration, and he wants the form of payment and an ID, so I give him the credit card that I used to reserve the room, which was actually Dad's credit card (I'm on all of those accounts), and my ID.

He says, "Oh, this card, this is a different card."

And I said, "That's the one I reserved it with."

And he says, "OK, well, this has a different name on it."

And I told him, "Yes, well, that's my dad."

Then he says, "Oh, well, is Sydney here?"

I just kind of looked at him for a second and said, "Well, he's in the car, but he passed away last December." (Laughs.)

This guy's face was priceless! His eyes just opened huge, and he didn't know how to respond to that. He mumbled, "Um, OK."

I finally said, "Actually, I'm taking his ashes out to Colorado."

And he said, "Oh! Thank goodness!" I think he must have thought I actually had a dead body in the car that had been there since December! Anyway, funny story! I know I gave the little strange man at the front desk quite a tale to tell his family.

I'm sure I must be getting near the Texas state line. It seems as if I've been driving for a long time. All this driving alone has given me the opportunity to reflect on Dad and our life together, especially our many trips to Colorado. They told me my first visit to the Centennial State was when I was around four months old. Of course, I don't remember that one, but I do believe that I was bitten by the Colorado bug at that time.

One of my favorite sayings is "The mountains are calling, and I must go!" Colorado is a part of me. I can't really explain it. I have friends who feel the same way about the beach. I do love going to the beach with the sand and sun and the water peacefully rolling in and out. But there is something so special to me to be standing among the pine and aspen trees, with a backdrop of beautiful and fabulous mountains. I cannot describe the smell—the best I can say is that it is the most wonderful smell of nature with pine needles scattered all around and clean, fresh air that is thin from the high altitude. You can feel this amazing air going into your lungs and pushing out the ugly city air that resides there. And the sounds…oh my…they cannot be replicated on any sound machine. You can hear the absolute sound of silence, with an occasional wind breeze and rustling of the aspen leaves. There will be a scurry of a chipmunk and the flight or calling of a bird enjoying the glorious, most peaceful place. And I cannot forget the sound of water…from a trickling stream to a fast-moving river. That sound promotes relaxation, happiness, and peace. Heaven on earth!

I made it! Texas state line! Each time I cross a state border, it's one step closer to my destination. Let's keep this car going…

> *I'm now in Texas, and I'm about twenty to twenty-five miles from Amarillo. I didn't know it was possible, but it has gotten flatter than it was in Western Oklahoma. There's not any hills, per se. Not much to look at. Every now and then, there is a tree. But I'll tell you, everywhere that I'm looking around here are these enormous windmill-type white wind turbines. It's almost like they are the state crop of Texas! At least up in this area Northern Texas. There's really nothing else, except for some straw, that I can see growing. There are some sort of fields,*

but they don't really look good at all. But I'll tell you what, these little white windmill, turbine things are really popping up. They're really fun to watch!

Texas—the Lone Star State. It became a state on December 29, 1845. The capital is Austin, and it is the second largest state in the US (behind Alaska). The state animal is the Texas longhorn, and the state flower is bluebonnet.

Texas produces the most wind power of any other state in the US. A wind turbine is a device that converts the wind into electrical energy. These turbines that I am seeing everywhere are white, with a very tall pole (around three hundred feet!) and three huge blades attached to some sort of generator at the top. It's almost like watching a choreographed dance—the blades spin so gracefully. I can almost hear some classical music playing!

The primary crops grown in Texas are cotton, corn, rice, and wheat. But the most famous thing Texas is known for is their cattle. They actually lead the US in cattle production. I saw a fact somewhere stating that Texas raises eleven million cattle each year, which puts them in the highest beef-growing categories in the US and around the world. That's a lot of cows!

I'm actually in the part of Texas called the Texas Panhandle. It's the northernmost part of Texas and the narrowest part of the state to cross. There aren't a lot of cities in this part, with Amarillo being the largest. It's nothing but plains, with hardly any trees. I was told that if I go farther south than Interstate 40, I would run in large canyons and rivers, but I don't have the time. All I know is that this highway I'm on is dull, to say the least. I have to keep reminding myself that mountains are coming, and tomorrow I will be standing in the middle of them!

Now I'm nine miles from the state line of Texas and New Mexico, and just in the last ten to fifteen minutes, I've noticed the terrain has changed completely. It's not flat anymore. Now it has a little bit of some, well, I'll just call them hills or mesa tops. It's more of what I think of when I think of New Mexico. The actual landscape now is desertlike. It obviously can't be farmed, and there's no homes. It's just very low little bushes. I guess these must be what turn into the tumbleweeds. But it's very windy coming through here. It's kind of pushing my car around a little bit.

New Mexico state line just ahead!

Third state of the day. I'm almost as far west as I plan to go on this trip. In a couple of hours, I will turn to the northwest and edge closer to Colorado. I will be spending the night tonight with my Uncle Phil and Aunt Carole. They live in Los Alamos, which is just northwest of Santa Fe.

Phil is Dad's younger brother by three years. They grew up in Salina, Kansas, with their younger sister, Julie. Phil has a doctorate in physics and eventually moved to New Mexico, where he worked for the Los Alamos National Laboratory. The purpose of the lab is to solve national security issues using scientific advances. Yes, he needed security clearance, but most of his work was not classified. The purpose of Phil's group was to develop technical equipment (for gamma ray and neutron measurements) and procedures that determined amounts of uranium and plutonium in spent reactor fuel, sealed storage containers, open containers in glove boxes, stuck in ducts and pipes, drums of waste items, etc. The purpose was to keep nuclear materials where they should be and not put in the hands of "bad guys." It was an international effort that took him to Russia (twelve trips), France (twelve trips), Great Britain (three trips), South Korea (twice), and Spain (twice).

The lab's website (www.lanl.gov) states that they actively protect our nation against all nuclear threats. That's the short version. When I was reading through their website, it got quite complicated. It was organized during World War II for the purpose of designing nuclear weapons. It was a top-secret place for bomb design during that time and the Manhattan Project. Their primary job was the design and coordination, and the bombs were built in other locations. They created different atomic bombs, but two of them are particularly famous—Little Boy and Fat Man, which were used in 1945 to attack Hiroshima and Nagasaki. Of course, that was before Phil's time there (he was only six years old), but they continue to this day to protect us with new scientific developments. I remember touring the lab (at least as far as they allow visitors) with Phil, and I was quite impressed!

> *I'm in New Mexico now, and I just saw a sign by the side of the road that read Icy Bridge…and it's ninety-seven degrees…so…just saying…*

It's hot. Very hot. I guess I should expect this in the desert in August. I'm used to heat being from Kansas and Missouri, but back home, we have the same heat plus humidity. The humidity is low here, but don't get me wrong, it's still hot!

My family from Dad's side were a unique bunch. They would all give the shirt off their backs to help someone, but they were the most hilarious people I've ever encountered. Fortunately, I have inherited that particular gene. Our sense of humor is what they call dry. It's kind of an indirect, tongue-in-cheek humor said in a serious way, but humorous for sure. It's delivering the funny statements without showing any change in the emotion or facial expression. Not everyone has that specific mutation in their brain so that they have the ability to understand our comical statements. My daughter doesn't. She will look at me like I'm from another planet after one of these jokes flies out of my mouth. Luckily, my son does have this gene, and with the straightest face, he will say something so funny I will have to hold my sides with laughter. I put no blame on those who don't possess it. If you don't have it, you won't comprehend it. But those of us who do, a simple dinner can turn into a tears-rolling-down-the-face, wetting-your-pants, falling-out-of-your-chair event. A lot of these stories will emerge later in this book, but I'm just building the foundation and preparation. Dad and Phil and their dad, my grandpa, Leroy, could get on a roll, that's for sure. Once I became old enough, I was right in there with them!

> *It's so funny to think about that where I am, in New Mexico, I'm about thirty miles from Santa Fe, but just looking around at the terrain and the land-*

scaping and how it is so completely different than Missouri and St. Louis and all those areas around there. It's just so strange to believe that the country is so diverse, as far as all of this. I should know... I've been driving for two straight days, and I've only made it not even half of the country yet. It's huge, but it's so different. I'm starting to get into an area where there are a little more of the hills. I see some things up ahead that could be some of the lower ends of the Rocky Mountains perhaps. There aren't as many of these mesa hills. There still are some, but it's really starting to get a little more rounded hills. I know the elevation is going up. The last city I checked about an hour ago was at 4,900 feet above sea level. I'm climbing! I'm getting more into the mountain area, which I'm just so excited to get to. This desert area is kind of cool, but I'm done with it. Been looking at it all afternoon. It's just funny how it's so completely different than merely three states over.

Phil gave me good directions to maneuver through Santa Fe and Los Alamos. It's been many years since I have visited them at their home, so none of this looks familiar. Thank goodness for my GPS. It took me right to their house! Phil was outside waiting for me, as I had called him when I passed through Santa Fe.

Los Alamos is a beautiful city that sits just over seven thousand feet above sea level. It's located on top of some of those mesa tops, with steep canyons around it. They say that was why they were chosen as the place to build the National Lab—it's harder to get there, so it protects the secret projects that go on there. They even have a ski mountain! It's called Pajarito Mountain Ski Area. I've actually skied there. It's not quite to the scale that you might think of with the large ski resorts in Colorado, but it does have forty ski runs and seven lift systems. Phil says that most winters they get enough snow, but occasionally, they have to make their own snow. He takes advantage of a local ice rink in a narrow canyon where it's largely shady. It is open-air, but the ice is refrigerated. The season runs from mid-November to late February when the sun is low and blocked. He has always been athletic and loves to hike, ski, skate, and walk. He's had to slow down the last couple of years because of health issues, but it doesn't stop him!

I'm pulling into the driveway and ready for a fun evening of catching up! Tomorrow morning, I will finally be in Colorado…cannot wait!

Me, Uncle Phil, and Aunt Carole

Chapter 5

Leroy and Mary

The Beginning of a Wonderful Life

Leroy Martin Rinard was born on September 5, 1913, in Salina, Kansas. His parents are Alonzo and Anna Rinard.

Alda Mary Kelly was born on January 13, 1915, in Seneca, Kansas. Her parents are William and Eva Kelly.

These are Dad's parents. My grandparents. Because they fell in love, Dad and I exist. As do my kids, Alex and Nicole. Just for that reason alone, they are wonderful people. But take the rest of us out of the picture, these two incredible human beings have an enchanting life story to tell.

Leroy was named after his father, Alonzo Leroy Rinard. "Martin" came from his grandfather on his mother's side, Martin Lebert. He was the youngest of three kids and just as ornery as the older two. They formed a neighborhood "gang," and from the stories that have been passed on down the family, they could get quite mischievous.

Leroy had quite a sense of humor, which has been passed along to his children and, ultimately, me. It is dry, but the results can end with streaming tears down the face and clutching sore abdominal muscles. That is, if the participant also has this unique sense of humor. Otherwise, we get the opposite response. I have been given the strangest look when I let fly one of my off-the-wall comments. But that's ok. It's their loss if they don't find the funny in it. I'm always laughing inside my head.

Leroy graduated from Salina High School in 1930. He was only seventeen years old, because he had skipped a grade in elementary school. His sister, Jeanette, said this about Leroy, "His wit made one feel good being around him. And we also enjoyed many serious discussions about life. Many of our thoughts were the same. Definitely a Lebert German, he had brown hair and blue eyes, was tall, athletic, handsome and clean-cut. His greatest asset was his personality. Everyone liked him. He had a way that made you laugh with his wit. He had much natural ability and could succeed without much studying. He did well in business and his contact with others."

After high school, Leroy attended Kansas Wesleyan College of Business. He met a friend named Merle, who talked about some of his special talents, "His superior typing ability [80 to 90 words per minute on a manual typewriter] and shorthand skill was awesome to those of us who were still struggling to make 40 words per minute."

Alda Mary grew up in Neuchatel, Kansas. When she was young, Alda was very bashful. She would cling to her mother's long skirts. Her father would make her sit on the curb downtown while he talked with his friends. Of course, they liked to tease her. Her father explained to her that if she would stop reacting, they would quit teasing her as much. Eventually, she worked on it, and he said, "Snookie [he always called her that], you have not only learned how to take it, but you can sure dish it out, too!" He was really proud when she learned that lesson. He always wanted her to grow up and learn how to take care of herself and not be dependent on others. Alda would bring home a couple of library books after school each day. Then she and her father would sit across from each other around the pot-bellied stove between the dining and living rooms, and they would read them together. He would push her not to follow the herd and to make her own decisions that made the most sense to her.

When the family moved to Onega, Kansas, Alda felt like an outcast at school. She finally determined that she would not only prove that she could do things as good as the others but that she could also better them. She often did, and she was valedictorian of her eighth-grade graduating class as well as her senior class. She earned a scholarship to attend Brown Mackie School of Business at Salina, Kansas.

At college, Alda Mary stayed at the home of the principal of Leroy's school. She was easily recognized as the prettiest girl in school, as well as the most vivacious. It didn't take long for Leroy to find her.

Leroy worked for Senator Sparks in Washington, DC, as a stenographer after he graduated from Kansas Wesleyan School of Business in 1932. Senator Sparks was up for re-election and held a Halloween party at the business college in Salina, and Leroy attended to help with the preparations. Leroy and Alda's first date was this Halloween party, and they never separated after. The senator lost the re-election, so Leroy moved back home to Salina. He took a job with Salina Supply, which was an independent wholesale distributor of residential and commercial plumbing supplies, HVAC equipment, and water/sewer pumping equipment. He started in the warehouse and soon worked up to responsible office work as an estimator. He would estimate the cost of all the plumbing supplies shown on the blueprints of a structure to be built. During World War II, he worked on blueprints for plumbing items as the Army built the new Smoky Hill air base for pilot training. This job kept him out of the Army and the war.

While they dated, Leroy attempted to correct Alda's name. She pronounced *Alda* with a short *a* sound, but Leroy said she should pronounce it like *ALL-dah*. She finally gave up hearing about it and started going by her middle name, Mary, for the rest of her life.

> Marriage Announcement—*Onaga Herald*, April 4, 1935:
>
> Miss Mary Alda Kelly, daughter of Mr. and Mrs. William H. Kelly, of Onaga, was united in marriage to Mr. Leroy M. Rinard, son of Mr. and

> Mrs. A. L. Rinard, 310 West Ash St., Salina, Kans [sic], on Sunday afternoon at the St. John's Lutheran Church. The ring ceremony was read by Rev. Benjamin R. Lantz. Attendants at the altar were Mr. Clarence Rinard. The bride was lovely in a blue crepe dress with darker blue accessories and yellow jonquils. The bridesmaid [Jeanette Brandt] wore a shoulder corsage of sweet peas.
>
> Guests at the church wedding were: Mr. and Mrs. Wm. H. Kelly, parents of the bride; Mrs. Ruth Fields, sister of the bride, and her three children, Edward, Byron and Earl; Carl Quentin Kelly, brother of the bride, of Onaga; Mr. and Mrs. A. L. Rinard, parents of the groom; Miss Jeanette Rinard, and Mrs. B. R. Lantz.
>
> Following the ceremony, light refreshments were served at 117 West Ellsworth Ave., where the bride and groom will be at home.
>
> The bride has been employed by the Kent Oil Co., and the groom is with the Salina Supply Co. An interesting sidelight of the wedding ceremony was the fact that the groom has been baptized, confirmed and married by Reverend Lantz.

Mary's boss told her that after she married, she would have to quit her job with him, as that was how women did in those days. So she quit. He quickly changed his mind and called her to come back to work. But Leroy refused to let her, wanting to be the man of the house.

Leroy kept a journal of their first year of married life. Two weeks after the wedding, he wrote, "Friends and relatives gathered at our house for a shower at a most inopportune time, since it was right after one of the dust storms which had been raging for the past month and we did not have our house straightened up very much. However, we received many nice little gifts which, while they came in handy, were not especially needed, as we had about everything we wanted. The 'social lights' went well, however.

"Up to this time we had been forced to live in the kitchen and bedroom, since it had remain constantly too chilly to use the rest of our house, for we had practically nothing to burn in the furnace."

They planted a garden with potatoes and tomatoes, and Leroy adopted two two-month-old kittens, Malty IX (yellow) and Malty X (black). Leroy had worked as a soda jerk in high school and always liked ice cream malts. Before he was married, he'd had a sequence of cats, naming each one Malty. Phil remembers an electric shake mixer mounted on the kitchen wall. He liked malts very thick and actually burned the motor out.

On Decoration Day, they rode their bicycles (accompanied by both kittens) out to "the old schoolhouse west of town on the old State Street road and spent that afternoon there enjoying our first fried chicken." By late June, they "put up half a bushel of cherries and got a short 7 quarts, a pie, and undetermined amount eaten whilst we pitted and stemmed them." They built awnings and started sleeping on the back porch for the summer.

One evening, while erecting an antenna in the attic, Leroy managed to poke one foot and leg through the ceiling in the upstairs hall, filling the entire upstairs with plaster and dirt.

On July 19, 1935: "We went to Kansas City on the Union Pacific Streamliner to spend part of our vacation with Jeanette. Jeanette's boyfriend Walt Brandt came over and we went to Tower Theater, but were run out of the theater by a terrific odor which arose, we believe, from the smell of the bodies and feet of the vaudeville performers, when the smell was wafted out over the audience by the cooling system. We had a swell time, however, just 'bumming around' in Walt's car after the show. I started drinking lots of beer in Kansas City."

On July 22, 1935: "A family reunion was held at Oakdale Park. Lots to eat." A week later, they visited Dr. Brown, who gave Mary directions about "everything," meaning pregnancy.

By August 27, 1935, they moved to 323 North Columbia Street. By September 30, they acquired a baby buggy from Sears, Roebuck and Co. "What a thrill it gave us after assembling it!" he wrote.

On December 11, Leroy played a basketball game on the Gibbs Clothing team, losing to the Lee Mercantile team. He was met with

Wayne Stanley's bony elbow that crashed into his mouth and broke his front tooth halfway up. It was his last basketball game and cost $30 to get a porcelain tooth replacement. "What a Christmas present!"

Around Christmas, one of the Malty cats had disappeared for two days. Then next morning, he was waiting for them on their back porch. "Pop called up and advised that he had picked up the li'l rascal down on Santa Fe at 1 o'clock in the morning, and he called the police and they gave the cat an escort home." That was when Leroy's father Alonzo Rinard walked the night beat as a merchant policeman.

On January 27, 1936, Leroy was promoted at work and suffered chronic headaches. He visited Dr. Heck and got a pair of eyeglasses for $19.40. "We consider it an investment which will pay for itself times over and is right in line with my new job, which I like better every day."

On February 4, 1936, his son Sydney (my dad) was born at 3:32 p.m. at Asbury Hospital, weighing eight and a half pounds. "Mary did not feel a pain, except for the first few before she got to the hospital," he wrote. Ten days later, the new family returned home in an ambulance provided free to them as an advertisement for Rush Smith Funeral Home. "Sydney cried a little of the way home and then went to sleep the remainder of the journey. He behaved splendidly all night and we shall probably soon be used to waking up and feeding him at intervals during the night." He noted it had been another month of sub-zero temperatures. "The worst in a generation. We are certainly growing tired of seeing zero every day."

Mary always liked to tell the story of taking infant Syd to the doctor because she had to wake him up for the 2:00 a.m. feeding she knew infants needed and should cry for. The doctor told her to relax and enjoy her extra sleep. Syd would let her know when he was hungry.

Mary transformed into motherhood and applied her business skills to make ends meet during those lean Depression years. Each month, Leroy collected his paycheck from the Salina Supply Co. and cashed it to bring home to Mary, who then portioned it out for the month's needs and managed to find spare change for insurances and savings bonds for the children to use later in their college education. Every penny was registered and accounted for in a ledger book through the years.

*****

My Mother's Desk
Syd Rinard

As I was growing up, it was very common to find my mother sitting at her desk in the corner of the living room in our small house at 816 Merrill. I seldom took note of what she was doing there. If I ever thought about it at all, I probably assumed she was writing letters or something. Now I know that she was indeed writing letters and notes and such, but she was also doing more. Much more. I'll get back to that, but first I will describe the desk.

It is not clear when they bought the desk. It may have been bought new, early in 1935, before or after their wedding, along with other furniture they bought after hours one evening from a salesman they knew at a store in Salina. I think it was Montgomery Ward. Or it may have been a desk that was bought in December 1942 after getting a nice bonus. Whenever they bought that desk, I suspect that Mom was especially fond of it.

The desk itself was nothing unusual. It was a fairly small piece of furniture, but it stood tall and was finished in a dark walnut color. It had four turned legs, with enough space for the user's knees to fit underneath when seated. The sloped front lid pulled open and was supported in the flat position for writing by strong hinges located at both sides. Under the lid were two drawers, each as wide as the desk and deep enough to hold a book. Inside the desk were more small drawers and pigeonholes to store small items. People used to refer to this type of desk as a "secretary" or writing desk.

While she was growing up in Onaga, Kansas, her family did not have a lot of room for extra furniture, and she probably had to use the dining room table as her desk. Now in her own home, she had her own desk in its own location. It must have been wonderful for her. She could sit at it anytime she chose, open it up, and take care of family business or enter her own world of imagination. She did not write essays or books, but she managed her family's finances, kept lists of addresses, birthdays, Social Security numbers, etc.

No one else sat at that desk very often, if ever. We all knew it was risky because we might disturb the order of her notes or lose something. Dad was clumsy and would probably have broken something if he had tried to sit there, and we kids didn't have any reason to sit there. It was Mom's desk, and it was a window into her own world.

The main instrument that Mom used to store her information was her financial accounting book she kept in one of the desk drawers. The book is a hardback Stirling No. 96 "Cash" book, made for accounting, with lined blank pages intended for recording financial transactions. It has 500 numbered pages and is 12 inches tall, 7 1/2 inches wide, and 1 inch thick. It fits nicely in either of the two big drawers in the desk where she stored it after each use. It is still there.

She entered almost every penny of the family's income and expenses in the book. But for her, it was more than a simple factual accounting book. She used it to document her family's activities and its history. She did this not with text but with notations she carefully made along with the detailed financial records.

The book therefore served as a sort of diary where she made daily notes that were important to her. She wanted to remember little details that made up our daily lives. The key word here is "little." No expense was too small to include in the book. The first page was dated April 1935, and it included not only Dad's salary of $85 per month (which included a $5 per month raise for getting married) but also showed that they had spent 5 cents for thumbtacks. Every expenditure was neatly listed, no matter how small. If the expenditure was for a movie (or "show"), she often included its title and occasionally even the actor's names. She often identified which family members saw the movie.

The last entry she made in the book was on page 467. It was dated December 1956, nearly 22 years after she began using it. By this time, the book was literally falling apart from use. She then started another book, similar to the old one, except it only had 80 pages in it. She used the new book through 1958. She entered January 1959 then crossed it out. After that, she used a similar scheme using 3-ring binders to continue to document the family's expenses and activities.

The book also provided clues about Mom's personalities. Examples:

- She always had a strong sense of responsibility, and she especially felt responsible for her family's well-being. When we kids were young, she watched over us like a mother bear, feeding us and teaching us, and always ready to protect us from harm. Since these efforts required financial stability, during those hard times, she controlled the family finances with an iron fist. All major decisions about spending were made by her or approved by her. She kept her eye on future needs and made sure there would be enough money available when needed. The book was her main tool for this. She not only kept track of income and expenditures but she made notes in it that identified their purposes. It was always important to her to have all the information available and accurate so she could make her decisions with confidence.

- She was extremely orderly. The contents of the desk were meticulously arranged with everything in perfect order. Stamps, paper clips, envelopes, pens, ink, and similar items each had a place in the desk. She knew where everything was.
- This high degree of organization was no accident. It reflected her extremely active and structured mind. She wanted her information organized and readily available. The desk and its book provided her with storage and working space for such activities. (If computers had been available then, she probably would have used that technology because it allows super organization, but she really did not like complicated devices and probably would have fought it.)
- She was frugal (sometimes to a fault!). People used to ask them when they were going to buy a car. Dad's answer was that his first car was still "ore in the mountain." They wanted to minimize their debts, and in Salina, bus service was excellent, so buying a car would wait until they could buy one for cash, with no loan to pay off. That event did not happen until 1951. The family really needed a car by then, and the book showed that they could afford one. Then, and only then, they bought their first car, a new 1951 Plymouth. They paid cash for it. After that, they traded their car in for a new one every two years to avoid major overhaul costs.

Mostly because of Mom's discipline in handling the family finances, Dad's adequate but hardly spectacular salary was stretched further than anyone realized. She planned and saved for future needs, especially future college costs for the kids. We lived very comfortably, but not as luxuriously as we could have if she had been willing to spend more of the money we had at our disposal. Wary of banks and risky investments, she preferred to put their savings into government bonds and later into certificates of deposit (CDs) that were insured by the government. She skillfully moved sums of money between bonds, savings accounts, and active cash, depending on the needs. Only late in life, when I had to help her because of her failing eyesight, did she grudgingly allow me to move her money out of her beloved CDs (which could no longer provide enough interest income for her needs) and into other types of investments recommended by our financial counselor. Her main concern then was that she did not thoroughly understand how such investments work.

She still had her beloved old desk, but it alone was no longer able to serve her fully in such matters. She kept the desk until she died. I found it cluttered with unanswered Christmas cards and the like, but it was still organized, with postage stamps and pens ready for use.

I still have the desk. It is a constant reminder to think carefully before spending big money on things that may not be worth it, or at least to be responsible.

The book is still in the desk drawer where she kept it. Its binding has almost completely come apart. Its pages are loose, but they are all still there. Its contents still define our family history. I have reviewed the entire book and have selected excerpts from it for review by anyone interested. I arranged them chronologically on a "time line" from 1935 to 1956 as noted by Mom in the book. I added my own recollections of some of those events plus related events that I remembered because of Mom's notes.

I enjoyed doing this project. I felt responsible to use Mom's book and its desk home as a resource to deepen the family history a little while I am still able to do it. As the only survivor of the early years before the other kids were born or when they were still too young to remember, I am now the only witness to some of these events and the circumstances surrounding them.

Human history is ultimately dependent on human memory, which is never perfect. But fresh eyewitness history is always better than hearsay or after time has elapsed, so this "time line" is Mom's best memory of these events because it was written as they occurred.

(Written December 31, 2005)

> *Lori's side note: My grandma's desk now sits in my bedroom. It is still filled with some of her important things but mainly her large cashbook. I love to read through the fragile pages and take a step back into time. It is so fascinating to see what things used to cost and what was important to families. I treasure all of this. When Dad gave me the desk about ten years ago, he made it clear that it was to be taken well care of and to make sure it always stays in the family. My daughter Nicole has said she wants to keep the desk after I'm gone.*

*****

Dad was the oldest child (born February 4, 1936), then Phillip came along almost three years to the day after Dad (born January 31, 1939). Julia was born almost two years after that (November 13, 1940).

Grandpa wrote in his journals later, "Many years ago when our three children were kiddies and we live at Charles Street, I used to make up a story to tell to them each night when they went to bed in a common bedroom. Did you ever make up a story of sufficient interest every night, night after night, year after year? I tried all kinds of variances—serials, re-runs, trite empties, etc. Finally, I hit upon the use of 'And what do you think happened next?' whenever I exhausted my subject. Eagerly the kids broke in with their ideas as to what had happened, thus completing my story satisfactorily and getting me off the hook. Sure enough, finally the particular night came when, having matured sufficiently and no doubt gotten a bit bored with my tales, that familiar question was greeted with utter silence, that of the tomb. This went on for a minute or two, then Julia could contain herself no longer. Snickers burst through her confining palms. The boys joined her in derisive laughter. I think that was the end of their nightly bedtime stories. They had a lot of their mother in them!"

Mary, Leroy, Sydney, Julia, and Phil

During the fall of 1948, the family moved to a new home at 816 Merrill Street in Salina in the growing southern district of town. They acquired a loan from Leroy's parents to make the down payment, moved, and when the former home on Charles Street was sold, they repaid the loan.

Mary became active in her children's school and church activities—Boy Scouts, PTA, and Sunday school. She also became involved in the League of Women Voters for many years. City councilmen, the mayor, and even state representatives learned to pay attention when Mary appeared on the scene.

In the 1940s and 50s, both Leroy and Mary were active in Salina's St. John's Lutheran Church. Not just service attendees but

ONE LAST TRIP

Mary taught Sunday school to junior high age and Leroy led an adult group (The Builders) in Bible studies. His books on religion had lots of marginal notes in his hand. When the church janitor took a vacation, Leroy was the one who helped keep the church tidy. When a pastor was gone briefly, Leroy got to sub and give a sermon. We know he really enjoyed that!

Leroy became active in the Junior Chamber of Commerce (Jaycees) for many years and served as their president and also was on the board of directors for the YMCA. He assisted in sports as a coach of Phil's church youth basketball program at the YMCA. He also worked out with coworkers there to play volleyball and handball for years, determined never to lose. One night, he limped home, obviously hurt and embarrassed. He admitted that when he tried to step on the other player's foot, he tripped and fell flat on his face. The foot he had stepped on was his own, it turned out!

Leroy was also active with youth baseball leagues during summers, and Mary became the scorekeeper for the teams. He drove a specifically fitted truck for the Exline team to their out-of-town games and treated players to Cozy Inn hamburgers after local games, whether or not they won. During the American Legion League, he served as public announcer for games held at the Blue Jay Stadium in Oakdale Park.

They bought their first car, a Plymouth, in 1951 just in time for rain that never stopped, creating the flood of '51 that surrounded Salina for all but one highway. They were able to use the new car for family vacations to South Dakota and San Antonio (to visit Leroy's brother Clarence and family).

Television was not on Mary's list or budget or much interest. But Leroy had always been a movie fan, and TV was like a movie theater at home. Phil doesn't remember any discussion on the topic, but one day a boxy Emerson TV showed up. Leroy had been in Chicago at a supplier's convention and bought it (on his own, most likely). It wasn't in Mary's money ledger book, so he probably saved his allowance he was on to pay for it. Mary's account book shows a 1953 payment for the tall antenna on the roof needed because the only station they could ever get was eighty miles away north of Wichita. Dad was a junior in high school, and Phil was in eighth grade. Mary quickly adapted and warmed up to the TV.

I remember Grandpa's competitive nature. The stories I've heard about his handball and volleyball playing were notorious. He would do anything to win, and if that meant breaking someone's body parts, then so be it. Because of his determination to win, he eventually wrecked his knees. He was even like that with me when I was young. I remember playing board games with him, and if by some odd chance it looked like I might win the game, he would stand up and topple the table so the game would be preemptively over. He didn't do any of that to be mean. He didn't have a mean bone in his body. He just wanted and needed to win.

Leroy became a regular blood donor through the years, having a rarer blood type. He was called for emergencies and always answered willingly to help save someone's life. So the family often received gifts from grateful recipients. He had hoped to will his body organs to science when he died, but that did not work out. Dad also was a faithful blood donor, visiting the American Red Cross every eight weeks. His donor card was filled many times, and we lost track of how many gallons he gave. Phil is also a frequent blood donor, donating more than 120 pints of blood over the years. It must run in the family, because I donate blood regularly as well. Every time I do, I think of Dad and his generous gifts of life.

Grandpa was an avid writer. He was very spiritual and a deep thinker. This was an alter ego to his crazy and funny personality. I have an entire binder of his writings, along with Dad's, and they will be compiled into another book. Sometimes when Leroy was first married, his father would need assistance with his job as merchant policeman. Leroy would help him by walking the beat. On July 21, 1941, after working one night, he wrote this poem:

> I found God last night.
> I found Him in the turmoil of the busy city streets.
> Sophisticated glamour could not hide His subtle feats
> God was there, all right.
> I found God last night.

He showed His Presence to me in the wonders of the dark,
In stars above and moonlight, too, and meteoric spark
He gave us this sight.
I found God last night.
He flourished in the stranger's fleeting smile as he passed by,
The friendly smile of greeting born of love for Him on high
Love makes faces bright.
I found God last night.
I found Him in my pillow, wet with penitential tears.
In comfort He has given me these many sinful years
May my soul requite!
I found God last night
Though prayer remained unspoken, for I could not even start.
I knew that it was uttered from the anguish of my heart
It reached Heaven's height.

On June 6, 1959, Leroy's family left Salina for Beatrice, Nebraska, after working for the Salina Supply Co., for twenty-five years. He became the division sales manager for the Dempster Mill Manufacturing Co., and they built a ranch home at 1709 Sara Road in a new subdivision there.

In 1961, Leroy accepted a new managerial job at Cedar Rapids Pump and Supply Co., and the family moved to 440 Mayberry Drive NW in Cedar Rapids, Iowa. When the company sold out to Globe Machinery, Leroy remained on the staff in the same capacity until his retirement. He took daily walks from their home that bordered farmlands, a total of four miles from the subdivision out west to Stony Point Road and back home. Adventures occurred that he shared. "I carry a fist-sized rock in each hand," he said once, "to ward off any attacking dogs. Today as I walked along the shoulder of the road, a large cement truck came tearing toward me. As it passed by, it created such a gust as to blow my hat off my head. Instinctively, I grabbed for the hat to hold it on my head, but it had already gone. And my hand [with the rock in it still] came down most cruelly on my head. God, how it hurt! Imagine knocking oneself out on a walk!" But during these walks, his mind wandered freely, so sometimes he became disoriented and confused in directions to find his way back home.

At Cedar Rapids, Mary continued her avid interest in the League of Women Voters and made first-name inroads with politicians there. One day she knew that the mayor had been dawdling to sign papers that Mary felt were important regarding a project she endorsed. So she marched into his office, determined, and ignored a conference he was holding with another individual. She rummaged through papers on his desk and found the document then held it up. "Are you going to sign this into law or not?" By now, the mayor knew that the fastest way to rid of her was to go along with whatever she wanted, for it generally turned out that she was right. So the mayor signed it in front of her. They shook hands, and she walked out.

Mary loved to travel. Leroy didn't always enjoy the touring, so she sometimes would go alone. After she began to have eyesight problems in early 1970, she continued to travel on her own through tour groups to Europe, using her business sense dividends to pay for the travel. In November 1970, she traveled to Spain on the Mediterranean coast out of Malaga.

She enjoyed that vacation so much that in October 1973, she talked Leroy into joining her for a return trip to Malaga, Spain. Leroy had learned the Castilian dialect of Spanish in high school years, which he found useless in the Mediterranean coastal Spain today. Castilian refers to the primitive Old Spanish language, a predecessor to modern Spanish. Now it refers to the specific varieties of Spanish that is spoken in Northern and Central Spain. It also differs from the Latin American Spanish. He got so much spirit from the tour that one night at a going-away party, Leroy climbed on top of a table to do a Spanish dance with a rose clenched between his teeth. Too much sangria!

In the fall of 1974, Mary spent six weeks in Europe, and in 1975, she vacationed in Germany. In the summer of 1977, she and Leroy traveled to Greece. In 1979, Mary toured Great Britain, including the Lancaster Castle, where one of her Quaker ancestors had died in the dungeons during persecution days.

One of Grandpa's characteristic traits was to delay helping with repairs around the house. His favorite response would be, "I'll do it

ONE LAST TRIP

next Saturday." Then when the day arrived and he was reminded, he would say, "I said that I would do it *next* Saturday, didn't I? Today is *this* Saturday." Consequently, his choice of Saturday never arrived.

Infamous date in Rinard history: On November 26, 1981, the Rinard clan met in Cedar Rapids to celebrate Thanksgiving together. We always avoided going to Iowa for Christmas, as the weather was too unpredictable. We would sometimes do Christmas at the same time, with Grandma even putting up the tree and doing gifts. Her Thanksgiving dinner was traditional and delicious, with all the fixings. When we were stuffed to the gills with turkey and dressing, she would transform what was left of the bird into turkey salad and send jars of it home for all of us to enjoy for sandwiches for days to come. After dinner was over that evening, it was decided to take family photos. As Dad and Phil struggled to set up their tripods and timer-operated camera, Julia grabbed her small movie camera to capture the awaiting family.

Flash back a few hours before dinner. Grandpa and I were sitting at the kitchen table laughing and having fun. I was fourteen at the time. There was a can of potato chips sitting on the table, so I opened the can and pulled out two chips and put them in my mouth, forming a duckbill. Grandpa started laughing so hard he almost fell out of his chair. Being the jokester that he was, he tried his best to duplicate it but struggled so hard to get it right.

After dinner, we managed to get a few nice photos taken before everything got out of control. Aunt Julie said, "It's movies—move and show action." A spontaneous result was to clown around in typical Rinard fashion. Grandpa grabbed the can of chips and passed them out to everyone to make the duckbills. Everyone attempted this feat, and that would eventually lead to holding fingers with the thumb and index finger in a circle over the eyes, Junior Birdman fashion, they called it. For five minutes, the film rolled while the antics made family grab their sides in uproarious laughter. We all got a copy of it, and I laugh loudly watching it, remembering that crazy evening! That filming captured the last time the complete family was together.

Thanksgiving 1981

Leroy turned seventy years old on September 5, 1983. We had a big family reunion in St. Louis to celebrate the weekend, as well as Dad and Mom's twenty-fifth wedding anniversary.

ONE LAST TRIP

Grandpa's seventieth birthday (1983)

For their fiftieth wedding anniversary in March of 1985, the entire family gathered at our house in Kansas City for a small party. We had made them a scrapbook memory book, and many friends included cards, notes, and stories from throughout the years. Dad put a note in: "You gave each of us something more valuable than we can imagine—your example. By your example, we saw the real meaning of such words as responsibility, morality, dependability, fairness—the list could go on and on. And over all this, you planted in us a faith in things on a higher plane than our existence here on earth."

On January 6, 1986, Leroy suffered a stroke and passed away from the complications on January 23. He died at St. Luke's Hospital in Cedar Rapids, Iowa. He was cremated, and Mary took his ashes on his daily four-mile walk and scattered them along the way.

>Obituary for Leroy Martin Rinard—*Onaga Herald*, February 2, 1986:
>
>Leroy M. Rinard, 72, of 440 Mayberry Drive, NW, Cedar Rapids, IA; died Thursday, January 23, in St. Luke's Hospital at Cedar Rapids, following a short illness. He was born 5 Sep 1913 at Salina, KS; and married Mary Alda Kelly there 31 Mar 1935.
>
>Mr. Rinard was a Lutheran, a graduate of Kansas Wesleyan School of Business, and was in the wholesale plumbing and heating business most of his life. He moved to Cedar Rapids in 1961 to manage Cedar Rapids Pump & Supply and was with the Globe Machinery for seven years before retiring in 1979.
>
>Surviving in addition to his wife, are a daughter, Julia Scott, Bloomington, IL; two sons, Syd of Shawnee, KS; and Phil of Los Alamos, NM; a sister, Jeanette Brandt, Kansas City; and one granddaughter.
>
>The body was cremated. A memorial service was held Sunday, February 2 at Faith Lutheran Church in Kansas City. Mr. Rinard was a brother-in-law of Mr. and Mrs. Speck Kelly of Onaga and Mrs. Ruth Fields, Havensville.

A family memorial service was held at Faith Lutheran Church in Prairie Village, Kansas, on February 2, 1986. This was our home church, and our pastor did the service. A memorial stone was placed in Gypsum Hill Cemetery in Salina, Kansas, in our family plot.

Leroy's sister, Jeanette stated, "In our youth there were many discussions about religion between us, and I knew then religion would always be a number one priority in his life. I think he always felt his calling was to be a minister. But perhaps God knew he could be just as effective as a layman, and he certainly was with his gift of words and great personality. He was so well liked and had such a caring way that I am sure he helped many people in their quest for God. When one sees that all through his life he did what he could do to further God's kingdom, we know it was true. He was truly a good man."

In 1988, Mary sold the house on Mayberry Drive and moved into an apartment, also in Cedar Rapids.

Mary took her most memorable vacation in 1990. She traveled with a senior bus tour to New Orleans at the time of Mardi Gras. They stayed on the fringes of the French Quarter. I wish I could have been a fly on that tour! I can imagine Grandma dancing and laughing at the world's biggest party! While she was there, she decided that when she died, she would like to have a New Orleans sendoff with "When the Saints Go Marching In."

At my wedding, May 7, 1993

In January of 1995, we celebrated Mary's eightieth birthday. All her children flew in, including me and Kevin. I was seven months pregnant at the time with my son, Alex. It was cold and snowy, but we had the best time with the usual Rinard craziness. We ate a huge meal at the Amana Colonies and helped her with some projects around her apartment, but it was a little bittersweet because it was near the anniversary of Grandpa's death.

Even though her eyesight was failing due to macular degeneration, she continued to research our family history and made a few trips to Canada to visit some places of her roots. She found a place called Backus Mills and, after some research, discovered that the people who it belonged to were part of the family. Early in the 1800s, the Backhouse family left Leeds, England, and settled in the forested wilderness of Toronto. *Backhouse* meant a separate kitchen building to keep the living spaces cooler and not get burned down. They farmed, created a pond for waterpower, and built a gristmill. England had used up its own tall trees for ship's masts, so the Backhouses built a sawmill and provided planks and tall tree trunks to England and most famously for some heavy-duty locks at a new Canadian canal. Around 1900, the matriarch changed the family name to a more respectable Backus. Today the complex of buildings is preserved as a national historic site—Backus Heritage Conservation Area. You can visit the Backhouse Historic Site, which includes fifteen historic buildings—the Backus family homestead, octagonal schoolhouse, country church, local history museum, and the 1798 Backhouse Grist Mill, where they produced stoneground flour. There is the Conservation Education Centre and a large park offering fishing, picnicking, and camping. You can read more about it by going to this website: www.lprca.on.ca

Mary and Phil, his wife Carole, and Julia traveled to Port Rowan in Ontario, Canada, for an annual family reunion to meet some of our descendants and tour the gristmill and home sites throughout the countryside. This is where Mary's grandfather separated from the family and moved to Kansas to start a new life. This trip fulfilled a lifelong search for her roots that were unknown until then.

In August of 1995, Mary's health began to decline after a fall during a walk broke her shoulder. It did not heal properly, and she lived with chronic pain. She experienced a light stroke the next summer, so she agreed to move to Kansas City to be closer to Dad. She

ONE LAST TRIP

lived in an apartment in a retirement community. Here, she befriended a man named Garland. He drove the van to take residents shopping and was a general helpmate around the facilities. He provided religious activities for the residents, and Mary loved his singing voice.

After a small heart attack, another fall with compression fractures, and becoming legally blind from the macular degeneration, she suffered a massive stroke on May 10, 2003, and died peacefully shortly afterward.

A memorial service was held by our family for Mary at the Garden Villa Retirement Apartments in Lenexa, Kansas, where she lived. Her friend Garland conducted the service and ended it with "When the Saints Go Marching In," as Mary had once requested. We took her ashes to the Kelly Family plot at Neuchatel, Kansas Cemetery, and buried them next to her father's grave site.

I miss these two special people so very much. They made me laugh. They displayed generosity and humbleness. But most of all, they taught me what love is. I can't wait to see them again one day.

Grandpa and Grandma, August 1982

CHAPTER 6

Day 3
Tuesday, August 7, 2018

New Mexico, Colorado (Ouray)

It is Tuesday morning, and I have just left Los Alamos, New Mexico. I stayed at my Uncle Phil and Aunt Carole's house last night. It was really fun to see them, as it's been quite a while since we've been together. We had a nice visit. We got to catch up on a lot of stuff and tell some old stories. My Aunt Carole made me a homemade meal, which was pretty awesome! It was nice to sit down and have that. And she made cinnamon rolls this morning, so I cannot complain about the food. It's been pretty good! They were very nice to have me there. Phil even checked my tires this morning, to make sure they were all filled up. Plus, he drew me a map of how to get out and where the good gas stations were, so God bless him. He was taking care of me! I stopped at the gas station that he told me to, filled up, got a drink, and now I'm heading north to Colorado! My first stop will be Durango. I'm about three and a half to four hours away from there. It's a very pretty day… sun shining, no clouds, about seventy-eight degrees, but there's no humidity, so it's really dry. I'm going to have to get used to this. I couldn't ask for a nicer day. It's kind of an odd landscape here. The mountains are close by, but we're still in that desert mesa type of landscaping.

My Aunt Carole has advanced degrees in home economics. She is so talented in crafting and cooking. She taught at Emporia State University in Kansas until she and Phil moved out west. She does needlework that is showcased all over the country, and she designs and constructs costumes for the Santa Fe Opera. I remember when I was younger how she would cook up a storm for us when we went to visit. The thing I remember most were her homemade sopaipillas. We would watch her make the dough, toss it in the hot oil, and be amazed every time it would puff up like a pillow! She would cover it with cinnamon sugar, and we would eat them all up with dripping honey. My mouth is watering just thinking of them! Dinner last night consisted of porcupine meatballs, green beans, pistachio fruit dip, and ice cream for dessert. Phil said he specifically requested the meatballs. This was a dish Dad loved as well. They consist of ground beef, rice, and seasonings. Once they are formed into meatballs, they're cooked in a skillet or baked in the oven then covered with tomato sauce. My mom used to make these a lot, and I haven't had them in years. I really enjoyed them at this meal, and it brought back many memories. When I got married, her gift to me was a typed recipe book of her favorite and best recipes. I really treasure that! With her permission, here is her recipe for the sopaipillas:

Aunt Carole's Famous Sopaipillas

1 cup *less* 2 Tbsp. warm water
1 pkg. dry yeast
3 Tbsp. sugar
1 tsp. salt
1 egg

2 Tbsp. shortening
3 cups flour
Fat for frying
Honey

Rinse a medium-sized bowl with hot water. Measure warm (115°F) water into it. Sprinkle with yeast. Add sugar and salt. Stir until all are thoroughly dissolved. Beat egg and add together with shortening and half the flour. Beat hard 2 minutes or until smooth. With hands, work in the remaining flour. Continue working (kneading) until dough is smooth and elastic. Place dough in a greased bowl, turning once. Cover with cloth and allow to rise in warm place until double in bulk. Punch down. At this point, the dough may be covered with plastic wrap and refrigerated for up to four days. Allow dough to come to room temperature. Using 1/4 to 1/3 of the dough, roll on floured surface until 1/4-inch thick. Cut into 3- or 4-inch squares. Fry in hot (375°F–400°F) fat, turning until puffed and light brown on both sides. Drain on paper towels. Serve with honey. Break open and pour honey into hollow.

My visit with Phil and Carole was wonderful, as we exchanged a lot of stories about Dad. I really wanted Dad to get one more chance to be with his brother. We talked about the family cemetery plot in Salina, Kansas, and how I will be spending a day there on my way home. I plan to visit the plot and talk with the office about getting a memorial stone for Dad. Phil printed off a map of Salina streets for me and highlighted where the cemetery is (including where our family area is in the cemetery) and where the two houses are that they lived in when they were growing up. I will be driving by those for sure, and I will be spending some time with Dad's best friend, Jack. I feel that will be a fitting way to end this trip!

I am now back on the road, and my excitement is building as I head toward Colorado! I've got a couple of hours left of New Mexico driving then have scheduled a couple of stops before I call it a day. The first stop is Durango, where I'll find a grocery store and stock up on a few things. I will stop off at Silverton, where the passenger narrow gauge railroad ends (it begins in Durango). That is a special place for Dad—he loved the old steam locomotives. This stop is an absolute must. After Silverton, I will finish the drive at Ouray, where I have a bed-and-breakfast reserved.

> *I exited off the main road to make a stop because I saw this really neat pull off. It's called Echo Amphitheater, and it's part of the Carson National Forest down here. It's this really cool mountain feature that looks like a round amphitheater carved out of the middle of it. It's big…really big! Reading the sign briefly, it has to do with the water that has run off the top of the little mountain there and formed this round amphitheater carved right into it. When I pulled in and I was getting out of my car, I was grabbing my camera and saw this older gentleman. He was near me, standing by his little station wagon. He said something like, "Are you interested in paintings?" And I said, "No, I'm here to take pictures." We got to visiting, and he's actually an artist. He went to the Art Institute in New Mexico back in, I believe he said, 1941. He told me he's ninety-three years old. He was so cute. He was wearing jeans and a cowboy hat, and he just drives around and shows people his paintings. Evidently, he was quite a salesman as well, because I bought one from him! Just a cute little painting, it wasn't that much money. Then when I bought it, he gave me a second one for free. He said, "Just pick one of these. I'm just going to give you one of these for free." He was very sweet. We talked for quite a long time. I told him what I was doing with Dad, and he shared that he did a similar thing when his wife passed away a few years ago. He's from this area, but he travels around, and he gets inspired by the scenery. And he loves to paint. He still paints, even to this day. He*

had his paints and stuff set up in the back of his car. When I gave him the money for the paintings, he called it his traveling money so he can get gas to drive around. It just shows that you can meet the most interesting people when you're traveling, and it's fun to hear their stories. All you have to do is look for those opportunities!

The Echo Amphitheater is located near Abiquiu, New Mexico. It is carved into a sandstone cliff. You can walk a short paved walkway from the parking lot to get very close to this enormous amphitheater, where you can yell and hear the echoes all around it. There is a legend attached to it that it's the site where a group of Navajo executed a family of settlers and that it's their blood flowing down from the top and staining the rock. There are actually some vertical stripes made by streaks of minerals that looks like blood. The entire cliff area is formed from horizontal striations, which make it really easy to see these bloodlike markings. The walk was really pretty, with all kinds of plants and wildflowers. It was an easy walk, which was good, as this really is the first day I've been in the altitude and not used to it yet. The different layers of the cliffs are stunning and so interesting. I'm glad I made the quick decision to pull off here and check it out! That is what is nice about traveling alone. I can stop whenever and wherever I want, and no one will complain!

I was just listening to the radio, and they were talking about how yesterday there was anywhere from golf ball-sized to baseball-sized hail in the corridor between Colorado Springs and Denver. I was just sitting here thinking that most likely, if I had driven the Kansas way to get here, I would have been there right at that time. Yikes! God had his hand in this to keep me safe! I know he's going to keep me safe now, because obviously he brought me around the southern route to avoid that. Wow! That's big hail…scary stuff! I haven't seen any bad weather at all. I've had sunny, beautiful skies. Yesterday, as I was driving west, I did see off to the north that there were some really dark clouds, so maybe that's from that storm system. I don't know...but thank you, God, for keeping me safe!

I do feel God's hands guiding me on this trip. I have not had any fear, car problems, or even close calls. I believe that every decision I have made so far, even before I left home, has been directed by him. I am confident that I am doing the right thing, the thing that God has asked me to do. When you follow God's directions, he will keep you safe!

I also feel Dad with me. I feel his smiles and his laughter, and I know he's so happy that I am taking him to rest eternally in the most beautiful spot on this earth. My heart is full of love and happiness, not sorrow. He is also protecting me, just as he did in life. I will never forget this trip, and I can only smile every time I think of it!

We just crossed over the border to Colorado! We have made it to Colorado, and I'm so excited. And I already feel the difference. It's like I'm home, and I'm ready to have some fun!

Dad, we have made it! The trip that I've been planning since January. All the preparations, reservations, and double- and triple-checking everything has finally paid off. We are in Colorado! I am going to take you to your favorite places one last time! This is an honor for me to be able to do this for you. You brought me here all those years, now it's my turn! I love you, Dad! I hope you're having a fabulous trip!

Colorado—the Centennial State. It became a state on August 1, 1876, and named for the Colorado River. The state animal is the Rocky Mountain bighorn sheep, and the state flower is the Rocky Mountain columbine. The capital is Denver. Colorado has forests, plains, mesas, canyons, rivers, and desert lands but is most known for the fabulous Rocky Mountains. It has over fifty mountain peaks that rise above fourteen thousand feet above sea level. Somewhere around 70 percent of everyone who lives in Colorado live on the east side of the Continental Divide, which is also called the Front Range. The Continental Divide goes along the tops of the Rockies. On the west side of the divide, water runs to the southwest via the Colorado River and eventually into the gulf of California. From the east side of the divide, water flows the other direction toward the east coast. I will be spending almost all my vacation on the west side of the divide. The areas are beautiful and not as crowded.

> *I'm in Durango, Colorado, right now. I stopped at a supermarket to pick up a few things so I can just stay in my hotel tonight and eat a quick dinner...some sandwich stuff, things like that. I am heading up towards Silverton and eventually will get to Ouray. I just went through their historic downtown area, and I'm going to get back out of town and work my way up to Silverton!*

Durango was built around 1880 to serve the San Juan mining district. The Durango and Silverton Narrow Gauge Railroad starts here. There are some famous sites near here, including Mesa Verde National Park and Chimney Rock National Monument. If I had more time, I would visit these places, but for this trip, I have to keep going to get everything else in.

> *I just got outside of Durango, and I noticed that up ahead the mountains were difficult to see. It's sunny out, so I figured it's probably smoke because of the forest fires or the big fire that was near Durango. I think it's called the 416 Fire. It's been burning since the beginning of June out this direction, so I thought maybe that's what it is. And now I'm a few miles closer to it, and I can smell it. So it's filling the valley here with smoke. I don't plan to get out and walk around until I get through this. I believe once I get*

ONE LAST TRIP

to Silverton, it should be all cleared up because it's not in that area.

Colorado has had a very dry summer so far, and they had a mild winter, so there have been quite a few big fires burning around the state this summer. The 416 Fire started just a few miles from Durango and has been burning substantially on the west side of Highway 550, which is what I'm driving on right now. As of right now, it is pretty much contained, and I don't see any real evidence of it, except for this bit of smoke in the valley. They had this highway closed for a while, but I'm glad to see that we are all clear and I can get through with no problems!

I am enjoying this drive. I'm getting deeper and deeper into the mountains. The roads are starting to get hillier and curvier. This is fun driving! One thing I'm noticing is that every now and then, especially when the road is climbing, there is a lane added to the right for slow-moving traffic. It's a great thing to have, as there are a lot of large trucks and campers out here, and they just can't keep the same speed as cars. Also, people are friendly drivers. That's a nice change from where I come from. Drivers who are aware that they are slowing traffic down will pull off to let everyone pass. I've been doing that myself, as I am enjoying the scenery and the drive and am in no hurry to get to my next point.

I see I am getting close to Silverton. I finally feel that I am officially on my vacation! Not that what I've done and seen so far doesn't count, it's just that this town is where Dad's heart and love was, outside of Tincup. This is a place where I can bring Dad, and we can make one more memory.

I just popped in to take a quick drive through Silverton...just to kind of check things out. I'm heading up now to Ouray. I couldn't check in to my bed-and-breakfast until five o'clock, so I needed to kill some time. But I've decided that the lighting is kind of weird—it's 4:12 p.m. right now—and I don't think I'm going to get very good photos on this

Million Dollar Highway drive…mainly because of the sun being in a weird place. I'm going to drive back down here again tomorrow and see if I can get some good morning pictures. I'll check out the train schedule too and see what time the trains come in. But it is just as gorgeous as ever here. I love the smell. I love the pine trees. I love the aspen trees. I love these little windy mountain roads. I'm in my happy place!

I spent a few minutes in Silverton. I first stopped at the visitor's center to gather some information about the area and the train schedule. By the time I got here, the trains had all left to head back to Durango, so I didn't get to see any of them. Since the trains are what Dad loved the most, I knew I had to come back tomorrow morning to see them. I parked my car and did a quick walk around so I would know exactly where I needed to be to have the best view of the trains coming in. I haven't been here in at least ten years, but everything was surprisingly familiar. I knew exactly where the tracks are and all the landmarks I remembered.

Silverton used to be a silver mining camp in the 1870s. The elevation is nine thousand feet above sea level. There is no mining done there anymore, and it's mostly a tourist area. What is neat about Silverton is that they have not upscaled their little town. It has the feel of the older west, when it was bustling with miners. It is a very charming town, and although its main economy is tourism, it doesn't feel that way. Depending on what time of day you are there determines the number of folks you will run into. A few of us will drive there as a destination, but the main tourists come in on the trains. They spend a few hours in town shopping for souvenirs or grabbing a bite to eat. Everyone who lives and works here is very nice and welcoming. There are some people who stop here while they are in the middle of multiday hiking, mountain biking, or motorcycling across the area.

They are most famous for being the end destination for the Durango and Silverton Narrow Gauge Railroad. There are other things to do here if you have the time. You can tour an old mine or an old mill, and there are dozens of fun restaurants, cafés, and bars. Of course, I love just walking around and capturing it in photographs!

It's a no decision that I will be back tomorrow. I have plenty of time in my schedule tomorrow and really want to spend quality time here and not feel rushed. So I'm turning my car back onto the highway and heading north to Ouray, where I'm staying the night.

The section of Highway 550 between Silverton and Ouray is also called the Million Dollar Highway. It was built in the 1880s to transport ore from Silverton to Ouray. It is considered to be one of the most scenic drives in America. I believe it to be one of the most beautiful drives anywhere. The only one I can think of that's equally as spectacular I will be driving in a couple of days. This road has everything wonderful—mountains, trees, waterfalls, and rock formations. The Million Dollar Highway is about twenty-five miles long and a part of the San Juan Skyway Scenic Byway. The last ten to twelve miles closest to Ouray is so incredibly beautiful, but the road can be challenging and sometimes a bit scary. It goes through a gorge and has steep cliffs and narrow lanes. Some places don't even have guardrails. Sometimes the road is cut right into the mountainside. If you look closely, you can see some old evidence of mines sticking out through the rock. Every curve in the road gives you a new amazing view. There is a pass called Red Mountain Pass that you drive over, and the climb up and down have a lot of what are called hairpin curves. The highway is open all year, but there are snow sheds built into parts of the road to protect it from snow avalanches. There are a couple of folklores of how it was named. One of them is that it cost a million dollars a mile to build. No one really knows for sure. But the truth is that it is absolutely spectacular and breathtaking!

I am taking my time driving this amazing road. There is so much to see and take in and places to pull off and get some fabulous photos! I'm in no hurry and feeling glad that I will be driving this again tomorrow. It's just too pretty to only drive once!

I just pulled off at a lookout where you can see an area called the Red Mountains. It was an old mining area. There is some really neat mining stuff that was left here. Some little structures...things like that. The soil on the top of these mountains are these spectacular different colors of reds and oranges. Hence, that's why they are called the Red Mountains. Just gorgeous!

The Red Mountains are a set of three mountain peaks in the San Juan Mountains, about five miles south of Ouray. They are called that because of the reddish iron ore that rests on the surface. They are tall—all of them are over twelve thousand feet. Because I was here in the late afternoon, the sun was at just the perfect angle to pop those amazing bright reds and oranges. It is called the Red Mountain Mining District, and the old mines are still here, although they are no longer working.

I parked in the pull-off area where I had a really great view of the entire area. The main mine at this area is called the Idarado Mine. They say it was still doing a small amount of mining even in the 1970s, but it is closed for good now. But you can still see quite a bit of the remaining structures—a large wooden trestle, tunnel entrance, and several old wood houses. It is so interesting to see, and I love to imagine how it looked and sounded a hundred years ago when it was in full swing! I am very intrigued by mining history, especially from the late 1880s with the big gold rush consuming our country. This was a neat spot to stop!

Right before I arrived in Ouray, there is a big curve around a mountain and a large pull off on the left. I parked there and walked over to the edge, and from there, I saw a fantastic view looking down over the town of Ouray. You could see everything, as it's a neat little town nestled right in a valley surrounded by mountains. The main street is easy to find, and the smaller grid-like streets radiate from it.

ONE LAST TRIP

Ouray

We've stayed here many times when I was growing up and also as an adult with my own family. We always stayed at the same hotel, and I remember some of the funny nights we had here with Mom and Dad and Stacey (one of my best friends who used to travel with us to Tincup). Mainly, our experience with having an actual bathroom with running hot water so we could take a really good long shower after being in Tincup for several days with only pumped almost freezing well water. We would steam up that bathroom so much you couldn't see anything! The town is full of natural hot springs, and every hotel had hot tubs filled with this amazing spring water. Ouray also has a huge public swimming pool in the city park filled with all-natural spring water that we have used a time or two. Both the hotel hot tubs and the swimming pool were so relaxing and always just the right temperature. We could also catch up on our TV viewing as Tincup had none. Our city girl would come out of us for that evening, even though we adored roughing it in Tincup.

I thought about staying in that same hotel from the past, just for the memories, but my online search discovered what looks to be a very charming bed-and-breakfast near there. I've stayed in B&Bs before, but it's always been with Kevin, never by myself. However, this place seemed to be calling my name, and it has the top reviews, so I'm going to give it a try.

As I'm driving into town, so many memories are starting to flood in. And just like with Silverton, the streets are all absolutely familiar, and I don't even need a map to find my way around. The last time Kevin and I were here by ourselves without the kids, we rented a jeep for the day and ventured up and around Engineer Pass. This drive was terrifying yet spectacular at the same time! The pass is close to thirteen thousand feet above sea level, way above the tree line. It's narrow, rocky, and steep. At one point, we were face up the mountain and spinning our wheels, thinking that this was how it was all going to end for us. Luckily, Kevin used his excellent driving skills and the lowest gear in the jeep, and we crawled our way to the top. The view from the summit was indescribable; however, breathing that incredibly thin air was quite difficult. On the way down, we maneuvered through the woods (once we got down to an altitude they could grow again!). We had to drive the steep path down over enormous boulders on the trail, and at certain points, I had to get out of the jeep to help steer Kevin safely around. I've never experienced such a bumpy drive, but it was so much fun that we didn't mind the sore backs and bodies once we returned back to town.

It has been a long day, and I'm ready to get unloaded and put my feet up and relax for the evening. I have pulled up to my bed-and-breakfast, and I have to say, my first impression is wow! This place is so quaint and charming. I can't wait to get inside!

Chapter 7
Sydney Rinard

The Early Years

Sydney Rinard was born on February 4, 1936, at Asbury Hospital, Salina, Kansas, weighing eight and a half pounds.

According to Mary's cash ledger, in February of 1936, they spent $0.90 to send two telegrams and $1.25 for cigars. The hospital bill was $57.80. The doctor charged them $60.00.

He was named for the hero in Dickens's *Tale of Two Cities*, Sydney Carton.

His brother Phil (my uncle) was born on January 31, 1939, and his sister Julia (my aunt) was born on November 13, 1940.

Dad was baptized at St. John's Evangelical Lutheran Church in Salina on April 12, 1936, and confirmed on April 2, 1950. St. John's was where the entire Rinard clan had attended church for each generation that lived in Salina. Grandma told stories of Dad drawing cartoons in the margins of the church bulletin during the Sunday service. Grandpa was always busy each Sunday with ushering or other jobs to help out, so Grandma had to find a way to keep three little kids quiet for an hour. She usually resorted to animal crackers and keeping them all separated from one another, or giggling would be inevitable.

Dad's Early Years

Phil recorded his recollections of Dad:

> I assume his baby immunizations were the same that I got three years later:
>
> - Whooping Cough (at 6 months old)
> - Smallpox (at 9 months old and at 6 years old)
> - Diphtheria and Tetanus (at 1-year-old and at 6 years old)
>
> Like all kids in those days we went through the standard childhood illnesses of the era before immunizations common today were developed:
>
> - Whooping Cough (I [Phil] had it near the age of three, despite the immunization), I got Measles twice at age 4 and 5, Mumps at age 6, and Chicken Pox at age 6.
> - Dad had Chicken Pox in June 1945 while at the same time I [Phil] had Measles. We recovered and were both well for only one day before swapping diseases.
>
> Doctors in the mid-1940's came to your house when you had these childhood illnesses. Dad [Grandpa] would bring home some simple dime-store toy or joke booklet each day we spent in bed; they were welcome treats.
>
> Of greater concern in those days was polio. The chances of getting it were not great but the consequences of getting in were horrendous [paralysis, expensive recovery with months or years in an iron lung, death]. I remember when my parents bought polio insurance from a sales-

man in our living room. I've seen an ad in an old *Salina Journal* newspaper for polio insurance for $5. That was much more money than in today's dollars and our parents bought it for all three of us [$15 total], given the huge expenses that could arise without it. *(Lori's side note: $15 in 1948 = $158 in 2018, the equivalent of spending $474 today for their insurance.)*

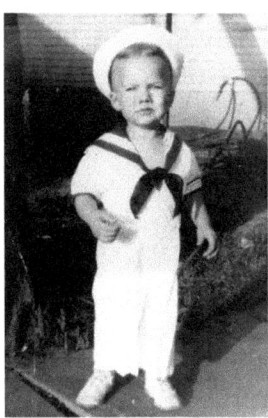

In June 1940, four-year-old Dad was roller skating with some neighborhood kids on their sidewalks one night. They were skating very fast into the fireplug on the corner by Dad's house, grabbing the top of it, then swinging around and returning back where they had come from. In the dark light of the single streetlight bulb hanging in the street intersection, Dad finally missed grabbing the fireplug and hit it with his left eyebrow. He ran into the house with blood streaming down his face. Grandma took him to the doctor, and he stitched it up.

In July 1948, Dad, Phil, and Julia all got their tonsils removed the same day. The main reason was to remove Phil's tonsils, which were enlarged as a result of a recent bout with rheumatic fever. Dad's tonsils were not bad, but his adenoids were giving him trouble, and their removal was part of a tonsillectomy. Probably they included Julia in the procedure as a precautionary measure. The three of them spent the night before the surgery in the hospital in the same room. A lot of horseplay happened that night, not so much sleep. In the morning, Dad went first with no problems. They used ether, which Dad remembers smelling terrible. Phil took extra time due to stubborn bleeding, but otherwise, there were no problems. Not as much horseplay that night. They gave the kids their tonsils in little jars to take home. Dad drew cartoon pictures of the operating room.

Dad, Grandpa, and Phil

A favorite game for the kids to play with Grandpa was called airplane at bedtime. Grandpa would hoist one of the kids up onto his shoulder. They would stretch out their legs behind him and stick their arms out to the sides to become an airplane nearly six feet above the floor. He would carry them and zoom around the rooms. They would have to readjust themselves to get through the doorways. The flight destination always ended up at bed for a crash landing.

Phil, Julia, and Dad

Here is Dad's account of their movie watching in the 1940s: "In those days before TV, movies were the latest form of entertainment. We went to a lot of them, at least 1 or 2 per month. I remember lots of cowboy movies with Roy Rogers, Hopalong Cassidy, Gene Autry. And the classic Disney animated films. It was important enough to Mom [in her 1941 records] that she listed each one by title. One was special enough to list the actors and to note the fact that it was Julia's first movie."

During World War II, Salina was chosen for an air base to train pilots (Smoky Hill Air Force Base). Grandpa's work to help supply plumbing and heating equipment to this all-new base gave him a deferment from the military. He and Grandma taught first aid classes to enlisted men at the also new Camp Phillips (where German and Italian POWs were also kept). Church members would "adopt" servicemen and bring them into their homes. Dad's family had two such Army men stay with them. Dad and Phil also played with commercial wartime games. Playing cards or flash cards had outlines of German and Japanese airplanes; they were amused by the funny names but never spotted any enemy planes. Another game taught them to be bombardiers. Marbles as bombs fell through a tube (bomb bay) onto targets in the game's cardboard box showing targets. Happily, nothing ever actually exploded, just flipped over if hit. They never had to practice "duck and cover" exercises at school, as Smoky Hill Air Force Base was for training pilots in the middle of the country, not a base where attacks would originate.

Phil tells me, "I remember many happy times playing with Syd in the large playroom involving Tinker Toys, an erector set, and a collection of wood blocks of several standard shapes. We could build all sorts of things from our imaginations, tear them apart and build something else. Good experience for an engineer, and fun for me too!"

ONE LAST TRIP

Grade School Years

Dad went to K-6 grade school classes at South Park Elementary School. It has since been torn down. It was on another corner of the same block as their house on Charles Street.

Dad and Phil inherited two adult-sized bicycles, most likely their parents had used them in their earlier years. The family did not buy a car until 1951. A bus route went past their house on Charles, and they walked a lot. Their church was a three-quarter-mile walk and downtown was about a mile. Their bikes were different from each other. Dad's had two springs above the front wheel that were to absorb shocks. He would often hit something hard enough to jar the springs off their short mounts, and he would then wrestle them back in place before being able to ride further. This was an early example of his engineering mind toward equipment; cars were in his near future.

Dad had a lot of friends—Max Griffin (he was artistic, as was Dad), Richard Bills, Henry Gehrke, and Jerry Weis. Later, he became very close to Jack Gebhart. Jack was another car buff but lived a little bit farther away from Dad. Grandma ran a Cub Scout den that included most of the nearby kids and more. Dad was in Boy Scouts for about a year until dropping out because of a poor (if not suspicious) scoutmaster and a disastrous weekend campout hit by a storm.

Summers in Salina were brutal for heat and humidity. There was a large municipal swimming pool a little over a mile away from their house—not a bad ride on their bicycles when they got old enough. But when they were too young to go places on their own, their own backyard was a playground. Grandma would put out a sprinkler to water the grass, and the kids would put on their bathing suits and run around in the spray.

Popular yard games involved toy pistols, cowboys, and the like. Getting shot and killed meant falling down for a few seconds before a resurrection. In 1949, Salina celebrated '49 Days and the California Gold Rush. Salina didn't even exist in 1849, but the city was promoting itself as a commercial and fun regional center. The kids got new cowboy hats and kerchiefs and spring-loaded shotguns that shot nothing but made some noise.

Kids love candy, and Dad, Phil, and Julia were no exceptions. Grandma would buy a bag of jellybeans for the three of them to share. They would equally count out the jelly beans, then Phil would trade the black ones for other colors. It was a very precise process.

When Phil was too big to sleep in a crib anymore, he and Dad used a trundle bed. Dad had the main bed, and Phil used the half that could be rolled under Dad's part to save space during the day. One night before going to sleep, Dad kindly pointed out that if they had a flood, Phil, being a few inches lower, would drown first.

The living room of their house had a hardwood floor, and it needed waxing now and then. Grandma would spread a layer of wax around and then tie rags to the kid's feet. They had a great time "skating" around the room as if on ice. The corners didn't get polished very well, but they didn't care. Grandma later said that they didn't get carpeting put in because it wouldn't last long under their busy feet.

Dad and his friends liked to tie cloths around their necks and be superheroes who ran around with their capes flapping behind them. One day a couple of girls their ages walked down their sidewalk, and the heroes became mock villains who pretended to chase them. The girls screamed and ran away, they never saw them again. They played a version of kick the can after dark where a single-bulb streetlight hung over the intersection. They would start with the can under the light, then it would get kicked around and eventually into the dark.

Dad wrote, drew, and ate with his left hand but threw a ball and batted righthanded. Phil could shoot baskets with either hand, and their Uncle Clarence was left-handed as well.

ONE LAST TRIP

Sometime in late grade school, it was obvious that Dad could draw better than anyone else in the family. My grandparents sent him to a local person who gave art classes. Decades later, Dad said the judgment was that he could be an illustrator but would never be a "real" artist. He stopped taking lessons but continued to "illustrate," especially with his friend Max, who was equally as talented. The two would draw together for comedic fun. This talent got Dad in trouble in high school one time. Decades later, while looking at a photo of South Park Elementary School, Dad pointed to a corner window and told Phil, "That is the principal's office, but don't ask me how I know." Dad was definitely not a troublemaker, so we can only image how he knew that.

Dad started learning to play the violin in fifth grade. Great-Grandpa Kelly had a violin from someone who had won it in a poker game. He played it for a few years but never in a school orchestra. It was a great introduction to classical music, which led to a lifetime interest. Grandma gave all three kids piano lessons, but only Julia took to it. Dad and Phil had no interest (or talent) in it. Both Grandma and Grandpa could play the piano and would play duet pieces together every now and then.

When they would visit their Grandpa Rinard (Alonzo), he would keep comics for them on top of the refrigerator and bottles of pop inside. He would tell them stories about Kansas in the late 1800s as the Wild West days ended.

When Dad was in grade school, he was a sleepwalker. Grandma and Grandpa were concerned of just what trouble he might get into while walking in the dark. So he was given a flashlight to use while sleepwalking! It seems that one of his goals was to see what time it was, so maybe the light helped, if he actually used it. He eventually outgrew it.

The family used to visit Onaga, Kansas (northwest of Topeka). Grandma had grown up there, and her parents and younger brother were still living there. Unlike the flat streets of Salina, Onaga had hills. A block from their grandparents' house was an especially steep hill that just invited them to fly down in a red wagon or on roller skates. At the bottom was the main intersection in town. There was hardly any traffic, so it wasn't a threat to them, but in the center of the intersection was a bronze statue of a World War I doughboy, which had to be avoided if they hadn't been able to stop by then. Since the family didn't have a car, they would use a borrowed company car from Grandpa's work. The Kellys slept on feather beds and had a player piano that the kids loved to watch and hear. Great-Grandpa Kelly would drink his hot coffee by pouring it into a saucer then blowing across the broad surface to cool it. He wore a long sleeping cap over his bald head during the night.

The Kellys had two adjacent large lots. One had the house, and the other was a large serious garden. The house had no indoor plumbing as we know it. A pump handle at the kitchen sink drew very cold water from a well just outside the house. A one-seater outhouse was out back. During one visit, they had some pigs in a pen just below the outhouse, and on another visit, it was filled with chickens instead. During that visit, Dad and Phil would pick grapes off the grapevines in the garden and throw them one at a time into the pen to watch the chickens race around to get the fruit. They called it chicken football. Another time, the garden was filled with sweet, ripe strawberries, which they were allowed to eat at breakfast time.

In January of 1943, Dad and Phil went to a 1942 movie in Onaga that led to a joke between them forever. The movie was *The Black Swan* with Tyrone Power. They enjoyed the corny action show but thought it was funny that it was still playing in Onaga a year later. They joked that the film company had forgotten to come back to Onaga to get the film. Or perhaps Onaga was the last theater to receive and show it, so it was theirs to keep.

Junior and Senior High

Dad started junior high in 1948. He went to high school in the old Washington High School, then his last two years he attended the new Salina High School. Today they have added "Central" to the name because a second high school was later built in the south end of town.

ONE LAST TRIP

During the summer of 1950, Dad, Phil, and Julia turned their basement into a casino. Dad had this idea because he loved to build things. He built a dice "table"—a twelve-inch-by-twelve-inch piece of wood with a nail sticking up at each corner to which rubber bands were wrapped around. He also built a roulette wheel—a twelve-inch diameter wood on an axle with holes partially driven in the rim where a marble would land. They took an oatmeal box and cut large squares out of it and covered it with large screening so you could see inside of it. They mounted it on a tinker toy stand so it would freely spin around and you could see the dice inside. A children's toy racing horse game was used, and a slab of thick wallboard was crayoned with red and black numbered squares to hold poker chip bets. The three kids made phony money by hand (no computers or copy machines then). They would "mint" their money with rubber stamps and green crayons on typing paper that was cut to size. Their friends and neighborhood kids would come over for the day to have fun "gambling." Each Rinard kid would run one of the games. Grandma didn't mind because at least they were all at home and not out causing trouble.

Around 1950, Grandpa was able to start bringing the company's Jeep home for evenings and weekends. It had two front seats and small benches in the rear with an aluminum cab over it all. It was a stick shift with four-wheel drive (although that was never needed.) In January of 1951, Dad took his driving test. He told this story, "The driving part of the test for a driver's license concerned me because I had never driven a real car. I learned to drive the Salina Supply Jeep, which Dad brought home every night. It had a floor mounted shift lever, but all the cars had shift levers mounted on the steering column and I didn't know the shifting pattern. I was afraid the tester would make me drive one of their cars and I would fail. But I was able to use the Jeep, and there was no problem."

In August 1951, my grandparents bought their first car. It was a four-door 1951 Plymouth Cambridge sedan, light blue. It cost $1,823.53. For the next decade, they traded for a new Plymouth every two years—that was the lifetime of the tires and batteries back then. They would spend about $700 each time after the trade-in.

Occasionally, Dad and Phil would play a pinball machine at a sundry store a couple of blocks from their house. One time, Dad made his own machine out of wood. It wasn't fancy; he used materials he could find on hand, but I'm sure it worked in its own magical way. That same sundry store sold comics, and when *Mad* magazine came out in 1952, they were the perfect ages for them. They had issue number 1 and many others that they kept in a metal toolbox. They were heavily read and used and probably not worth anything to collectors. Unfortunately, in 1960, they got thrown away.

By high school, Dad was heavily into cars, especially learning about and fixing them. He seemed to just plunge into a task and keep with it until it was fixed. He learned by doing. He got his first car in 1952. His car stories are in a later chapter of this book. To pay for his expenses to maintain and work on his cars, he worked at the new Dillons grocery store on south Ninth Street. He mostly stocked shelves and bagged groceries. He would tell me stories about some of the customers he helped. One time, he had to deliver a large watermelon to a lady at her house, and all he had at the time was his bicycle. This was the time when he became close friends with Jack Gebhart, because of their shared interest in cars. Jack's story is written in a later chapter of this book.

Girls also began to come into Dad's life, along with the cars. Phil remembers two whom Dad dated often. Dad had kept friendships with one of them and one time organized a lunch with her and her husband, as well as Mom and Phil and his wife, Carole, while visiting Phil and Carole in New Mexico. They all had a great time reminiscing, with no issues or awkwardness.

Dad played football in high school for three years and was on the track team his junior and senior year. He also was involved in the drama department. He acted in the school plays and sometimes would work behind the scenes, no doubt building sets and props.

He was involved for four years in Hi-Y. Hi-Y was an organization to promote "high standards of Christian character." He was also on the scholarship team.

Getting a TV in 1953 was a life-changing event for the family. They waited until they could pay cash for it, as Grandma would never let them buy anything on credit. They added a tall antenna to the roof and got an inferior black-and-white picture on an Emerson set from a station eighty miles south at Hutchison, Kansas. They had seen TV in the windows of a downtown furniture store, where they watched a Red Skelton show and saw characters they had heard on his old radio shows. The very first night that they watched their own TV, Grandma and Grandpa were out somewhere, and the three kids were glued to see what would happen. The first show was a half-hour show with a pianist that had fancy script in the title that they took to be "Silver Ace." Since being an "ace" was a recurring joke with Dad and Phil, they laughed so hard until they figured out that the unscrambled title was actually "Liberace." Dad actually got to meet Liberace later in Wichita as a reporter for the school newspaper. They watched all evening until there was only a test pattern, and then they watched the test pattern. Back then, programming did not go twenty-four hours a day. They would watch *My Friend Irma*, *Omnibus* with Alistair Cooke, and later Jackie Gleason and Milton Berle. And of course, Sunday nights would be filled with the Ed Sullivan variety show.

A TV room was created in their basement. The massive TV cabinet filled one corner of the room, and extra furniture found spots for each family member to use. Grandpa had a recliner, of course. I still remember as a kid going down to the basement in his Cedar Rapids home and find he was sound asleep in his recliner in front of the TV. He would deny it, of course, saying he was just "resting his eyes." In the 1950s, television was strictly for entertainment, and they only had access to three different stations. *American Bandstand* with Dick

Clark was very popular with the teens back then and, of course, the *Mickey Mouse Club*. Game shows, or quiz shows, were popular, including *Price Is Right*, *This Is Your Life*, and *What's My Line?*

Dad's art teacher in high school was very well liked. Everyone described him as a wonderful person. On the opposite side was one of Dad's English teachers, Ms. Smith (not her real name). She had a reputation of creating unpleasant experiences for the students. Dad and his friend Max drew cartoons for the school newspaper. Many of the cartoons were of the teachers at the school. The drawing including Ms. Smith was very biting and did not go over with her very well. Her jowls and tough-looking eyes could have been exaggerated, and we don't know exactly what they had her saying. Needless to say, Dad ended up getting a low grade in her class. When Phil came along three years later, the older teachers had no difficulty remembering ancestors of his they had in classes decades earlier (including Grandpa and his brother Clarence). Because of the "misunderstanding" between Dad and Ms. Smith, Phil decided not to take her class and risk it, especially because he had a good reputation as a serious student.

In May 1954, Dad graduated from high school. According to Grandma's cash ledger, it cost $1 to rent his cap and gown.

Dad's high school senior photo (1954)

Dad's Homes

When Dad was born, they lived at 323 N. Columbia Street in Salina. In July 1938, they put a $500 down payment for a house at 528 Charles Street, also in Salina. This house had two bedrooms with a bathroom in between, a string of rooms for living, dining (with a bay window), and cooking. Just beyond these was a large porch that had been made into a simple room with a back door, a great playroom for the kids. A stairwell went into a basement. There was a coal-fired furnace that had been converted to burning natural gas with ducts for the hot air to go to the first-floor rooms. A corner of the basement had originally been the coal bin, receiving coal that came down a chute on the north side of the house.

Dad's second house

There was a tree in the front that all the kids liked to climb. There were bushes that lined the front porch. Their cat Puff liked to hide in them and then leap out at them when they walked by. It had some nasty thorns on it, and rumor is that when an annoying neighbor boy that they didn't like wouldn't go home, Dad and Phil threw him into the bushes and he never came back.

Grandpa said he never wanted to live on a corner lot again because it had double the snow to shovel. The boys were too young to help at that time.

A porch swing hung on the front porch outside of the master bedroom's window. Next to the swing, they built a cardboard box "house" for their cat Puff and then Puff II.

There was a garage in the back. They didn't have a car, so the garage was just for storage and playing. In the spring of 1948, they poured a new concrete driveway and installed a basketball goal on the garage. When they moved to their next house, they took the goal with them.

The sloped roof on the back of the house covered the enclosed porch that became a great playroom. There was a bent-over nail in the flooring, and Dad used to get his little brother to do anything he wanted by threatening to pull up that nail, which would cause the entire house to collapse. Somehow, Phil always bought it 100 percent.

In June 1943, Grandma and Grandpa had saved up enough money after six years of making payments to pay off the remainder. Approximate total paid, including loan interest:

- Down payment: $500
- Closing cost: $108
- First payment: $37
- August 1938 to June 1943 ($37 × 70 months): $2,590
- Payoff amount: <u>$660</u>
- Total paid: $3,895

Right before they moved to their next house, Dad had the idea of leaving a time capsule behind for the future generations. There was a loose brick in an odd end of the basement's south end. The contents can't be remembered, but a note was included. The intent was that it was supposed to last a long time, but the new owners found it right away. They called Grandma to say how cute it all was.

In October 1948, the family moved to their next home at 816 Merrill. Dad, Phil, and Julia were told to come to the "new" house after school instead of the "old" house. Dad has this memory: "That afternoon after school I rode my bicycle to the old house first since it was on the way to the new house. The door was unlocked, so I went inside. The house was completely empty. Everything had been taken to the new house. It seemed strange without furniture, yet basically familiar. I wasn't sad, but I had more than a little tinge of nostalgia as

I walked from room to room. The house was quiet, and my memories were like echoes, almost audible. I only stayed for a few minutes, then I returned to my bicycle and rode to the new house. Later the new owners called us and said they had found some 'treasure maps' and similar papers hidden behind some loose bricks in the basement wall. I had forgotten about those items. We had made them for some of our games with our friends."

Dad's third house on Merrill Street, Salina, Kansas

After going through the front door, on the right was the living room (with a fake gas-fired fireplace). On the left was Julia's bedroom. The master bedroom was across from Julia's toward the rear, with a floor furnace in the hall between them. The bathroom was between these two bedrooms. The kitchen/dining room was connected to the living room. A long stairway between the kitchen and master bedroom took you to the attic.

The full-length attic (with windows) was finished into a large bedroom for Dad and Phil. The north end was made into a separate room where Dad built an electric train table and a pinball machine. They loved the space, even with the sloping roof near the edges. A gas-burning radiant heater was put into a wall that didn't have a thermostat. Stray cats would find a way onto the roof and then come in a window so that they could sleep in a warm place on their heads and feet.

There was a full basement; access was on stairs beyond the kitchen in line with a back door. It was furnished with an office for Grandpa and a large laundry/storage room. After they got a television in the fall of 1953, it was put downstairs in the large common room and became a well-used spot. A tall antenna was put on the roof to get a signal from the one station eighty miles away. The direction could be changed with a motor on the antenna controlled by a switch in the basement. This was the standard technology in the 1950s long before any cable TV. The TV was a black-and-white picture Emerson simple console.

The garage was never used to hold a car. It stored Dad's car parts, a stack of old *Life* magazines, outgrown toys, and other miscellaneous junk items. The basketball goal was attached to the garage. There was a white-painted mark on the driveway fifty feet from the goal. Phil spent many hours practicing hook shots from that mark. He worked on shooting left-handed even though he was right-handed. This would give him more value as a player.

In the summer heat, their group of young cats found it coolest against the house by the fifty-foot white line. Inside, they had an evaporative cooler for the living room; it was cooler air but raised the humidity. Upstairs, the attic bedroom was miserably hot in the summers, especially with no breeze, making it hard to sleep at night.

The door at the back of the house had a vine-filled trellis that the cats climbed to start their way to the roof and the upstairs window. There was a wooden fence in the backyard. Beyond the fence was an alley for trash pickup trucks and a fifty-five-gallon drum where they burned paper trash (it was legal back then). They had a large weeping willow tree and a couple of elm trees in the backyard. In the front yard, there were large elm trees that arched across the street but were eventually killed by elm disease and had to be cut down.

ONE LAST TRIP

In February 1949, Grandma and Grandpa used the proceeds from the sale of 528 Charles and selling bond to pay off 816 Merrill. Approximate total paid, including loan interest, fees, etc.:

• Down payment:	$3,500
• FHA fees:	$195
• FHA payments:	$173
• Applied from sale of Charles house:	$6,328
• Balance due on Merrill house:	$1,600
• Total paid:	$11,796

Ice Cream

The Rinard family had and still has a tradition—ice cream. Especially homemade ice cream. It is the thing that has held the Rinard family together for many decades. We considered the newer electric ice cream makers "cheaters." There was something about the work and sweat of turning the handle that earned its rewards.

Generations of Rinards grew up with ice cream as the main staple in their house. I am proud to say that I have kept that tradition alive and have even converted Kevin to join our ranks. He now joins me every evening for some form of the frozen delight. Sometimes we don't even bother with putting in a bowl, we will just spoon it right out of the carton.

Grandpa had such a passion with ice cream that his preference was to grab the largest soup bowl he could find, put a piece of pie or cake in the bottom, then cover it with ice cream. Now his definition of a "piece" of pie was this: take a pie and cut it into four pieces. He was a big German man with a big appetite. He would then eat his extravagant dessert, and when he would notice that it seemed unbalanced or lopsided (meaning the pie and ice cream quantities were different), he would simply add more of whatever was lacking to "even it out." This could go on indefinitely. Grandpa was a bottomless pit for ice cream. A pint of ice cream was an insult to him. He tackled half-gallon sizes.

When Dad was young, the Rinards would gather on the back porch to churn homemade ice cream. Grandma had to prepare two batches—one for the men and one for the rest of the family. They would start the procedure by walking a half mile to Ashton's Groceries to buy the ice. The store sold it in blocks and had a machine that you could put the block into and convert it into chips. Grandpa would pull a red wagon to Ashton's to catch the chips for pulling home. When the two soldiers were living with them during the war, Grandpa made some ice cream for them. The three of them kept tasting it until it was all gone. Grandma had a fit and insisted that they make another batch for the rest of them!

Here is the process for making hand-cranked homemade ice cream:

- Prepare your recipe. There are many different ones you can use. We prefer the purity of plain vanilla.
- Fill the bucket of your hand cranked ice cream maker with ice and sprinkle with rock salt. The metal cannister (where the mixture will go) is in the middle, surrounded by the ice and salt mixture. Layer the ice and salt until it reaches the top of the bucket, and top it off with more salt to slow the melting process.
- Pour your homemade ice cream mixture into the cold cannister. Be careful not to let any ice or salt fall into the cannister when you open the lid. You could fill the cannister before you set it in the bucket. Just make sure the cannister is in the proper place when you add the ice. Place the lid over the cannister and attach it to the handle assembly.
- Crank it! This is not a job for the timid or weak. The handle needs to be constantly turned for about twenty-five minutes until that ice cream is frozen enough to eat. While you are cranking, you will probably have to add more ice and salt as it melts down. As the mixture turns to ice cream and thickens, it gets harder and harder to turn the paddle, so it is well advised to have several people lined up to take

turns when your arm starts to feel like jelly and lose all feeling in it. Plus, you could work up quite a good sweat!
- The finished ice cream is always soft serve and will melt fairly quickly if not eaten right away. We would fill our bowls then put the rest in the freezer to enjoy another time. After the paddle came out of the cannister, one lucky person got to lick it clean! It is definitely in the top ten best foods ever invented! But beware of brain freeze. It is one of the coldest substances that exists!
- The buckets were made of wood slats, so it was best to do the cranking outside, as the water from the melted ice would seep out through the cracks. If we made it in the winter, our basement floor would do.

Dad and Grandpa making ice cream

I have so many memories of making this wonderful ice cream. Anytime the family would gather, we would do our tradition. Sometimes we would just make it for ourselves. When Dad married Mom, she had a recipe that the family agreed was much better, and that became the prized one.

Vanilla Ice Cream (for five-quart freezer)
Mom's recipe—originally from her mother (Beulah Boehner)
5 eggs
2 1/2 cups sugar (heaping)
2 tsp. vanilla
5/8 pint (10 oz.) whipping cream
Whole milk

To prove how much ice cream is a part of our family, Julia (my aunt) wrote a poem about it:

While living on Charles St. corner,
we kept a creaky freezer
that lasted through a lot of use
of pumping and squeezer.
The ordeal was exciting as
Mother mixed the "soup"
and Dad gathered salt pellets
and ice nearby to scoop.
It took a mighty muscling
to keep the crank churning,
a lot of huffing, hustle that
required some team-working.
You'd think that we were panning gold,
about to have a strike,
as all impatiently waited
to savor that first bite.
Some melted drips of water oozed
to trickle down the side,
as carefully and anxiously
the elements replied
to directions to add some more
until the temperature
perfected to solidify
the "soup" to creamy stature.
When finally the churning stopped,

*the ice cream paddle was
removed as all grabbed spoons to taste
the first bit just because
it seemed the purest ecstasy.
The freezer then was packed
to wait a while to finish it
as empty spoons were licked.
The difference of the homemade brew
and store-bought imitation
was how one's facial nerves did hurt
from such cold infiltration.
A few bites of the homemade kind
resulted quickly to
produce a slap against foreheads
and grimaced painful hue.
If there is such a loving God,
may I deserve His say
to pack my body in ice cream
when death has had its sway.
And if I then awaken to
an after-world one day,
I'll have my ice cream there with me
to start me on my way.*

The Little Old Lady and the Milkman

One particular evening, when Dad was a teenager, the family was all sitting down to supper, and an offhand, yet hilarious, story was created. This, of course, was nothing new with the Rinards, as our sense of humor was and is one of our top family traits. But this tale got legs, and it always came up over the years at family gatherings. Now mind you, hearing these types of stories secondhand are nowhere near the level of hilarity as when it originated.

Dad wrote, "It was a spontaneous creation that got completely out of hand. It occurred during a meal at the kitchen table when we were all there. It would be impossible to recapture the mood of the moment that results in such things. Absolute fidelity to the actual events is highly unlikely, but I think I can approximate the process of creation. It started with an innocent comment from Mom about the milkman. He had trouble understanding her order sheet that was stuck in an empty bottle. He rang the doorbell, but for some reason it took Mom a long time to answer the door. That started it.

"Each new comment brought forth several new ideas, all feeding from some common pool of imagination. Not all suggestions were accepted as worthy, but most were. A significant amount of time was spent while we were laughing at each new twist. When the timing was right, we could be out of business for several minutes while we laughed our heads off at the latest development. I guess we finally finished the meal. You had to be there to appreciate it to its fullest."

Julia took the time to recreate, to the best of her recollection and input from Dad and Phil, the story of the old lady and the milkman. Nothing in this world can imitate the Rinard laughter when it gets going!

Why Milk Is No Longer Delivered to the Door
Created by the Rinard Clan. Written by Julie Rinard-Scott

One of our memorable delights evolved innocently in the 1950s as we all sat at the kitchen table one day when Mother made a comment about the milkman. That was when fresh bottles of milk from the local dairy were delivered to the front door stoop and left for us in the early morning on a regular basis. In the summer, we had to retrieve it early before the heat and humidity soured it, and in winter times, if we were too late, the milk froze and pushed the cardboard cap up and off the top to resemble a lollipop.

But now the current new story fun began this day through a spontaneous response to Mother's comment. She had left her change of order as a handwritten note stuck into the neck of an empty bottle on the stoop for the milkman to pick up in place of fresh filled milk bottles. The milkman could not understand what the note said and rang the doorbell.

ONE LAST TRIP

For some unknown reason, Mother took a while to answer the door. Perhaps she was caught in the bathroom, or perhaps she was in the basement pushing clothes through the wringer of the wash machine. Whatever the reason, she was slow to answer the doorbell this time.

"I'll bet he got pretty cold out there waiting for someone to answer," said Syd, the eldest son.

Younger Phil piped up, "Yeah, and suppose the door was locked and she couldn't find the key?"

"And what if she lived on the fourth floor and had to traipse down all those steps to get to him?" Syd continued. His body began to imitate a little old lady crimping downstairs, one at a time, hanging onto the railing and shouting in a crackled voice, "I'm coming! I'm coming! Hold your horses!"

Ring! Ring! "Anybody home?" shouted the milkman as he also pounded on the door.

Comments and chuckles emerged from everyone seated at the table as they got into the mood of the scenario. I hunched my shoulders and rounded my back like I was old and bent over with a beginning dowager's hump. Phil scrunched his face into beady slits of eyes that could not see well. Syd continued to comment on the slow descent of a little old lady down narrow rickety steps.

"What if she finally got down to the door," Phil then added, "and she found that she had left the key to the door upstairs on the fourth floor?"

Our eyes lit up with the new twist, and Syd said, "Then she had to go back upstairs to get the key." His head reeled back with laughter at the thought and what it implied.

Ring! Ring! "Lady, it's the milkman," someone called out. "I'm getting chilly out here!"

Now it became more difficult for the little old lady to climb back up four flights of creaky stairs. We added huffing and puffing to her dilemma, along with a few comments. "Impatient man. [Puff.] Youth have no respect. [Pant.] Wait till he grows old."

"Yes." Phil thought suddenly. "She was crippled, you see. That's why it took her so long."

"And she couldn't find her cane," added Syd with new delight.

This set the stage for imaginations to blossom fully as the story adjusted to fit each new addition. "And what if there was a door at each landing of the stairs?"

"And of course, each of those doors was locked too."

"Then each door took a separate key to open it."

Eyes began to roll, and tears of glee had to be wiped aside. "And all of the keys hung on a common ring, so she had to try each key, one at a time, in each door lock until she found the correct one."

"Yes, oh yes!" I shouted with new mirth. "And the poor milkman was still standing outside in the freezing cold."

"He probably stomped his feet for warmth and cursed under his breath, but he waited and kept ringing the doorbell and knocking. He could barely hear the little old woman's voice from inside telling him to wait."

I let a sigh release and shoulders dropped to relax a moment, still chuckling to myself at the thought. The moment slowed us down to catch our breaths before Syd resumed the next chapter of the Little Old Lady saga. "Finally, she got her key and her cane and made it back downstairs to the front door. When she unlocked it and got the door cracked open, crisp, cold air rushed in without awaiting an invitation. A scowl came over her face, and she barked, "What do you want, young man? Didn't you see my note?"

"I can't read your note. How much milk do you want, lady?"

"How should I know? I'm eighty-two years old. Don't expect me to remember such things," she replied. "I'll go check. You wait here." And she slammed the door in his face before he could say another word.

By this time, the weather had grown into a typical Kansas blizzard with sleeting snow in addition to the brusque gusting air that chilled a person to the soul of his bones. The poor milkman quit stomping his feet by now, defeated, and leaned his freezing body against the side of the house like a handle on a shovel. Tears started to form in his eyes, except they seemed to freeze before they could roll down his checks. Snow began to accumulate on his backside like a blanket.

For another interminable length of time, the little old lady stepped and puffed and panted, unlocking and locking each door at each landing until she reached the top of the stairs again. She paused to open one window briefly and yelled down to the awaiting milkman, "I'll be just a minute!"

But it took her five minutes to open her refrigerator and check to see how much milk she needed. One brow scrunched into a wrinkled furrow as she helped up her gnarled hand to count on her fingers. "Two quarts. Two. I can remember that."

She turned and shut the door then looked at those fingers and asked herself, "How many did I say I needed?" So she turned back, opened the refrigerator again, and bent over to repeat the investigation. "Oh yes, it was three. I remember now," she spoke to the air. "Three quarts. I can remember that."

This time, she held out two fingers in front of her as she tottered across the floor, leaning on her cane. "Three quarts," she told herself over and over as she looked at the two raised fingers. "I won't forget this time."

The trip down the stairs was repeated, step by painful step. She clung with one hand to the railing as she stepped down with one foot, gained a secure footing, then brought the other foot down to rest beside it before starting the next step. Again and again. Occasional faint raps on the door were heard to encourage her along. But then at her age, the little old lady could not be hurried. At each landing, she stopped to test her ring of keys in each door until the proper one was inserted to allow her passage.

Eventually, the little old lady reached the main door. She could hear the weather screaming outside and had to use both hands to pull open the door this time. Snow flew in like it was attacking her, and she grabbed the crocheted shawl around her shoulders to hold it tighter around her neck. "My goodness, young man," she said, "you picked a fine time to deliver my milk. Why didn't you wait until the storm was past?"

The milkman looked with sad eyes at the little old lady. "It wasn't snowing when I came here," he murmured without moving frozen lips. "How much milk do you want?"

The little old lady held up her hand to view how many fingers would indicate the number of milk bottles she wanted to receive. But she had just used that hand to grasp the front doorknob and fling it open. Her face now went blank. "I don't know," she said with an apology. "I'll have to go check."

Before the milkman could respond, the little old lady slammed the door in his face and yelled, "You wait here!" Then she started back up the stairs again.

Thus, the tale continued around and around. Each time she made her repeated rounds, a new twist was added into the plot of confusion and delay. She always went back and forth without delivering the message or receiving her milk order. No one felt sorry for the milkman, for he could have left the premises at any time. But that would have ended the tale and its evolving fun through the years of retelling.

This is our legacy to document, as strange as it seems. But why hide the truth? This is who we are, and we couldn't be prouder of it!

Dad, Julia, Grandpa, Grandma, and Phil (1953)

CHAPTER 8

Day 4
Wednesday, August 8, 2018

Colorado (Ouray, Silverton, Gunnison)

Today is Wednesday, August 8, just after nine o'clock in the morning, and I've checked out of my bed-and-breakfast, which was really a quaint, fun place to stay. I would definitely stay there again! It was built in 1995 but designed to fit in with the old architecture of Ouray. There are thirteen rooms to stay, and each one has a private bathroom. Mine had a beautiful four-poster bed that I had to use a step stool to get into! In the evening, I sat out on the beautiful covered front porch, listening to the sounds of the mountains and enjoying the crisp air.

So this morning, I'm first heading up to see a small falls, then I'm going to work my way back down to Silverton, because I would like to explore there a little bit more. Hopefully, I will be there when the trains come in. I know Dad loved that. So I'm going to do this little hike and head back over the beautiful Million Dollar Highway.

Ouray, Colorado, was established in 1875 by prospectors searching for silver and gold in the mountains all around it. At its busiest, it had more than thirty mines. It was named after Chief Ouray of the Utes, a Native American tribe. In 1887, the Denver and Rio Grande Railway arrived in Ouray and carried passengers until 1930. The entire Main Street through the center of town is registered as a national historic district, with most of those buildings built in the late 1880s.

I have been to Ouray so many times in my life. It really is one of my favorites places to spend time. Like Silverton, Ouray has managed to keep its old-fashioned Victorian-era charm. Two-thirds of the original building are still standing and have been restored. They don't have any fast-food restaurants, shopping centers, etc. Everything in town is locally owned, and they rely on tourism. Since it is nestled down into a deep valley, potential growth is not an option. The elevation of Ouray is 7,800 feet, and on three sides, the mountain-tops are over 13,000 feet above sea level. It has a 360-degree fabulous view of the Rocky Mountains. In the summer, you can see waterfalls, go hiking, go four-wheel driving, or swim in a sulfur-free hot springs pool. In the winter, Ouray offers an ice park where you can go ice climbing, back-country skiing, snowboarding or soak in the hot springs pool, which is open all year.

> *I walked up to Cascade Falls in Ouray, and it's an easy walk luckily, because I'm still getting used to the altitude here. But it wasn't too bad. It's very pretty. I was a little disappointed with how much water was not coming out of this falls; it was more like a trickle. I've been out here before when it was really coming down pretty hard. But it was still pretty... got some good pictures.*

Cascade Falls Park has a couple of trails to hike, but I limited myself to the Lower Cascade Falls trail for today. It's pretty easy, and at the end of it is the base of a waterfall that brings the snowmelt down from the mountains. The trail is less than half a mile long, and there's a couple of benches to sit down to rest or enjoy the scenery. If you are adventurous, you can walk across the rocks in the stream from the falls. I've done that in the past, but not today! I wasn't in the mood to start my day off getting wet shoes! Today there was not a lot of water coming down the falls due to the dry summer they've had so far and a mild winter last year. Over the years, I've seen the falls much heavier. However, it counts as my first official waterfall of this trip, and I'm glad I came up to see it!

> *Now I'm on the Million Dollar Highway heading back to Silverton. I stopped at a pull off where we've stopped many times in years past. Again, one of the waterfalls had no water coming out of it. It's a bit unfortunate, but the scenery around it does not disappoint!*

Things have changed a little bit on this highway in the last ten to fifteen years. When my kids were little, we would stop here and get out of the car to explore. The road curves to the left and then a quick right, and we would pull off just before it turned left. We could get out and see a beautiful view into a valley surrounded by stunning mountains. To the right, there would be a tall rushing waterfall coming from near the top of that peak. Today it is dry. We would then get back into the car, drive to where the right turn begins, and get out once again. Here, we could walk down just a bit to a big stream of melted snow coming down the mountainside. The water would be moving very quickly then go under the road to yet another waterfall into the valley. We would climb around by the stream then work our way down until the water dropped off. The sounds of that water gushing past us was deafening and fabulous! Unfortunately, they have permanently railed off the area where you can get down to the water. I guess someone declared it too dangerous. Maybe, but it was so much fun!

> *I just saw my first deer! She crossed the road up ahead of me. I was able to pull over, because I wanted to try to snap a picture, but by the time I got out of my car, she was up in the woods. So they're here!*

Mom always looked for the deer when we traveled. She just loved them. I also find them to be beautiful, graceful animals, and I'm on a lifelong quest to take the perfect photograph of one. Even though I get them in my own backyard occasionally, there is just something different and special to see them when I'm traveling, especially when we have the fabulous Rocky Mountains as our backdrop! Mule deer are the most common in Colorado, but white-tailed deer and elk also live there. Mule deer are usually about three feet tall at their shoulders and can weigh up to three hundred pounds. They are usually brown in the summer and turn grayer in the winter. Their ears are large and mule-like (how they got their name), and they have a short, narrow tail. It is estimated that there are close to half a million of them in Colorado.

> *I just saw another one! Yep, she was just by the side of the road, staring at me. I guess she was waiting for the cars to pass so she could get across.*

The odds are improving that I will get that award-winning photo of a deer! I'm sure I'll run into many this week.
Next stop: Silverton!

> *I just left Silverton. It's about 2:20 p.m. I stayed longer than I was planning to, but I just couldn't leave! I couldn't do it. I don't know, I just had the feeling that I needed to stick around there for a while. And I'm glad I did, because I arrived there in time to watch the first train pull in, which was great! But before that, I took Dad's ashes and set them on the train track then got a picture of him on the tracks. I know that's corny and all that, but you know what, it really touched me, and it was very emotional. And very awesome. I got the pictures… and, Dad, you got to sit on those train tracks there in Silverton, right where the trains are coming in, which I know you loved so much! I didn't get the best*

photos of the first train coming in because me, being a dork, tried to video with my phone and take pictures with my camera at the same time. Yeah, that didn't really work either way really. My video is a little sketchy, and the photos were not great. I asked one of the conductors when the next train is coming in, and she told me it was going to be around 1:15 or so. This was at 11:45 a.m., and thought, Yeah, I don't know. I probably shouldn't take the time here. *Evidently, it's not their normal running schedule because back towards Durango a couple of weeks ago, they had an avalanche, or something like that, that covered the tracks. They got the tracks cleaned off, then the next day, something happened, and all of the soil and rock and stuff that were under those tracks in the same spot eroded away. So it damaged the track, and they are in the process of fixing them. Because of this, they had to re-route the train trips and bus the passengers to another location to get on the train rather than Durango. Anyway, long story short, normally they have three trains coming in each day. Today they are only running two.*

 I decided to grab a sandwich at this fun little local sandwich shop, sat out on a picnic table out behind the shop, and ate my lunch. Great sandwich, and I had a really fun talk with the owner! After lunch, I decided to walk around a little bit more, and by that time I realized, it was already one o'clock. I might as well stay. So I did! I found the perfect spot and watched the second train come in. This time, I captured the amazing photos I was hoping for! Right before this second train came in, they brought back the first train to load up the passengers. They back them up after everybody gets off and store it down the way at a depot near the visitor's center. They turn the train around and back it into the center of town to re-load the passengers. About ten minutes before train number 2 was to arrive, train number 1 was brought back in, but it came in backwards, so after it picked up all the people, it could leave straight away. I did get some neat video of that and some good pictures as well. During all of this, I was visiting with different people, all very nice, and I noticed everyone was eating ice cream. I needed ice cream. I ran into a little local shop to buy some T-shirts and gifts, then I went next door to the ice cream shop and got me a cup of strawberry ice cream. I have to tell you, that was the best thing I've eaten all week. It was so good!

Silverton

Ahh, Silverton. So far, you have been my most emotional and special stop.

Let me tell my experience in better detail from the beginning.

Last night, I went online and checked out the train schedule. It was important that I be in Silverton in time to watch these magnificent machines arrive. With Dad being a mechanical engineer and knowing everything about how all engines work, he would watch with joy and amazement every time one would come into town or leave or sitting at rest, getting ready for its next part of its journey.

ONE LAST TRIP

The Durango and Silverton Narrow Gauge Railroad began in Durango in August 1881 and was completed through Silverton in July 1882. It was originally built to haul silver and gold ore from the San Juan Mountains, but it wasn't long before people discovered how wonderful and beautiful the view was between the two towns. It has been in continuous operation for over 130 years, although now it's strictly passengers. In the 1960s, the Durango-Silverton was registered as a national historic landmark. The movie *Butch Cassidy and the Sundance Kid* was filmed there in late 1968. It just so happened that they were filming at that exact moment when I was there with Mom and Dad actually taking this train ride. Even though I was just shy of two years old, they said I was with all the other ladies on board smashed into the one side of the train where Paul Newman and Robert Redford were working! I'm surprised that train didn't tip over! So I can officially say that was my first movie star sighting! Not bad!

The locomotives that pull the trains on this route today are still 100 percent coal-fired and steam-operated. In honor of Dad, I feel I have to get a bit technical here. These locomotives are fueled by burning a combustible material (coal) to produce steam in a boiler. The steam then moves the pistons that are connected to the train's main wheels. The steam also operates the whistle, the air compressor for the brakes, the water pump in the boiler, and the heating system in the passenger cars. The exhaust steam goes up through a chimney, which creates the famous chugging sound of the steam locomotive. That is the simple explanation. The actual detailed procedure is actually quite complicated to me, although Dad tried to teach me all about steam engines dozens of times while I was growing up. But for this purpose, I made it as easy as possible to understand.

I arrived in Silverton around eleven o'clock. The schedule I picked up at the visitor's center yesterday and their website showed three separate trains arriving from Durango each day. The arrival times in Silverton are 11:30 a.m., 12:15 p.m., and 1:00 p.m. The departure times from Silverton to head back to Durango are 1:45 p.m., 2:30 p.m., and 3:00 p.m. It appeared I would have several opportunities to see them. There are two sets of railroad tracks that bring the trains right into the center of town. Literally, they end right before an intersection that automobiles use and are in the middle of the surrounding shops. You are allowed to walk right up to them and even touch the trains. I parked my car and headed straight to the tracks area, thinking that a lot of people must have gathered to view the arrival of train number 1. Surprisingly, there were only a few scattered people milling around, not seeming too interested. Not me, however! I could hardly wait for this exciting event!

    I had brought with me Dad's ashes box and the small glass jar with extra ashes. Since I had a little time before the train arrived and nobody was really around, I decided that this was the perfect time to get Dad out and include him. I placed both containers on the railroad tracks. I took some photographs, and I said a quick prayer and told him to enjoy this moment! The emotions overtook me right then. I felt a rush of happiness and sadness at the same time. But mostly, I felt peace. I also felt Dad standing right next to me, with the biggest smile and total approval. I couldn't help but have the tears start to flow. I'm not a crier, per se, but this trip was designed to bring honor to a man who was always my hero. My tears were healing and beautiful. It was perfect.

ONE LAST TRIP

Since the train was scheduled to arrive any minute, I picked up his ashes and positioned myself in the perfect spot and waited. And waited. No train. I asked a man who was there with his two young kids if he knew what time it was supposed to arrive, and he said he wasn't sure but thought he had heard that the schedule might have been adjusted for some reason. He had talked with a couple who were waiting for family members coming in on the train. We finally heard the wonderful train whistle coming from the curve in the valley, so I knew it was almost here! Moments later, I could see the engine coming around the bend toward me, with steam shooting out of the top and that glorious *chug-chug-chug* sound. Since I was alone and I wanted to get great photographs *and* video, I thought I could somehow set the video recording on my phone and hold it while I took pictures with my big camera. It's amazing how our brains can think we are so capable of such impossible tasks. That beautiful train came barreling in, and I got crooked video (some train and a bunch of grass and gravel) and close-up photos of small parts of the engine or one of the passenger cars. Hmm…not my best work! But oh, that sound. The shaking of the ground as I stood just feet away from it. The power. Pure joy. Pure excitement!

Once all the passengers had exited the cars, I found a conductor to find out what time the next train would be coming in. I found it really strange that train number 1 was so late, as they are never off their schedule, even by a minute. She couldn't tell me exactly but thought it would probably be around one thirty and then started calculating and said it could be closer to one fifteen. This threw me off because my schedule said it would be twelve fifteen. My original thought was that I really couldn't hang around that long as it pushes the rest of my day's schedule off. So I took a bunch of photos of the train sitting on the tracks and figured that would be it for Silverton for today.

Something inside of me was saying, "Nope, you are going to stay here." I couldn't explain it; I just knew that I was supposed to hang out here for longer. I guess it was Dad nudging me. He wasn't ready to go away from the trains yet. So I found someone who explained why the train schedule was off. In July, a slope near some of the tracks near Durango were flooded, which washed out and sent down a bunch of rocks and debris. The tracks were damaged and are in the process of being repaired. This caused the trains to not be able to make it into Durango. In order to continue the service, they are busing the passengers to another town, where they get on the train to Silverton.

Another fun memory of Silverton and the railroad tracks is with the kids. Every year, when we would all come here, they would place pennies on the track before the trains came in. Then after it arrived, we would go on a hunt around the tracks to find the smashed coins. We always tried to leave some sort of marker to make it easier to locate them, but it was always a challenge. When we did manage to find them, they made fun souvenirs!

I figured I had plenty of time to eat lunch. I had packed myself a peanut butter sandwich, but right by where I had parked, there was a cute little sandwich shop. That sounded much better, so I went in and placed my order. While I was waiting, I visited with the owner and a couple of guys who had stopped in Silverton while trekking across Colorado. Later in the day, I was talking with a man who was here with a bunch of friends from Maryland. They had been traveling by motorcycle. He said it had taken them three weeks to get here, and after this, they were starting their trip back home. After my sandwich was ready, I headed outside to a picnic table and enjoyed lunch.

Afterward, I realized it was close to one o'clock, so I began to head back to the tracks. I did a quick walk around town on the way and came across a little place that was set up as a mini sluicing/mining company. It actually was a fun place for kids or adults who want to try their hand at gold panning. We had found this place ten years ago or so with the kids, and they had such a fun time trying to "strike it rich"! You would purchase a bag of dirt and rocks and run it through their small sluice. A sluice is a sliding gate for controlling the flow of water. The water would run though the dirt in a screen, and it would separate the dirt from the rocks. Then you search through the rocks by hand to hunt for the gold. It's a great treasure hunt. We didn't become rich, but it was so much fun, and the kids still remember it even today. It brings the feel of the gold rush to the present day, and it shows the temptation and excitement that the old miners must have felt as they continued their quest to become rich.

There was a pretty little walking path just outside of town that I walked while waiting. It took me to the river that goes past the town, and there were some neat old railroad parts on display. Once I heard the train whistle, I got back to the tracks and saw the first train coming back in, only backward! After they drop off the passengers, they back the train up past the depot on the outskirts of town. It will sit here until it's time to load the people back up for the return trip. They bring it in backward so it's ready to go straight out once loaded up. I thought it was funny but did get some great video! About ten minutes later, the familiar whistle was heard once again, and I crossed the track to get a better view. Once it arrived, I was able to take some great photos with the two trains side-by-side, facing different directions. I also stood for a few minutes and watched the engineer of the train stand on top of the engine and take large rags and polish the big bell and the steam gauges.

I knew it was time to start heading out.

As I was walking through the crowds, I noticed a whole bunch of people were eating ice cream. With my family history of ice cream addiction, I needed ice cream, and right then. The ice cream shop was right by the end of the tracks. I first went into a little souvenir shop to buy a few things then walked next door to the ice cream shop. The line was long, but I didn't care. Once I knew I needed ice cream, nothing was going to stop me. I bought a cup of strawberry ice cream and headed back to my car. At that exact moment, that was the best ice cream I'd ever eaten!

I stopped at the gas station just on the edge of town to fill up and get a drink and some ice. I also had to scrape off the community of bugs that had somehow found my windshield. I noticed a large handmade sign taped in the window of the store that said, "Thank you firefighters!" They have been working tirelessly all summer trying to contain all the fires around the state and have done a fabulous job!

As much as I didn't want to, it was time to leave. But as I leave this fun, historic town, I take with me so many new memories and emotions, and I know I will definitely be back again. Thank you, Dad, for instilling in me the wonder and excitement of the Old West and the history and life from that era and for your constant efforts to teach me the internal workings of the great steam locomotives. I did try my best to understand!

> *Now I'm heading back across the Million Dollar Highway one last time here, and I'm going to do another hike in Ouray. Then I'll head out and end up in Gunnison, which is where I will be spending the night.*

Back on the Million Dollar Highway. I'm feeling a bit sad as I know this is the last time to drive on it, at least on this vacation. I also know that I will be back. This part of the world is a second home to me, and there is no doubt in my mind I will be seeing this absolutely beautiful road in my near future!

> *I just pulled over because I saw a pretty stream off to one side. I parked in a graveled pull off, and as*

I got around the car, I looked up and there was a deer right there in the clearing in front of me. Clear as day, just staring at me! Not super close but close enough that I could see her very well. There she was. She stood there for a really long time…almost as if she was posing for me! The backdrop was incredible!

My new four-legged friend had made me really happy. It was the perfect photo opportunity, and if I had blinked, I would have missed it. It made me think that sometimes the most perfect situation is placed right in front of you, but you have to be open to the unknown to reap the rewards. It's just like God's plans—you have to be ready for anything, but you can never stop seeking!

I see Ouray again in the distance. I have one more hike I'd like to do today there. It's actually a two-part hike—one easy, one more challenging. Dad and I have walked this hike several times, and each path has a different, yet just as beautiful, view of a powerful waterfall. Let's go check it out, Dad!

I just left Ouray, which was kind of bittersweet because it's such a pretty place and I just didn't want to leave. But I need to move on my journey. I'm sure I'll be back again, so it's ok. I visited a park called Box Canyon Falls and took two different hikes there. The first one was a simple thing down to the falls itself. You could walk down and get right next to it and just hear it—it's so incredibly loud and powerful. That water is coming down out of the falls so fast. It was really impressive. Then I backtracked and walked to an upper hike, which ended up on top of the falls. There is a bridgeway up high over the falls, so I could look straight down and see where I was before. This hike was quite a bit steeper and a lot more tough, especially when I'm still getting used to this altitude. But I did it, and I'm glad I did! You can overlook the entire town of Ouray from one side of the bridge. And from the other side, you can see through the valley where the water is coming from that goes down in that falls. So very pretty. There were tons of little chipmunks and these little cute squirrels running all over. Someone called them little ground squirrels, but I'm not sure. I'm going to have to look that up. But oh my goodness, they were so cute, and they were not afraid of us at all.

Box Canyon Falls Park is the end of the journey for Canyon Creek, narrowing down and spilling thousands of gallons of water a minute over the falls. On the lower hike, you walk down a path that leads to the spot where the water comes flying out. It's an eighty-five-foot waterfall that dumps from a narrow slot into a canyon surrounded by steep walls. The sound is deafening, and if you want to be impressed, it does not disappoint! You can continue to climb down a large series of steps to reach the bottom where the water ends up and works its way down toward the town. The water is so powerful that you can actually feel it through your body, and the water spray will touch your skin. Back in the day, this water was used with mining operations, and in one area, you can see some old mining equipment that had been brought in to use. When the mining dried up, they decided it would be too difficult to remove the equipment, so they just left it there. In a couple of areas on the path, I could lean over and see it resting along the side, rusty and falling apart.

The second hike I took was the High Bridge Trail, which is a half-mile round-trip and rises about two hundred feet. That may not sound bad, but this was the first time my heart got pumping fast, and breathing became difficult! I'm in pretty good shape, but this altitude is a killer for us Plains states folks! Once I got to the top of the path, there was a suspension bridge that crosses the gorge. On the right side, I could see the beautiful view of the entire town of Ouray.

On the way up the trail, there were some signs that pointed out the existing mining buildings, ore tailings, and other landmarks on the other side of Ouray to look for while you are at the top. One of the landmarks is Cascade Falls, which I had seen early this morning.

When I looked carefully, I could see the water falling from it, even though it is very light this summer. I was impressed and amazed when I saw the old mining buildings. They were so incredibly high up the mountains, and I had to wonder how they could ever haul equipment up and down that slope, especially because they didn't have the conveniences and technology that we enjoy today. I have so much respect for those miners and their families who sacrificed daily, working extremely dangerous and difficult jobs. Most of them never made it rich, only the lucky few who owned the rights to the mines and land. They wanted to provide for their families, and they worked hard and long hours knowing that any day could be their last because of a cave-in or accident. They were so brave.

Looking the other direction from the suspension bridge, I saw the most spectacular view of a deep valley through the mountains. At the bottom was a perfect river of melted snow tumbling down toward the falls, flowing around the rocky curves, and glistening from the sun. On the other side of the bridge stood an opening to a tunnel. It was short enough that I could see the end of it, and the pathway did continue through it. I had to check it out! As I walked about halfway through, I saw some abandoned pipes on the ground. They looked to be made of something like concrete and were partially broken. The ceiling was too low to stand up fully, so I walked bent over. I tried to imagine what it would have been like in this tunnel and others like it over a hundred years ago during the height of the gold and silver mining. I bet it was bustling and loud. It would be fun to go back in time for one day to experience the sights, sounds, and smells of this fascinating era.

The chipmunks and squirrels are the main attraction in this park. They scurry around and are not afraid of people. They seem to enjoy the attention and will pose for the pictures we are all trying to get of them. The chipmunks are least chipmunks, and they are the smallest squirrels. Including their tails, they are only seven to nine inches long, and they have five stripes along their body, with two of those extending onto their heads. That's how you can tell a chipmunk from other squirrels—they are the only species that will have stripes on their face. The other squirrels here are called golden-mantled ground squirrels. They look a lot like chipmunks, but they are larger and don't have any stripes on their heads. They do have wide stripes on their bodies and a shorter tail. All of them are extremely cute, and show-offs! I did take a large number of pictures of them. It was hard not to stick a couple of them into my backpack and bring home!

> *Now I am heading towards Gunnison, where I will spend the night tonight. Tomorrow I go to Tincup. Today I will be passing by Blue Mesa Reservoir on the way. It's a pretty lake, where a lot of people fish and go boating. But I'll just be passing by there without stopping, since I won't be getting into Gunnison until about 6:30. When I get there, I'll grab something to eat and relax in my hotel.*

Blue Mesa Reservoir is an artificial lake that was created by a dam on the Gunnison River in 1956 to help make power for the area. It is the largest lake in Colorado. It has three main basins, and it extends about twenty miles. It's really popular for boating and fishing for trout. It also has several campgrounds, and in the winter, you can actually go ice-fishing! I do notice that the water level is down significantly, again due to the dry summer and winter. It is very pretty to look at, and since it is extremely long, I am enjoying driving along it for quite a while. It's getting late in the afternoon, and I'm tired. It's been a very long day. Wonderful, but long. I'm ready to grab a bite and get to my hotel and put my feet up and relax!

Tomorrow is a very important day. It is the day I have been planning for. Tomorrow I will arrive in Tincup and bury Dad in the most peaceful and beautiful place!

CHAPTER 9
College and Early Marriage

Dad graduated from Salina High School in May 1954. In the fall of 1954, he left home to attend Kansas State University (K-State). He was the first in his immediate family to go to university. In the extended family, Uncle Clarence (Grandpa's brother) had attended Kansas State College (K-State's previous name) for architecture. Clarence's son John, who was the same age as Dad, attended Texas A&M. Other than those two, that was all regarding university studies to that point.

Grandma's cash ledger shows that between June 1954 and May 1958, they paid the following for Dad's college expenses (they cashed bonds and used salary bonuses for this):

- In 1954–55, they spent a total of $1,040.
- In 1955, until November 27, they spent $486.50.
- After that, they put $510 in Dad's checking account, $250 in his savings account, and $2,400 in cash.

Dad chose mechanical engineering as his field of study. In 1954, K-State had around seven thousand students. Today they enroll about twenty-three thousand.

Kansas State University was established on February 16, 1863, in the town of Manhattan, Kansas. K-State was opened as the state's land grant college under the Morrill Act in 1863. It was the first public institution of higher learning in the state of Kansas. The original name was Kansas State Agricultural College, and it was founded during the Civil War.

The state of Kansas was admitted to the United States in 1861, and that year, efforts began to get the school established. After two failed attempts to get enough votes from the state to form the college, the third time was the charm, and the city of Manhattan donated the Blue Mont College building and surrounding grounds for the new university. K-State opened in September 1863 and became the second public institution of higher learning in the US to accept both men and women equally in the US, with fifty-two students in total—twenty-six men and twenty-six women. Twelve years later, they moved the main campus to its present site. Three years later, in 1866, the University of Kansas in Lawrence held their first classes.

The first years they had debates whether it should stay an agricultural school or become a full liberal arts school. They would develop a home economics program for women, one of only two colleges to offer it.

In November 1928, K-State was accredited by the Association of American Universities as a school where the graduates could move forward and study advanced graduate work. In 1931, they changed the name of the school to Kansas State College of Agriculture and Applied Science. In 1951, the name was changed again by the state legislature to Kansas State University of Agriculture and Applied Science. Since then, the "Agriculture and Applied Science" is usually dropped from the name, and it is simply called Kansas State University, or K-State for short.

Fun fact about the architecture of K-State: the campus has more buildings built before 1910 than any other campus in Kansas. Most of the structures are built from native limestone. Anderson Hall, built in 1885 and houses the administrative offices, is listed on the National Register of Historic Places.

Today it is considered a public research university, one of 115 others with the highest research activity by the Carnegie Classification of Institutions of Higher Education. K-State has sixty-five academic departments in nine colleges—agriculture, architecture, planning and design, arts and sciences, business administration, education, engineering, human ecology, technology and aviation, and veterinary medicine. Their grad school offers sixty-five master's degree programs and fifty doctoral programs.

Intercollegiate sports began at K-State in the 1890s. The sports team are known as the Wildcats, and they participate in NCAA Division I and the Big 12 Conference. The school color is royal purple. There is a large Greek system with social fraternities and sororities as well as leadership and service fraternities. They are also known for their distinguished lecture series. The Landon Lecture Series brings in high-profile speakers, primarily current or former political leaders. Seven US presidents (including George W. Bush and Bill Clinton) and ten current or former heads of state have given lectures there. In other lecture series, speeches have been made by Martin Luther King Jr., Dr. Benjamin Spock, and Buckminster Fuller.

Dad was driving his 1946 Studebaker at the time so he could drive himself to and from Manhattan, which is a seventy-six-mile drive. He found a place to stay that was a large old house on the edge of campus. A widow, Mrs. Rogers, offered room and board for twenty guys. There were two rooms for four guys in the basement and many rooms in the upper stories of the house. In Grandma's cash ledger, June 1954, she entered a payment of $10 to Mrs. Rogers for the boarding house. That was a down payment to hold a space. They would pay her a full semester at a time when school started, which was around $200. Dad's notes attached to her entry said, "Large old house, held about 20 boys plus an additional 10 or 15 who just ate there."

Dad and his friends who roomed there decided to become an official school organization and called themselves (and the house) the Kasbah. I have never been able to establish why they chose that name, but from my limited research, I have found that the word *Kasbah* is another word for *fortress*. In Morocco, every village has a Kasbah where the ruling sheik or king would live. This Kasbah would offer the highest vantage point to watch for unwanted visitors. Having a Kasbah built was a sign of wealth. It could also simply be a large home or complex for one or two families.

Because they became an official school organization, it allowed them to participate in school events, including Greek Week. Greek Week is an annual event at the university where fraternities and sororities (and men's houses like Dad's) come together for a series of events to promote unity, competition, and fun for the entire organization. This included the annual chariot relay races. In ancient Greece, chariot races were one of the most popular sports. It was a contest between two-wheeled small vehicles with a driver, pulled by two-, four-, or six-horse teams. These races were prominent in the ancient Olympic games. Between four to six chariots would compete in a single race. The chariots would be made light but fragile and could get into some serious collisions, including the deaths of the drivers.

In the spring of 1956, the Kasbah was paired with a sorority for Greek Week and the chariot race. Dad and his friends built their chariot with the hopes of winning the creativity award. They all were smart with engineering knowledge but filled with quirkiness and humor, hoping to give everyone a great show. The sorority they were paired with was Alpha Chi Omega, and the young woman who was chosen to be the rider was named Joline Boehner. She was selected because she was one of the smallest, lightest girls in the house, and it would be easier for the guys to pull her. She is also my mom.

Dad designed the chariot for the Kasbah, making it look like a Model T Ford sitting on bicycle wheels. They created a fake radiator and placed dry ice and water inside it, making steam flow up and out. Originally, they had planned to only keep the dry ice inside it during the promenade parade, but they forgot to remove it, and during the first running of the race, the cold water flew up and out into Mom's face throughout the race. After the race, they were informed that the lane markings had some irregularities, so the chariots had to race a second time. So once again, they pulled the heavy chariot around the track while Mom held on.

There were two categories of awards for the chariots. One was for winning the relay race, and the second was awarded to the most unique chariot. Dad's chariot won the second category.

The Kasbah and Alpha Chi Omega chariot
Mom and Dad (*second from right*) with their trophies

Dad did more than win a trophy for his chariot that day—he won Mom's heart. They became an instant couple, and as the saying goes, the rest is history.

Mom describes their first kiss as so sweet and tender, and she knew at that instant that she was madly in love with him. No question. He was the most gentle, caring, and considerate man. He was funny and smart and very handsome. She was going to spend the rest of her life with him.

First date faux pas: the last french fry. The first time they went on a date, they ate at a burger joint near the Alpha Chi house then went to the movies. Mom had a big love of french fries, and while she was eating, she found a particularly perfect one. She set it aside to enjoy it last. At one point, Dad saw the french fry and thought it looked good, so he grabbed it and ate it. Mom stared in disbelief, thinking, *He just took it.* She didn't want to cause waves on their first date but later made sure that he knew it was not acceptable to take her last french fry. She was upset about it for the next sixty years, and Dad never did dare to do that again.

Alpha Chi Omega formal (1957)

When Dad became a senior, his younger brother Phil joined him at K-State.

Phil writes, "Syd and I seriously reconnected during the 1957–1958 school year at KSU. As usual for the little brother, I hung around and learned from my big brother. I rode with him between Salina and Manhattan, and The Kasbah a pre-selected place to stay and a roommate I already knew well. I took the path he had pioneered [although majoring in physics rather than engineering.]

"We had one of the basement rooms, away from the noisy crowd upstairs. We slept in bunk beds, as we had in Salina the first year or so just after we moved to 816 Merrill. Still being the little brother, I got the safer bottom bunk. Meals were bad jokes but I didn't lose any weight. A stray cat adopted us and spent some time in our basement; he rejected the end of a hot dog brought from the dinner table, as had we. The cat preferred being outdoors over inside the Kasbah.

"Syd was dedicated to his studies but had some distractions. He took off every other weekend to go to Kansas City where Joline was now at the KU Medical Center finishing a degree of Medical Technology."

Mom grew up in Coffeyville, Kansas, right along the Kansas and Oklahoma state line. She was born February 24, 1936, and was an only child. Her father, Jesse, was a chemical engineer who also graduated from K-State, and her mother, Beulah, was a schoolteacher. Grandpa worked for Sherwin Williams paint company as a chemist. Grandma taught a variety of grades, sometimes several in one classroom.

Mom graduated from Field Kindley High School with honors in 1954 and became a student at K-State. She studied medical technology. She told me she had really wanted to become a doctor, but back then, it wasn't easy for women to get into that field. Besides Alpha Chi Omega sorority, she was a member of Alpha Delta Theta honorary medical technology fraternity, Phi Kappa Phi (honor society), and the Purple Pepsters. She was also a member of the Royal Purple court.

Phil writes, "There was an evening when Syd was talked out of studying. A Kasbah buddy of mine was Dirck Praeger and we saw that that movie theater was showing an Italian Hercules movie that sounded so stupid it would be funny. Only Syd had a car so we pestered him until he went too. The movie fully met our expectations for fun [some background music was merely a very, very slow version of 'Home on the Range'].

"Dirck and I diverted Syd yet another time. Dirck or I asked a question involving the low, false ceiling in our basement room; is it possible to jump and touch your head on that ceiling? You naturally hold back to avoid hitting your head, but the three of us [including Syd] all gave it tries. Finally, Dirck or I [history is uncertain these days] not only touched the ceiling but drove through the soft fiberboard, leaving a hole the size of a man's head. [Mrs. Rogers never inquired; she never came into the rooms, hiring a woman to wash our sheets.] Quickly this became the goal of a game where you bounce a tennis ball off the concrete floor and have it go into the hole in the ceiling [where it couldn't go far]. This went on for days or weeks—who knows anymore? The Kasbah was razed decades ago so all these treasured relics are long gone."

ONE LAST TRIP

"Neuman Ball" head hole at The Kasbah

    Dad had told me this story many times, and he talked about how they called the tennis ball game Neuman Ball. They had a fun fascination with Alfred E. Neuman. He was the fictional mascot and cover boy of the humorous *Mad* magazine. His famous catchphrase was "What, me worry?" I'm sure that had something to do with the name of their "game." In Dad's version of what happened, he said he was trying to study while Phil and Dirck were attempting to touch their heads to the ceiling while jumping. He got so frustrated with their crazy attempts that he said he would show them how it's done. Not only did he touch the ceiling but his head also kept going right through. Thus, Neuman Ball was created.

    Dad belonged to Pi Tau Sigma and Sigma Tau honorary mechanical engineering fraternities and was a member of the student branch of the American Society of Mechanical Engineers.

    Mom tells me, "I remember the first time Syd took me home from K-State to Salina to meet his family. I knew immediately that this was a family I could love, enjoy, and feel completely at home with, although I was a little curious about Phil, who was kept in their attic." Grandpa penned this, "Back when Julia was in high school and so was Phil, Syd was dating a girl in college [Joline Boehner, whom he subsequently married] and brought her home to Salina several times to meet all of us. Now, Phil was a very quiet, studious, reticent fellow who spent ninety percent of his time in the bedroom upstairs. It seems that about the only time Jo ever saw him was when we called him downstairs for the meals, at which he ate abstractedly, responding mainly in gutturals, his mind deeply engrossed in his studies of physics, etc. It was not until later years after she and Syd were married that Jo revealed to us that she thought Phil had mental issues or something was wrong and that we simply kept him in the room upstairs practically all the time."

K-State graduation (1958)

When it was close to graduation, Dad had two separate job offers. One was with a vending machine company, which he thought would be a fun job but was concerned about the future of the company. In those days, most likely the job you accepted at graduation was the company that you would retire from. He chose the other job offer, working as a mechanical engineer at Burns & McDonnell in Kansas City, Missouri. Their work was mainly engineering but did architectural, environmental, and consulting as well. It was a wise choice, as the other company did eventually go out of business, and he would have had to relocate. He was with Burns & McDonnell until the day he retired.

Burns & McDonnell began in 1898 by two engineering graduates. They chose Kansas City as their location because it provided the most potential clients in a two-hundred-mile radius—towns that would need water and power systems. They were bought by a large steel company in 1971, then a group of employees bought the firm back in 1985. They are a full-service engineering, architecture, construction, environmental, and consulting firm. Today they have seven thousand employees and do projects all around the world.

Dad worked almost exclusively on power plant projects. He designed HVAC systems and controls. He had a passion for these coal-powered plants and was a proponent of developing new ways of providing energy, including trash-burning systems. He was promoted through the ranks to manager, and after a few years in that position, he decided to go back to working as a design engineer. He wanted to get his hands dirty with the designs, not managing people. He became very respected among the leaders and peers and was a very important man within the company.

Dad started working for Burn & McDonnell right after graduation in May 1958. He and Mom were engaged by this time, and Mom was already living in Kansas City while she finished her internship at the KU Medical Center then went to work for Dr. Atchison, a general practitioner.

That first summer, Dad would write letters home to Grandma and Grandpa to keep them updated with news about his new job, apartment, and wedding plans. He did not have a phone for a while. He would add fun cartoon characters occasionally.

> JUNE 7, 1958
>
> HI —
>
> I HAD SOME TIME SO I DECIDED IT WAS ABOUT TIME TO LET YOU KNOW I'M STILL ALIVE. (IT'S A WONDER IN THIS HEAT!) THE JOB IS SWELL (A LITTLE BORING NOW — STILL DOING WORK FROM THE BOTTOM UP, YOU KNOW) IT'S AIR CONDITIONED BUT IT'S HAVING TROUBLE WITH THIS HUMID WEATHER. STILL PRETTY NICE.
>
> I STILL HAVEN'T FOUND A PLACE TO LIVE YET, SO I'M STILL HERE AT MY OLD PLACE. THIS TOWN IS IMPOSSIBLE TO FIND DECENT ROOMS IN, BUT I 'SPECT WE'LL FIND SOMETHING SOON. I HOPE SO. I'M SURE GETTING TIRED OF SPENDING EVERY EVENING RUNNING AROUND WITH THE CLASSIFIEDS!
>
> OTHER THAN ALL THIS, EVERYTHING IS FINE. I DON'T NEED MONEY (YET, THAT IS.) I'M FINE, THE CAR IS FINE (BUT DIRTY AND IT RATTLES IN THE DASH) AND JO IS FINE. BUT WE'LL SURE FEEL BETTER WHEN WE FIND AN APARTMENT OR SOMETHING. OH YES, I THINK THE WEDDING MIGHT BE AUGUST 24 OR SEPT 7. THAT'S THE MOST DEFINITE SO FAR (DON'T KNOW WHERE OR ANYTHING, OF COURSE!)
>
> WELL, I'D BETTER MAIL THIS NOW BEFORE I SWEAT ALL OVER IT. GAD!
>
> SYD
>
> PS. — MY ADDRESS NOW IS 3930 MERCIER, K.C. MO

Letter from June 7, 1958:

Hi. I had some time so I decided it was about time to let you know I'm still alive. (It's a wonder in this heat!) The job is swell (a little boring now—still doing work from the bottom up, you know). It's air conditioned but it's having trouble with this humid weather. Still pretty nice.

I still haven't found a place to live yet, so I'm still here at my old place. This town is impossible to find decent rooms in, but I 'spect we'll find something soon. I hope so. I'm sure getting tired of spending every evening running around with the classified!

Other than all this, everything is fine. I don't need money (yet, that is). I'm fine, the car is fine (but dirty and it rattles in the dash) and Jo is fine. But we'll sure feel better when we find an apartment or something. Oh yes, I think the wedding might be August 24 or September 7. That's the most definite so far. (Don't know where or anything, of course!)

Well, I'd better mail this now before I sweat all over it. Gad!

Syd

Letter from June 17, 1958:

I talked to my employer Monday morning about my little "love note" from the draft board, and he said he wanted to write them a letter. He took my number and everything, so maybe you'll hear from the board soon. I hope so. (Dad was eventually found to be exempt from the draft because he worked for an engineering company, and he would be a bigger asset staying there.)

We found an apartment!!! It's really sharp. It's small (1 bedroom), unfurnished except for kitchen, but almost new with all utilities included but electricity. It's got a shower (and tub), radiant heat in the floors (like Daddy likes), and a new refrigerator and electric stove, real nice, and venetian blinds on the windows. It's part of a motel-like arrangement but I think it's real nice and private. Oh yes, it's only $87.50 per month, which is a real deal believe me.

I'm fine, kind of anxious to find out about the army business for sure, and I'll probably always be hungry. Better close now. See you soon.

Syd

Letter from July 14, 1958:

Don't faint—I'm not sick or broke or anything! Just thought I'd let you know I'm still alive and kicking.

Actually I've been busy building the radio cabinet. Tell Phil I've got the sound box done and it really works.

I don't know if I told you but I think Jo has decided Sept. 6 would be better (Saturday) since everyone could get back home easier. (Of course, an extra day for the honeymoon too). She had her picture taken and it will be in the paper soon…

Letter from July 18, 1958:

I finally have a phone! It's number is Emerson 3-2165. Not bad, huh? Now you can call me when something comes up or you're in town. If I'm at work, just call Burns & McDonnell and ask for me. I'm a big wheel there.

LORI RINARD GAMBILL

Letter from July 20, 1958:

Hi again! Jo and her folks just left, and I'm to write you and tell you to make up the list to send invites to. Right now she wants the number so she can get them ordered. I gave her an estimate (enclosed) and told her to allow a few extras.

We had quite a weekend here with her folks. Saturday she and her mom shopped for wedding stuff I guess (at least her dad and I were ordered to go amuse ourselves elsewhere occasionally). Last night we fired up the new charcoal burner on some steaks her folks brought up.

Letter from August 18, 1958:

Well, I got my blood test at the medical center, but they said that a doctor has to sign it to make it ok since I'm getting married in Kansas.
It looks like you'll be stuck with the rehearsal dinner Saturday. I don't know where it will be or how many, but I don't think there will be too many. Just the wedding party and family prob'ly (I hope). And I'll be more than glad to help foot the bill, now that I finally have an income!

ONE LAST TRIP

Letter from August 20, 1958:

Just a note with the soon-to-be-much-needed moolah! When Joline and girl friend or mother arrive Friday, money will begin the outward flow. We're going to get the rings, my suit, ties, etc. for the guys in the wedding and (if there's anything left) whatever else comes along. Got to be done tho, I guess.

Letter from August 31, 1958:

Just got back from Coffeyville. We got the letter (& the license) ok, so everything's about all set.

We got the motel rooms reserved, and I have one Friday and Saturday nights so you can use it to change clothes. We also made arrangements at the eating place for the dinner. There will be about 25 in the party, and the meal will be $1.50 each, which come to about $37.50! Steep, but it could be worse I guess.

Well, everything seems to be set finally. I'll see you at the motel Saturday morning, if I'm alive. The room's in my name, so you should be able to find me. See you then.

Syd

Marriage Announcement

Joline Bea Boehner was graduated from Field Kindley High School and K-State, Manhattan, with a B.S. degree in medical technology. She also got a certificate in medical technology at the KU Medical Center, Kansas City, where she interned. She was a member of Alpha Delta Phi honorary Medical Technology fraternity, Alpha

Chi Omega sorority, Phi Alpha Mu, Phi Kappa Phi honor societies and the Purple Pepsters.

Sydney Leroy Rinard was graduated from Salina High School and K-State with a B.S. degree in mechanical engineering. He belonged to Pi Tau Sigma and Sigma Tau engineering fraternities, also the student branch of the American Society of Mechanical Engineers and works for the Burns & McDonnell Engineering Company, Kansas City, MO.

Prior to the marriage was a rehearsal luncheon hosted by Mom and Dad at Tony's Café, Coffeyville.

Reverend Robert Scott married the couple. The altar was decorated with pedestal baskets of pink gladioli and white mums. Sara Jo Pursley was soloist. Joline wore a white imported Chantilly lace gown over blush pink taffeta with a basque scoop bodice, scalloped scoop neckline, and long sleeves that tapered to points over the hands. The bouffant floor-length skirt was enhanced by a watteau back that flowed into a court train. She carried a bouquet of blush pink roses with pink streamers.

Mary Louise Mowery was maid of honor. Julia Rinard and Frances Rooney were bridesmaid and junior bridesmaid. They wore rose peau de soie with blush pink silk organza harem overskirts with matching headbands. They carried crescent bouquets of pink carnations outlined in rose petals of peau de soie. Cousins James and Jerold Reid were candle lighters.

September 6, 1958

They honeymooned in the Missouri Ozarks then settled in at their apartment in Kansas City, Missouri. It was cozy, but they loved it.

Dad learned good budgeting skills from his mom, and he also kept a very detailed notebook of deposits and money going out. It's so interesting to see how different everything costs today compared to the 1950s.

Dad's birthday (1959)

On August 6, 1960, they broke ground on their very first home at 7216 Beverly, Overland Park, Kansas. Dad designed the house and helped the builder during all phases of construction. It was a three-bedroom, two-bathroom ranch, with a full basement and a big fenced-in backyard. It had two very large cottonwood trees—one in the front yard and one in the back, and in the back corner of the yard was a large apple tree. Along the back fence were honeysuckle bushes, which smelled amazing, and we could pull the center out of them and taste the sweet goodness inside.

Phil was still single and in graduate school at K-State at the time they first moved into the new house. He didn't live too far from them, so he would come over to visit, to celebrate their birthdays and during the summer to make homemade ice cream.

ONE LAST TRIP

Dad and Phil

Dad, Mom, and Phil

For nine years, they led a happy, fulfilling life. Then on May 19, 1967, their life changed forever.

I came along.

Chapter 10

Day 5, Part 1
Thursday, August 9, 2018

Colorado (Taylor River, Taylor Reservoir)

Today is Thursday, August 9, and I just left Gunnison. It's about 9:30, and I'm heading to Tincup. This is exciting! This is the day I've been planning for a long time. I'm going to take Dad to the Tincup Cemetery. The Protestant Knoll, of course! I'm going to bury some of his ashes there so he can be a part of that place forever. It is one of his special spots… Mom's special spots…my special spots. It's just such a beautiful and peaceful place. So many fun, wonderful memories there. I should be there in about a little over an hour. So, Dad, let's enjoy this ride!

I'm very excited for today, not just to bury Dad but also because I believe that this is the most beautiful part of the country that I've even been in. I've been to most of the lower forty-eight states and seen some spectacular and lovely places, but there is just something so special about this part. Maybe it's the memories with Mom and Dad over the years. Maybe it's the way the aspen tree leaves rustle and the way the water in the river and creeks trickle and tumble down and crash around the rocks. Maybe it's the clear, crisp air—warm this time of year but low in humidity. Maybe it's the wildlife scurrying around searching for their next meal or playing chase through the woods. Maybe it's the people and how everyone here is so friendly. Maybe it's a combination. I do know two things about this place: it fills my heart with joy and happiness, and I feel God all around me.

> *I'm driving along this little road that follows the Taylor River, which I think is the most beautiful drive from Almont to Taylor Park Reservoir. That is where the river originates. They have a dam there that lets the water out from the lake. It's just absolutely spectacular! Gorgeous! Just tons and tons of trees—pine trees and aspen trees mixed in. I just saw a bunch of people getting ready to go on a white water rafting trip. I don't know, but I bet the water is probably pretty cold! I don't think I would want to do that.*

The Taylor River runs directly from the Taylor Park Reservoir. The lake sits at 9,300 feet above sea level and is bordered by the Continental Divide. That provides a most stunning backdrop to this large two-thousand-acre lake. The reservoir was created in 1937 by the construction of the Taylor Park Dam. The dam sits 200 feet high and 675 feet long. It was built to help with water shortages in the Uncompahgre Valley. By the late 1920s, farmers had grown so many acres of fields that there wasn't enough water for their crops. Their need for a better water storage infrastructure is what spurred the reservoir to be built.

Taylor Reservoir is a prime fishing destination. Here you can catch lake trout, rainbow trout, brown trout, and northern pike. In years past, we have rented a motorboat and puttered around the lake, trying our hand at fishing. My son Alex thought he was pretty awesome when, at age eleven, we let him have a try at the controls! The Taylor River also offers some great fishing opportunities, especially if you like to go fly-fishing. You can try to snag rainbow, brown, and cutthroat trout. There is a marina on the lake where you can rent a boat and buy fishing equipment.

Just as you begin to head down to drive along the river, there is a magnificent pull off where you can read about the mountain range in the background and snap some beautiful photographs. I have been here in the early fall, and you can get a stunning view of the bright-yellow aspen trees climbing up the mountains to the tree line. Today I'm about a month ahead of that awesome transition of the leaves, but even in their green state, it's just breathtaking!

Taylor Reservoir

The summit of Cottonwood Pass is just a few miles east of the reservoir and can be accessed by a county road during the summer months. Once the snows start, it can become very treacherous, so it is usually closed from October to May. This pass goes over the Continental Divide from Taylor Park to Buena Vista. In all the years I've been traveling here, starting in the 1970s, the Buena Vista side road is 100 percent paved, and once you head down the Taylor Park side, the road is mostly dirt/gravel. They are kept very well maintained, so they are comfortably passable for even a regular passenger car. By the end of the summer, the road can develop washboard areas from all the melting snow runoff and summer rains crossing the roads. It can get bumpy but fun! The Cottonwood Pass summit is

12,126 feet above sea level. The east side of the pass (by Buena Vista) is where water flows in the direction toward the Atlantic Ocean and is located in the San Isabel National Forest. The west side (near Taylor Park) flows in the direction of the Pacific Ocean and is located in the Gunnison National Forest. The mountain range where the pass is located in is called the Saguache Range. Once you have reached the summit coming from Buena Vista, the road to Taylor Park is fabulous. You drive on sheer cliffs near the top, then once you work your way down a little, you drive through dense trees and hairpin curves all the way down to the reservoir. Many places there are pull offs that you can stop and see the lake in the valley. You have to pay attention the entire way down. I highly recommend the drive to anyone who loves to see amazing views and enjoys the excitement of a challenging road. I love driving it!

I remember one year Kevin and I left the kids with our parents and came out to stay for a week in late September. We wanted to come out that time of year so we could have a chance to see the beautiful aspens turning golden. One day we decided to take a drive up to and over Cottonwood Pass to see the views. It was sunny when we left our cabin, but by the time we got about half-way up the pass road, the weather had changed drastically. Clouds had rolled in, and the precipitation started. It was just rain, so we decided to keep going. It didn't take long for that rain to become more solid, especially the higher the elevation we were climbing. I was driving my two-door Ford Probe (not four-wheel drive), and Kevin began to have a freak-out session. I, of course, was determined to continue on, not letting a little snow or ice stop me. By the time I had cleared the tree line and we were nearing the area with the shear drop-offs, Kevin was hysterical, and I agreed that we needed to get back down the mountain before we slid off and rolled down. The problem was, we were to the point where there were no pull offs to turn around, so I had no choice but to get all the way to the top. By this time, it was snowing so hard on top of the ice that we had just had that I could barely see ahead of me. I had to crawl foot by foot to the top, gripping the steering wheel so tight I couldn't feel my fingers anymore. At one point, Kevin had stopped yelling, so I glanced over and saw him staring me down with a look like I'd never seen before or have seen since. I can only describe it as pure anger or pure terror or both. I don't know. Like somehow this was my fault. But in the end, we made it safely to the top where I could turn around and begin the slow, careful trek back down. By the time we were halfway down, the sun was back out and the roads were fine. Kevin didn't speak to me for an hour or two. He said it was the only time since he's known me he thought about a divorce! Ha!

A few moments ago, I passed by where White Water Resort used to be. It's the resort where we used to stay every time we traveled here once we couldn't stay in Tincup anymore. They had cabins, actual log cabins. I believe they were built in the 1940s, if I'm not mistaken. Each cabin had full bathrooms and electricity, but of course, they did not have TVs, and we didn't have cell phones and stuff like that when we stayed there in the 1980s and 1990s. But I stayed here many, many times with Dad and Mom, and we had so much fun just relaxing by the river… and it was so peaceful. And of course, Mom always had to take rocks! So poor Dad was always hauling these rocks all over the place. Anyway, it was a really neat place.

  We would stay there for a week, and I remember on every Wednesday night, they had a big cookout for everyone who was staying there. The owner of the place made these huge cast-iron skillets of potatoes. She was famous for those. And they would grill steaks for everybody. It was delicious and amazing! All of the other guests would bring a dish to share… so it was kind of a big potluck. It was really fun. You got to meet a lot of really neat people. Sadly, the people who owned it for all of those years retired and chose to sell it. Some private group or party came in and purchased it, and it was so sad to see that all of the cabins have been torn down. I don't know what they use it for now, but it's such a shame because it was a really neat resort. I totally miss staying there!

White Water Resort was located on the Taylor River about eleven miles north of Almont. The resort sat right along the river surrounded by Gunnison National Forest. A couple of dozen cabins were scattered throughout the small resort, and each was completely surrounded by pine and aspen trees, offering privacy and serenity. The cabins were true log cabins, either a stand-alone or a duplex. The stand-alone cabins featured a sleeping area with a queen bed, a full kitchen, a small bathroom with shower, a dining area, and a loft with a double bed. There was a log ladder in the middle of the room that you would use to climb up to the loft. My kids loved the climb and had fun sleeping up there. The ceiling was too short for adults to stand up. One visit, my daughter had a panic attack when she discovered a couple of spiders up there. She still has an arachnid phobia even today! The duplex cabins had a living room, full kitchen, two bedrooms (one with queen bed and the other had a full bed and a set of bunk beds), and a full bathroom with tub/shower. We would bring all our own food and make meals there. I remember the struggles in learning how to light the gas stove and oven with a match. All the cabins had a small porch and bench, with most of them facing the river, and a picnic table to enjoy eating or playing games outside.

A clubhouse sat at one end of the resort, offering a lot of different social activities. There was a huge fireplace in the center with big comfortable chairs around it, perfect for reading or enjoying conversation. There was an old upright piano that was free to use by anyone who felt brave enough to play a song for those who were within listening distance. My favorite part was the billiard table. Over the years, I played many, many games of billiards with Dad, Mom, Kevin, Alex, and Nicole. Not that I was any good at it, but oh, how many laughs and memories do I have from around that table! There was also a smaller area that had a big television and tons of movies that they would show at guest's requests. They had an entire bookshelf full of books and games that were available to all.

They had a large outdoor center area for recreation. There, they had picnic tables, grills, and a small playground. I remember they had enormous rocks that the kids loved to climb on and around. They were big enough for a game of hide-and-seek.

Once a week, the owners would throw a large cookout for all the guests at the resort. They would string a huge tarp over all the picnic tables, and on the enormous grills, they would cook steaks, taking orders on how everyone preferred them, and season them perfectly. Our wonderful host would also make her famous potatoes for all to share. Year after year, I always looked forward to those potatoes! So simple, tender, and steaming hot. Somehow, they tasted so much better when someone else cooked them in cast-iron skillets in my little haven in the center of Colorado than when I tried to replicate them at home. All the other guests would bring a dish to share with everyone. We had everything from salads to pastas to desserts. I remember Mom would always make her green rice casserole or a fruit salad. Everyone brought their own plates and silverware and went back to their cabin with full bellies and great memories.

In 1994, the current owners at the time compiled favorite recipes from their guests into a cookbook. I am including the famous potato recipe (although I warn it just won't be quite the same as when I was blessed to experience them!). You will have to adjust the amount of ingredients, unless you are cooking for a very large group of hungry people.

Peggy's Potatoes

30 lb. peeled potatoes, sliced
Crisco
9 onions, sliced
Salt and pepper

Put sufficient amount of Crisco in skillet so they don't stick. Have grease hot when putting potatoes in. Add onions and salt and pepper to taste. Turn when they reach a nice golden brown. Don't turn any more than necessary. Serve to hungry guest. Enjoy! (From the cookbook "White Water Resort on the Taylor River, Almont, Colorado—Peggy's Potatoes," copyright 1994, Cookbook Publishers Inc.)

The resort sat right along the Taylor River. Actually, the river was lower in elevation, so to access it, you had to walk down to it using well-carved-out paths made through the dense trees. But that wonderful roar of the water could be heard from anywhere on the resort. The noise is so calming and beautiful, and you could just sit on your bench and enjoy the blissful sounds of nature. Every now and then, a raft would float by with the brave ones who didn't seem to mind the cold water.

We spent a lot of time wandering around by the river, taking pictures, collecting rocks, or throwing them into the water. If you felt confident, you could toss your lure into the fast-moving water and try your best to catch a trout for dinner. Dad and Mom had a special place by the river that they would sneak down and sit together on a large rock. Then of course, Dad had to carry other rocks back up the hill to the car for Mom's collection. Every year, she would try to figure out a way to get one of the large boulders home to set up in her backyard. Never mind that they were almost as big as the car! Ironically, when my daughter Nicole was eight or nine years old, she and Kevin had a special rock by the river as well. I would catch a glimpse of them sitting there together, enjoying precious father-daughter moments.

Kevin would also share time with our son Alex as they would practice their whittling. It was a great teaching moment for Alex, who was a Cub Scout at the time (and would eventually become an Eagle Scout).

Most people who stayed here during the summer were guests who would return every year. When you checked out, you were given the opportunity to reserve the same cabin for the same week the following summer. It was fun to reconnect with other vacationers whom you had spent time with in years past. The memories I have from those summers spent there as a child and all through the years when I eventually brought my own children there are so dear and precious to me. I thank God that he blessed me with it.

Me and Mom, White Water Resort (1993)

Sadly, about ten years ago, we received a letter from the owners saying they had made the difficult decision to retire. Instead of finding new owners or managers, they decided it was the right thing to do to sell the resort. We were heartbroken, as were so many who felt this place was a part of their heart and home. We had hoped that someone would buy it and continue to offer it as a resort, but unfortunately, the new owners tore down all the cabins and built a large home on the property. The only existing building they left standing was the clubhouse. We don't know if the buyers were a private homeowner or some sort of corporate project, but the resort no longer exists to make special memories for future travelers. I'm so glad I could be a part of it for all those years.

I have now passed the emptiness that was White Water Resort. I smiled from the memories but shed a tear for its loss. But that's OK. I have a very important job to do. I must keep going to my mission. I have been looking forward to this drive since I started planning my trip. The Taylor River Road. Every curve in the road brings another spectacular view of the river, forest, and mountains. Every so often, there is a campground. I can't imagine a more perfect spot to pitch a tent and sleep under the stars and among the serenity of the pine trees, listening to the water continuously run past. There are plenty of pull-off spots along the road to stop and get out. Fishermen grab their gear and either stand on the river's edge or put on their waders and go straight out to the center to dunk their hooks with hopes of catching the prized fish. I enjoy that too, but I prefer to grab my camera instead and aspire to snap the most perfect photographs that will adorn my walls at home. I will say it is difficult to take a bad picture. The scenery was designed and constructed perfectly by God's loving hands.

Taylor River

The river road is about a twenty-mile gentle climb toward the lake. The final curve opens up to a great view of the dam with the water roaring out of the opening, then just a bit farther, you are standing up above the lake, looking down on the peaceful water. The lake seems to be nestled majestically by the surrounding mountains. It is so quiet, and you can see the gentle trails carved into the water from the motors of the fishing boats. This is the only place in a large radius that you can get any kind of signal for your cell phone. If you look off to the right a ways, you can see a grouping of cabins that can be rented. They are usually filled with fishermen. There is one restaurant and a general store. Here, you can pick up basic supplies, food and drinks, fishing licenses, and souvenirs. There are two gas pumps to fill your car, truck, ATV, or dirt bike. We used to call the store Cranor's, as that was the name of the man who owned it back in the 1980s. He has since passed away, but we still refer to it as that.

After a quick stop at the overlook, I head over to Cranor's. I had seen an electronic sign along the river road that said that Cottonwood Pass was closed. My heart sank for two reasons. One, I've been very excited to take the drive while I was by myself so I could stop as often as I wanted to take pictures without the worry of irritating my family. Second, this is the route I was planning to take later today to reach Denver, where I am spending the night so I can pick Kevin up from the airport tomorrow morning to join me for a much-needed vacation together. I stop in at the store to use the bathroom (the only rest stop for quite a while!) and ask about what's going on with Cottonwood Pass. I discover the pass has been closed for the entire summer while they do improvements to the roads. They are re-paving most of the way on the east side from Buena Vista to the summit and are improving guard rails and parking at the summit. Great stuff, except it messes up my plans for sure. When I leave, I will have to backtrack all the way back to Gunnison (where I started this morning) and drive south and around to get over to Monarch Pass to cross the Continental Divide. It will add a good hour or two to my drive today, but that's ok.

I am now tucked back into my car, ready to take a step back into my childhood. This is it! I'm eight miles to Tincup. I'm so excited I can hardly sit still. I have made it!

The eight-mile drive is through a small valley. It's a flat road, all dirt and gravel. In years past, it has been a rough ride, but this year, it has been very well maintained and easy. I am still having to shift around to avoid some washout or potholes, but for the most part, it's good. In the late 1800s, this valley was filled with several other small towns, but except for a couple of lone surviving structures, there is no evidence left of them. I have passed a couple of cars and some motorbikes and ATVs, but I feel like I'm entering a private heaven, almost like God has presented me with this perfect situation. I feel in my heart that I'm being guided and protected by him, knowing that I am doing exactly what he wants me to do. I look over to the little box holding Dad's ashes, and I can feel his smile and excitement as well. I know he's sitting with God watching me do this for him. My heart is about to burst with emotion! We're almost there, Dad!

I make the final turn, and there it is—Tincup!

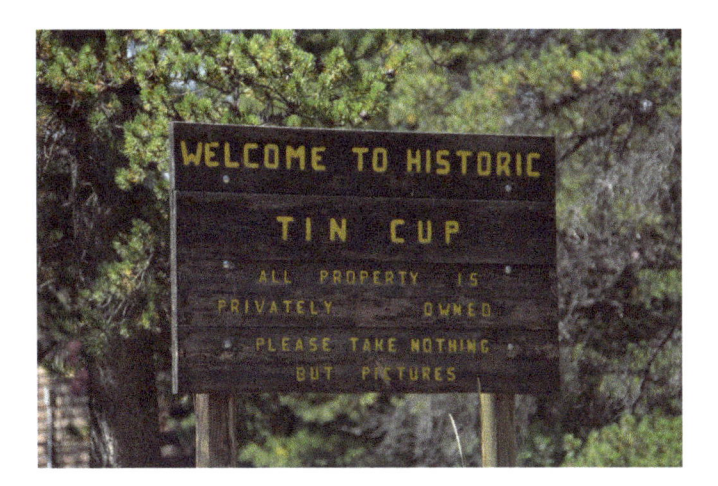

Chapter 11

Fatherhood

May 19, 1967. 1:14 p.m. That was the moment that Syd Rinard became a father.

He was so excited to have a child. He was thirty-one years old, and he and Mom had been married for nine years. They were doing financially well, living in their own house, and they had been able to enjoy just being a couple for some time. It was the perfect time to expand their family.

This was a time before ultrasounds were used in pregnancy so you would find out what gender your child was at the time of birth, not before. There were all kinds of ways that people would "predict" if you were having a boy or a girl—sweet versus salty cravings, carrying high versus low, morning sickness, heart rate of the baby. There was also the ring test. You would tie a ring to a string and hang it over your belly. If it swings in a circular motion, it's probably a girl, but if it swings side to side, you're having a boy.

According to Mom's obstetrician, I was going to be a boy. Evidently, he used the heartbeat method of prediction. So to everyone's surprise, I proved that doctor wrong. From day 1, I liked to keep people guessing! Mom was beyond thrilled, as she was hoping for a girl. Dad was happy too, although I know a teeny part of him was wanting a son. Didn't matter. It took about 1.3 seconds for me to become Daddy's little girl. He was smitten.

Mom and I have always been very close and still are. But there was a special relationship between Dad and me. Psychology states that the same-sex parent has the most influence on a child. I agree with that in most respects, but it doesn't count for the bond that forms between a dad and his little girl. Until the day he died, he was always looking out for me and wanting to protect and help me, even when he physically couldn't anymore.

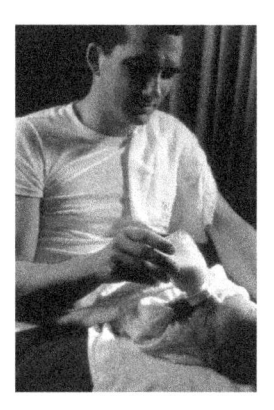

One week after I was born, I came home from Research Hospital in Kansas City, Missouri, and began the life that God had laid out for me. Of course, I don't have memories of those first years, but I have lots of photographs that document those times. Thank goodness Dad was a photographer like me and took many pictures throughout my life. These are precious records that I consider extremely valuable, and I have been systematically scanning them to digital storage so we never lose them.

My baptism

My first memories are from our house in Overland Park, which was the first house Mom and Dad had built. I had a bedroom filled with toys, and Dad always somehow found the energy to play with me after a long day at work. He built me a swing set in the backyard when I was around three years old. I spent many hours playing on it, swinging so high that the metal legs would lift off the ground.

We had two very large cottonwood trees in our yard. They were so big that we could play hide-and-seek behind them and were virtually invisible! We loved to take the cotton pods that fell and carefully peel them apart to make fun puffballs. We could play chase around the trees and not be able to touch the other person. I've rarely seen trees that were this large in diameter. We also had a large apple tree in the far corner of the backyard. The apples it produced were not really good to eat, but it had wonderful big branches that grew out each direction that were perfect for climbing. I spent many hours playing in that tree.

Every time my Uncle Phil would come for a visit when I was very young, he would bring me fun and unique toys. Since he was a physicist, he had access to cool things he could get from his work. The memory that sticks out the most was the series of balloons he would bring. These weren't your everyday, run-of-the-mill balloons that would pop the second it touched anything. These were heavy-duty, science-worthy balloons. We would blow them up with the vacuum cleaner and spend hours chasing them around the yard. Each visit, he would bring a balloon that was bigger than the last one. I was always so excited to see the treasure he would pull out of his car at each visit. Just recently, he mailed me a funny card he made showing what size of balloon it would be today if we had kept up the tradition. The photo was of the Hindenburg airship!

During Uncle Phil's visits or when Grandma and Grandpa Rinard would come over, we would always make homemade ice cream. I could hardly contain my excitement to make this heavenly treat, and I was always involved in its creation. Dad would let me help pour the ice and rock salt into the maker, and I would always get my turn spinning the handle. My little hands could hardly hold on to it, but no matter, I was determined to help. Once we couldn't move the paddle anymore, we knew it was time to pull it out of the churn. I was given a spoon and allowed to clean up the paddle once Mom would get as much as she could off it. Best treat ever, even if you have to endure the brain freeze!

I was definitely an outside child. In the summers, we would play in the sprinkler or the kiddie pool, and in the winters, we would build snowmen and have snowball fights. Dad was a master snow builder—his creations were masterpieces. The neighborhood kids loved coming over when Dad began to build—he was quite renowned!

We would go for bike rides as a family. Until I was old enough to ride my own bike, I would sit in a seat attached to Dad's bike. One time we were on a ride and I reached out to grab a leaf off a bush. Unfortunately, it was a rosebush, and a huge thorn cut right through my palm. Once I was bigger, I rode my own bike, and we would go to the local parks and find trails along lakes or through the woods.

Dad had always wanted a sailboat and to learn to sail, so he and Mom finally purchased a Sunflower sailboat. The Sunflowers were built from 1971–1983. It was about eleven feet long and held two people. It only weighed fifty pounds, so it was easy to transport. The boat was yellow, and the nylon sail was yellow and white-striped with a black sunflower printed at the top. The cockpit area was open like a canoe, and we had a wooden center seat across the middle. There was a large park nearby that was the best place to go sailing, and they took sailing lessons. Once they completed the lessons, they taught me how to sail as well. It's been many years, and I wish I still knew how. I felt so big and special when Dad would let me be in charge of the tiller. The tiller is attached to the rudder, which goes down in the water in the back of the boat. This is what steers the boat. The tiller is like the steering wheel, and the rudder is like the wheel of a car. It had a centerboard or keel (an adjustable plank in the center of the boat, which could be raised or lowered) that worked to keep the boat balanced so it wouldn't tip over. I learned how to maneuver the sails to work best with the wind. I have so many wonderful memories of us sailing on the lake. When we moved to our next house, our neighborhood was surrounding a small-sized lake. We took the Sunflower out on it a few times, but it was too protected by surrounding hills and trees to get good wind to sail.

ONE LAST TRIP

One of my favorite holidays was the Fourth of July. Dad and I would go the fireworks stand and purchase bags of fireworks. He was always extremely careful, and we had to follow strict rules while shooting them off. He taught us how to tie firecrackers together to get a bigger boom. He also showed us how to set them up under a tin can, and we would have contests to see whose can would fly higher. He would construct long tubes connected to wood handles, and we could shoot them through it as we held them up in the air. We would write our names in the air with sparklers and make "snakes" on wood boards. After dark, Dad would build neat platforms where he would light roman candles and spinners. He never let us shoot them by ourselves. He always supervised and no one ever got hurt. We would get together with all the neighborhood families and combine our fireworks, grill hot dogs, and have a great time. Some years we would climb into the car and go to watch a professional fireworks display. The next morning, we would gather in the streets with our brooms and clean up our mess.

Halloween was always fun too. Of course, getting dressed up and going out trick-or-treating was wonderful, but the night before, we would carve our pumpkins. This was an event. The pre-show was going to a nursery or pumpkin patch and choosing the perfectly sized and shaped pumpkins. They would sit on display until we were ready to carve them. Dad called it brain surgery. We would cut the top off them, being careful not to break off the stem. Then we would begin the "brain" evacuation. After they were cleaned out, we would draw our faces on them then carefully cut out each feature. Dad's creativity and artistry would always result in the most fabulous creations!

I also loved Christmas. Every year on the weekend after Thanksgiving, we would drive out to the country to a tree lot and spend hours finding the perfect Christmas tree. We would walk around the big lot, marking trees we were interested in with a long stick or branch sticking up so we could find it again later. When we would finally decide on the right one, Dad would saw it down with a small handsaw they would provide, then we would get it wrapped in twine and secure it on top of our station wagon. Once we got it home, Dad would take a hammer to make some holes on the bottom of the trunk to allow water to soak up easier then bring it into the house so we could decorate it. I remember I would sit on the sofa waiting for him to bring it into the living room. I was always so excited that I couldn't sit still! I would clap when it was up, and we would spend the rest of the day unwrapping ornaments and untying knotted-up tinsel and light strands. By evening, it looked spectacular, and I knew that the Christmas season was officially here!

On Christmas Eve, we would eat an early supper then get in the car and drive around looking at different Christmas light displays. We would go to some neighborhoods that would famously decorate the entire street. They would turn them on every evening, and cars would wait for what seemed like hours in lines that would wind around the streets to get a view of the displays. They would have volunteers that would hand out candy canes, and festive Christmas music would be piped up and down the streets. It would be this time while we were out enjoying the lights that Santa would come to our house. I always wondered how Santa knew that we were gone at that exact time. After we would get into the car to head out, Mom would "forget" something and have to go back into the house. While I waited for her, I would stare into the sky looking for Santa's sleigh, figuring that he had to be nearby. Sure enough, when we got home, I would scramble into the house, and the evidence was there. My stocking would be overflowing, and more gifts would be scattered around the floor. We didn't have a fireplace, and I never was concerned he couldn't make it into our house. I had the total faith of a child.

After the excitement of Santa's visit, we would get into our dress-up clothes and head to church for the late candlelight service. I always looked forward to that service, as our lovely church was lit up by dozens of candles and the music was beautiful. We always sang "Silent Night" while everyone held a candle and lit it from the person next to them, and they would turn off all the regular lights so we were bathed in the stunning light of the lit candles. It was magical. You could feel God's presence with us.

Christmas wasn't just about the presents for me, even as a young child. I had a nativity set that I would set up and act out the Christmas story with the figurines. I knew the meaning of Christmas. Dad was a very spiritual and religious man and had the strongest faith in God and Jesus. He instilled that into me every day. I was baptized when I was a month old and confirmed when I was fourteen. We attended church every single week, and I would go to Sunday school with my friends. I didn't always want to go, or I'd get bored, but I was there. And like it or not, the messages and lessons would seep into my brain and stick. Both Mom and Dad were very involved in the church. Mom played guitar in the worship group, was a member of the Altar Guild (they made sure that the church was set up properly each week), and helped out at Vacation Bible School. Dad would help out with ushering, church maintenance, and whatever other things they would need to get done. But his most wonderful contribution was his absolutely beautiful wood carvings and projects he made and donated to the church.

Dad was an avid woodworker. He owned pretty much every tool under the sun. He had his own workshop in every home they lived in. His pride and joy was his Shopsmith. Shopsmiths are multi-purpose woodworking tools. It included a table saw, lathe, drill press, disc sander, and a boring tool. Other accessories could be added, including a band saw, jigsaw, jointer, and belt sander. I believe Dad's had all these. This was not a small tool—it took up a large amount of floorspace, and his workshops were all designed around this beautiful machine.

Dad in front of his workshop (2010)

Dad used his talents to create beautiful masterpieces. He built furniture, candlesticks, and even small cat carvings for Mom. I still have a few pieces of his furniture that he built, as does my son. To others, it's just a thing, but to me, they are priceless. He was extremely meticulous, and the final products were virtually flawless. He offered to build some pieces for our church. Over a period of years, he created for them lathed plant stands and candleholders, special baptismal pieces, a nativity structure, and carved Alpha and Omega wall plaques. He made pew candleholders that were used in weddings and special occasions. About two years ago, the church building was sold to the city, and they tore it down to build a special park. Before the demolition, the church sold most of the interior fixtures, and we were blessed to be able to receive most of his items. We have split them up, and I proudly display a plant stand and a candleholder, which was most likely used as a unity candle stand for weddings.

ONE LAST TRIP

We did a lot of traveling while I was growing up. We always drove, and over time, we covered the entire country from Maine to California. I loved the trips as a kid, and it has continued into my adult life. I truly enjoy seeing new and different parts of the country, as well as international travel. When I was young, we would rent a pop-up camper that could be pulled by our station wagon. I remember those trips and the fun we had. We especially loved visiting Colorado. Mom grew up going there every year, and Dad soon fell in love with it too. We would go almost every year.

I remember one time when we were walking alongside a lake, and Mom kept telling me to be careful because I would fall into the water. I just laughed and said, "No, I'm not going to fall." Sure enough, it didn't take long for me to fall in! We would hike, play games, and build a campfire. Every lunch would be a picnic. We had a red metal Coleman cooler that was filled with goodies for sandwich making and drinks. We would pull off at a picnic table, set up the tablecloth, get the cooler and the food box, then create our masterpieces and fuel up our bodies. I actually still have that old red cooler. I don't use it anymore because it has some rust, but every time I look at it, I can remember all those picnics.

When I was six years old, we bought a beautiful piece of property across town in the city of Shawnee, Kansas. It was in a subdivision called Black Swan Estates. It had a small-to-mid-size lake with windy, hilly roads surrounding it. The entire subdivision was thick, deep woods. The builder contractors would only cut down the necessary trees to place the house and the driveway. The hills were steep, and the roads were narrow. It was the most wonderful place to live. Our property was at the end of the road at the bottom of Suicide Hill. It was named that because it was the longest, steepest hill in Black Swan, but no one has ever actually died on it.

Just as with their first house, Dad designed our new house, took out a construction loan, hired his own builder, and did majority of the work himself (with Mom and my help!). It was a ranch home with three bedrooms, a large deck right into the woods, and a walk-out basement.

Groundbreaking day

4650 Black Swan Drive

He made sure we had a beautiful huge stone fireplace, and the open-plan vaulted large family room had floor-to-ceiling windows with a view of nothing but trees. There was a long line of upper windows along the roofline that brought in extra light. The kitchen was large and beautiful as well, with a vaulted ceiling that opened right into the family room. Between the two spaces was a very large island, which is where we ate our meals, did projects, had talks, and solved all the world's problems.

Right off the front door to the right was a vaulted room that we used as a music room. Mom's piano was there, and we had comfortable chairs for relaxing. I spent many hours at that piano, taking lessons for nine years and doing countless recitals. Mom and I even played a couple of duets at church. The kitchen was on the left from the front door, and the family room opened up straight ahead.

On the right side of the family room was a hallway that led to the bedrooms. The master was at the end on the left, and my bedroom was at the end on the right. My bedroom was great—it was large and pink (my favorite color at the time). I had windows on two sides and a four-poster bed. Dad made me a desk that fit into one corner and a cubical organizing piece of furniture that had shelves and many drawers to contain all my things.

I loved my bedroom. It was where I could allow my imagination to run free, whether it was playing with dolls or contemplating my future. My friends loved coming over and having sleepovers. It was so peaceful there—no traffic going by, only the sounds of nature.

We never did finish the entire basement while we lived there, but he did finish out a lovely office/sewing room for him and Mom. There was also a finished bathroom down there, and he drywalled out a big playroom for me. I remember when we finished the bathroom and it was time to install the shower unit. Dad and a friend had to drag the large piece around the back of the house, downhill, and figure out a way to get it through the sliding glass door. After many tries, they ended up having to take off the door completely to give them that extra couple of inches needed.

ONE LAST TRIP

My playroom was awesome. I had a chalkboard that was Mom's as a child hung on one wall, where many hours of playing school were spent. I had a large desk that had come from Grandpa's old office and lots of office supplies to create to my heart's content. But the best part of my room was the ping-pong table in the corner. We played so many hours on it. If I couldn't find an opponent, I could flip one side up and hit by myself. I had a cat who loved batting the ball around with me. She wasn't quite competition ready, but she did enjoy playing.

The main part of the basement never got finished while we lived there, but since it was open and had concrete floors, I could roller-skate in it. There was a round stand-alone fireplace against one wall, but it was never completely installed, so it was never used. We also had an old black upright piano in the room that was Mom's. It really never sounded too good, and I don't remember that we ever got it tuned, so we never played it. Eventually, that room began to become the "storage" area, and our plans to finish it never happened.

Over the years, Dad built two sheds next to the house. The first one was built with the house and attached to the garage. The second one he built later, and it stood alone. I was always a bit cautious to go into those sheds because there were usually some sort of critters in there—from birds and bats to snakes to lizards to spiders. Living in the deep woods, we had our fair share of all those plus more. Dad was fearless, however. Whenever we would spot something we didn't like, he would take care of it—from squishing spiders with his shoe to chopping the heads off the poisonous snakes. He was our hero!

It took three years to complete the build on the house. Problems with the builders and Dad doing so much of the work himself (evenings and weekends) caused the long build. I always "helped" when I could. Once, I told Dad I wanted to help paint, so he gave me a can of paint and a paintbrush and told me I could do the inside of my closet. I now understand why. I was eight years old and probably wouldn't do quite the best job. But that day, I was bursting with pride! I worked really hard on that closet interior!

Moving day was an event. I remember the moment that moving truck pulled into our driveway and how excited I was to finally move into our new house!

I loved living there. The summers were fun because we were able to swim in the lake and the fresh-water pool that sat directly next to the lake. There were diving boards between the two hanging over the lake. A floating dock in the lake rested near the pool area, and it was fun to swim to it and dry off in the sun before swimming back. Being lake water, visibility was nearly zero, and every now and then, something would brush by your leg. Most likely a fish, but there were snakes out there too! We would float on rafts to get the perfect suntan. The pool was great too—it was long and narrow with the deepest end only being about five feet in depth.

Winters could be a challenge when a snowstorm would hit. Since we lived at the bottom of a very steep and long hill, we learned how and when to hit the accelerator in the car to boost it up the hill through the snow. We didn't always make it, but most of the time, we would. Dad developed and headed up the snowplow committee. He did the research for purchasing the right pickup truck and fitting it with the proper plow, salt spreader, and cover. He formed a team of drivers from Black Swan and did training sessions on how to properly plow and salt the streets. He was the contact person when the first flakes hit, and our streets were always very well cleared of snow. We never had to miss a day of school because of snow, sometimes to our disappointment! One time, the salt spreader wasn't working, so Mom and I rode in the back of the pickup, and while Dad drove, we tossed out handfuls of salt onto the road. I thought that was really fun, even though I ruined a good pair of gloves.

We lived on an acre and a half of thick woods, which required us to do a lot of upkeep, especially in the fall. The amount of leaves that we had to rake was unbelievable. Mostly we just kept the area around the house cleared, and we would rake them into large trash bins and drag them to an area of our property that sloped down toward a creek and dump them. They would compost and be gone by the next summer. Dad also cut all our own firewood from downed branches and trees. We never needed to buy any. He built a large woodpile off to the side of our house, next to a wonderful tire swing he made for me and my friends.

We always had cats when I was growing up. Mom loved cats and continued to adopt them over time. We always had at least two. Dad liked them too, but not as much as Mom, or so we thought. One time, we had a stray cat hanging around our house every day for months. She would come into our garage, especially on the cold days. We always suspected that she belonged to the family over the hill, but no one ever came looking for her. Dad would play with her and pet her during the days. Over time, he put out a warm blanket in the garage for her to sleep on. Then came a bowl of water and a little food. Eventually, he built her a spa-like getaway in his workshop (off the garage). He made a boxy cave-like area with a soft blanket and a lamp to provide heat in it because the nights were getting cold. Of course, that was it. She permanently moved in. She was his cat, and he was her person. After a couple of years, he brought her in to live in the house, although she spent most of her time in the basement. She was with us for many years. How did she know which house to hang around and whose soft heart would make him fall in love with her?

We quickly settled into our new house in the woods. Each season brought the forest around us amazing new beauty. I had acres of trees to play in, and my friends and I would go exploring for hours on end. If we hiked north far enough, we would come to a large field filled with horses. If we set out to the east, we would run into a flowing creek and wildflowers. If we walked far enough to the south, we would end up at the dam holding in the water to the lake. On some summer nights, we would pitch a tent and spend the night under the stars and trees, pretending that we were far out into the wilderness and that the bears and other creatures would be trying to get us. A snowy day would find us hurling ourselves on our sleds down the hills through the trees, weaving around them like an obstacle course, trying to avoid a collision. We would brave the curvy and very hilly roads on our bicycles, flying down the hills and ending up pushing our bikes up them. I would sit on the edge of the dam in the evenings and dream about what my future would hold. I was so blessed to grow up there and never took that for granted.

We had always wanted a larger family. A few years after I was born, Mom had a miscarriage. So in the end, it was just me as far as children. Evidently, God's plan was just for one. That spurred us on right before I started high school to investigate the possibility of having exchange students come live with us. The organization Youth for Understanding (YFU) was recommended to us, and after much research, we took the leap and became a host family. Our first student was named Birgit, and she lived in Germany. She would be living with us for an entire year. I was so excited at the idea of having a sister. There were many unknowns before she came, and we were nervous how it would work out. Our lives were about to change forever.

We picked Birgit up from the airport on a hot August day, and so our adventure began. She immediately became part of our family. She called our parents Mom and Dad, and we called each other sister. It was a wonderful year of teaching each other about our cultures. She attended high school with me. We were the same age, so we were in the same grade at school. We were like regular sisters. Most of the time, we got along great, and sometimes we would irritate each other. We did a lot of things together, but she developed her own set of friends and activities. When the time came for her to return home, it was the hardest day for all of us. Lots of tears and promises of future visits, both back here in the USA and Germany.

Dad, Mom, Birgit, and me (1983)

The experience was so wonderful and successful that we knew we had to have another one. Our second student was named Minna, and she was from Finland. Instantly, she was one of us. She and I were like peas in a pod. We developed an interest in Finnish culture and were looking forward to visiting there. She made closer friends with my friends, and we did most things together. We even double dated a lot. I had received my driver's license a few months before she arrived, so that made it easier for Mom and Dad in the fact that I could take us places. She was silly and loving and another perfect fit in our family.

Me and Minna (1984)

Because her birthday was right before the cutoff date for school grades, they placed her a year ahead of me in school. I was a junior, and she was a senior, which meant that she had the opportunity to graduate and receive a diploma from an American public school. About a month before she had to return home, Birgit came back for a visit. So amazing to have both of those wonderful women together with us at one time!

Soon after, we became so involved in YFU that Mom became an area representative for them. She would interview potential host families, help them choose their students, and guide them through the year. She loved doing this, and even Dad got involved.

So it goes without saying that we would continue to host students. My senior year, we welcomed Letizia from Switzerland. She is my firecracker sister—so full of love and energy. She is so passionate about everything, and her laugh could be heard all over the house. She wanted to learn everything she could about everything. She was also a senior, so we were able to experience all the fun and excitement of being seniors together, including graduation. She discovered she had a hidden talent for drama and was awarded the lead performer in our school's play *Medea*. She was fabulous!

She helped me with my preparations for heading to college in the fall. She had to return to Switzerland and finish school there even though she had a US diploma. For the third year in a row, we had a tearful goodbye at the airport. Again, promises for future visits. Happily, they all would come to fruition in the future!

Mom, Dad, and Letizia (1985)

ONE LAST TRIP

The fall after Letizia went back to Switzerland, I left home to attend Kansas State University. But that didn't stop Mom and Dad from the exchange student arena. They welcomed Juha, who was Minna's brother, to live with them my freshman year at college. Because I didn't live at home, I didn't get to know him as closely as the others, but I still felt he was my brother, and we would spend a lot of time together when I was home for holidays, weekends, and summers. It was really fun for Dad to finally have a son to live with them after years of women. He would joke that even our cats were all female. He needed a little extra testosterone to fill the house, even if it was only for a year. Juha was a senior at the high school, so we were able to celebrate another graduation.

Dad, Juha, and Mom (1986)

Dad absolutely loved these students. Each one was different, but he had special relationships with each one. He and Letizia would spend hours debating issues, politics, and the like. Her own father had passed away not too long before she came to live with us, and Dad quickly slipped into that role. She recently told me that unknowingly, it was exactly what she needed at that time. He loved learning Finnish culture from Minna and Juha and would try to recreate one or two at our house, especially around the holidays. He truly was, and continued to be, their Dad. No question.

He was just that type of guy, and even my American friends thought of him as their dad. He always made everyone feel welcomed, special, and loved. My house was always the one that was picked for events or sleepovers, and both Dad and Mom would make sure that they were successes and also fun. Laughing was a requirement. He would use that quiet, subtle way of his to get us rolling on the floor, holding our stomachs. He enjoyed life, and it showed.

He was thrilled when I chose K-State for my higher education. Kansas has two state universities—Kansas State University and the University of Kansas (KU). He always joked that I could go to either of them, but he would only pay for K-State. That made my choice easier. I knew he would have paid for me to attend college anywhere, but it was a running joke as everyone else in the family was a KSU grad. He was right with me when I moved into the dorm for the first time and made sure I had everything I needed and enough money to get through the semester. I didn't take my car with me, because Dad was pretty certain it wouldn't make it back and forth. He did buy me a new car at the end of my junior year as my early graduation present. One of his coworkers was selling it, and he thought it would be perfect for me.

When I look back on my childhood, I can't help but smile because it was so wonderful. Don't get me wrong, it had its share of hiccups and bumps, but overall, I couldn't have asked for more. I lived in a house filled to the brim with love, and that taught me how to be a compassionate, caring person. I rarely saw Dad get mad at anyone. He was a hard worker, even at home. I never saw him just sitting on the couch or watching tv. He was so busy with his projects, whether it be home repairs or improvements, building things in his workshop, tinkering with his cars, or teaching himself the newest computer programs. He was very intelligent and strong in his beliefs. He loved God and always wanted to make sure others knew God's love as well.

He was quiet when he needed to be, strong all the time, nice to everyone, and would give the shirt off his back to anyone who needed it. He didn't have to give it any effort—it was just who he was, deep into his soul. He learned it from his parents, who learned it from their parents. I learned it from him and passed it along to my kids. He taught me values, to always be kind, do not take "junk" from people, and to be a strong woman who can take care of myself.

ONE LAST TRIP

He always reminded me of his favorite phrase: "Don't let the bastards win." I take that to heart, even today. My husband thinks I'm too independent, but I know I'm just the right amount, thanks to Dad.

I was blessed. I thank God every day for that.

CHAPTER 12
Tincup, Colorado

One of Dad's sketches—Tincup cabin

Tincup, Colorado. Elevation, 10,157 feet above sea level. Gold discovered in 1859, incorporated as Virginia City in 1880, re-named and re-incorporated as Tincup in 1882. Population declined when mines dried up in 1918.

That's it in a nutshell. Simple? Yes, but this little town has grabbed my heart with its interesting story and unforgettable memories.

Brief History

In the fall of 1859, there was a man named Jim Taylor who was prospecting for gold in the town of Leadville, Colorado. Leadville is north of where Tincup would eventually be and on the other side

ONE LAST TRIP

(east side) of the Continental Divide. He and some friends had set up their winter camp just south of Leadville. He wanted to find a way across the Divide to search for better gold locations. One day he discovered a large river on the other side of Red Mountain Pass. It seemed like it could be a possible area to find some gold, so they trekked over the pass to test some of the soil. They were excited when they were able to pan some gold from a creek coming off the river. Taylor carried the gold back to their camp in a tin cup and named the area Tin Cup Gulch. Since it was winter, they could not mine and made plans to return to that area the next spring. They spent the following summer prospecting for gold by placer mining in the various streams running through the area. Placer mining is a type of mining that uses water to remove the deposits of gold, such as by panning. They built some shelters and stayed until fall. Once they left, the friends split up and moved on to other things.

For the next twenty years, other prospectors came to this area, but only seasonally. There were no year-round communities established mainly because of the tough winters. Jump forward to the late 1870s. Leadville had become very crowded with prospectors and miners with hopes of striking it rich. There were so many that some started to search out other locations around the state, looking for new opportunities.

In 1877, a man named Sol Bloom wandered into this location and had a feeling that this area was rich with gold. He was so confident that he built the first permanent log cabin in "Tincup." It was a one-room cabin that was very strong and still stands today. Someone has since bought it and restored it into a summer home.

In 1878, the mother lode was discovered on Gold Hill, which would eventually be called Gold Cup Mine. This was the start of the Tincup gold rush, and people began to arrive. By 1879, the area was called Tin Cup Camp, and the settlers here began to plan out the town. Construction of log homes and businesses were built quickly before the winter came. Some prospectors decided to give up mining and start their own businesses, including saloons and gambling/dance halls. According to the 1880 census, the population of the town was 1,495. That number included all the miners working in the surrounding areas. In 1880, the town was incorporated with the name Virginia City. Because there were already two other towns in the United States with the name Virginia City (in Nevada and Montana), the post office thought it was too confusing and told the residents it would be best to change the name. After a lot of debate, they decided to change the name of their town to Tincup. It was re-incorporated in July 1882.

Gold Cup Mine was also called Gold Cup Republic Mine and sits at over 10,700 feet above sea level. It was a three-mile trip southeast of Tincup. The mine produced gold, silver, and lead. It is no longer active. Most of the buildings are gone; however, a few structures have managed to survive.

Dad checking out the old mining equipment—Gold Cup Mine (1990s)

Gold Cup Mine

By 1884, Tincup had banks, hardware stores, grocery stores, and hotels. The actual population in town was around five hundred people. Tincup was actually a wild town, with over twenty saloons along the two main streets. Tincup also had a school and a jail and a newspaper.

In 1903, Tincup's town hall was built on the corner of Grand Avenue and Washington Street. It was built to be the center for government meeting and community gatherings. Church services were held here as well. It still stands today and is used for various events throughout the summers.

Tincup Town Hall (2018)

The main way to get to and from Tincup back then was going over Tincup Pass to a town named St. Elmo. It was only twelve miles from town to town, but not an easy trip, especially in the winter. Each day, passengers, food, mail, and mining supplies would cross the divide at Tincup Pass. St. Elmo had train service and stagecoach lines.

Tincup had a reputation for being a violent town. Two town marshals died in separate gunfire incidents. Because of the many saloons, there was a lot of drinking by the miners, which escalated into many fights, some violent.

A water system was built, including hydrants, but eventually stopped working because the pipes would break and the cost to repair them was too much. People used well water after that. There were two major business district fires, in 1906 and 1913. Both fires caused a lot of damage and destroyed large sections of the town.

Once the mines stopped producing ore, the population of Tincup declined, as the miners moved on to new locations to try to find their wealth. In 1908, the post office closed, and after that, the town shut down. By 1918, all the mines had closed.

For more detailed history of Tincup, I recommend the following books: *I Remember Tin Cup* by Eleanor Perry and *Colorado's Alluring Tin Cup* by Conrad F. Schader. They are both excellent books about the area.

By the 1950s, people began to purchase the surviving cabins. They renovated and restored them to make them into vacation homes. The town comes alive from May through October. Once the winter snows melt, residents can maneuver the streets to open up the town. The only businesses there today are a store and one restaurant.

The Tincup store is on Grande Avenue and at one time served as a gas station. The old gas pumps still sit outside the store, although they are no longer in use. Now it's the place to buy limited food or fishing supplies or to shop for gifts and souvenirs. I remember going there every day to get some candy or buy postcards.

Dad and Mom in front of Tincup store (1980s)

We bought "tin" cups at the store. You could also get these special cups from a Sarsaparilla stand just down the street that was open during a couple of summers. Someone had built this as the "Tin Cup Saloon." We could buy the tin cups filled with Sarsaparilla soda. It was such a wonderful drink, which tasted a little bit like root beer. It was a popular soft drink in the 1800s and was considered a kind of health tonic.

When you come to Tincup from Taylor Park, you enter the town on Grande Avenue. It's one of the main streets in town, although it's short. If you continue south on Grande, it takes you outside of town toward the cemetery. The cross street at Grande by the town hall is Washington Street. This was the main "drag" when Tincup was in its heyday. Here is where most of the saloons and businesses were located. The cabin we rented every summer was on Washington Street, about two blocks from Grande and on the intersection with Laurel Street. Our cabin was owned by a family named Brink, and they were the parents of one of Mom's friends. The first year we visited Tincup was in 1976, and we fell immediately in love with the quaint town. Each summer, we made it our vacation destination.

The Brink's cabin originally had three rooms. Along the way, they added a large family room and a back room with an unfinished bathroom. The original cabin had a kitchen and two other rooms. I'm not sure what each room was used for exactly when it was built, but I assume the front room was their living space and the middle and back rooms were the kitchen and the bedroom. The two fronts rooms are now both bedrooms, and the kitchen is set up in the back. There is a small covered porch off the front room with a little bridge over the stream that runs alongside Washington Street. This was probably the main entrance before the addition.

Brink's cabin (1976)

There is a door on the opposite side of the front room that opens into the second room, then on the opposite wall of that room is another door that opens into the kitchen. Our cabin did not have electricity or running water. It had been wired for electricity, and there was a small gas-powered generator we could run if we wanted or needed power. We usually would only use it once while we were there, if that. Once it got dark, we used lanterns and candles and put extra blankets on the beds at night as it could get quite chilly.

Our rule was, first person up in the morning would start a fire in the pot-belly stove in the large family room addition to begin to take the chill out of the air. We also used this stove to heat up a pot of water if we wanted to do a quick sponge bath or wash something out. One time, Mom had her feet resting on the bottom rung of it, and her shoes melted to it because it got so hot! We used it at night to make popcorn—the type that was in an aluminum pan with a cover. You can use them when you're camping—just set it on top of the fire or hot plate and watch the corn pop and balloon up. We would hang wet things around it to dry and roast marshmallows with it to make s'mores as well. It was the center point of the cabin, and I always wished we could take it home with us!

Dad sawing wood for the stoves (1976)

As for water, there was some plumbing coming to the cabin but no actual water supply to it. We would get all our water from the pump in the backyard. It was well water, and it came out of the ground barely above freezing—it was so cold!

Mom pumping water from the well (1976)

The owners had built a bathroom on the back of the cabin, with a small shower and toilet, but nothing was connected. Some of the other cabins in town were connected to water and electricity, but we didn't mind. It was fun to rough it.

The main landmark in the kitchen was the Buck's wood-burning cooking stove. Dad would get the fire going whenever we wanted to cook. There was an oven, but it took quite a lot of practice to do any baking as it was difficult to control the temperature from the fire. We usually just used the cooktop. We never tried anything fancy as far as meals. There was no refrigerator in the kitchen, so all our food had to be stored in coolers. Because there was no grocery store in Tincup, we would buy everything in Buena Vista on our way to the cabin. Midweek, we would drive to Gunnison to replenish our supplies.

The kitchen had a sink, but again, it was not hooked up to a water supply. We would pump water from the backyard into buckets and fill a dishpan to wash dishes, then we could empty it into the sink to drain. We usually heated up the water before we washed as it was just too cold!

The new addition was built off the kitchen. It was always unfinished the years we stayed there. The owners had plans to finish the walls, but it was never done while we visited. Every year that we would go, there would be something new added—furniture, decorations, etc. The beautiful woodstove was in the center along the back wall, flanked by windows. On either side of it were comfy chairs, and there were a couple of tables that we would use for eating, playing games, and doing puzzles.

There were a lot of laughs in that room. Dad always had funny and silly stories he would tell. We had hot meals together, including a recipe that Mom created and called Tin Cup stew. I remember that I used to drink the orange soda Orange Crush, which was a treat, because for some reason, I didn't drink it at home. I also remember that we would eat cinnamon fire Jolly Ranchers candy—they were our special Colorado treats.

There was a covered patio just outside the new addition. Many hours were spent here enjoying the crisp, clean air or watching a thunderstorm roll over the mountains toward us.

We would also enjoy the animals that weren't afraid of us. We had a lot of chipmunk friends who were suckers for the treats we would leave for them. They would even eat right out of our hands. We also had many hummingbirds. One summer, Mom bought a feeder, and we hung it by the patio. They were unusually bold, so once, Dad held the feeder, and they didn't seem to mind and just kept eating!

Dad and the hummingbird

This cabin sits on the last street of the town, so the backyard is wide open to nature, including the streams and beaver pond. There was a huge rockpile I loved to play on, and we could watch beavers swim around and work on their structures.

The centerpiece of the backyard was a fantastic barn. There were not a lot of barns in Tincup left when we stayed there. As a matter of fact, I don't remember any others. At least not as big and beautiful as ours. I'm sure there were more originally, but time and environment have a way of destroying these buildings. There were still remnants of a few horse stalls remaining and a loft high above. We played a lot in this barn. We didn't care that it seemed a bit precocious or that there might be other living things hiding out in the straw and debris. We could envision this space decades before when the town was alive and booming. They would have used this barn to shelter horses and carriages, probably for many families at once.

Our barn

Attached to the far side of the barn was our outhouse. Since the porcelain toilet wasn't connected to a water supply, this is what we used. It was a two-holer, meaning two people could sit side-by-side to do their business. The wooden seat had been worn smooth, so there was no chance for a splinter. There was a vent on top and enough cracks around the wood walls that kept the ventilation ok. If you needed to go during a rainstorm, you would expect to feel a raindrop or two coming through the cracks. And if you needed to go at night, you had to take a flashlight with you. It was one step above going camping or hiking and looking for a bush to use. But again, we didn't mind at all. It was part of the experience!

Unfortunately, in the years since we stopped vacationing there, a fire took down the barn and the outhouse. Such a shame to lose a part of history, especially where we had made so many fun memories.

My best friend from elementary school was Stacey. When we were in fifth or sixth grade, her family moved to Evergreen, Colorado (just outside of Denver). Every year we would stop by and pick her up, and she would spend a week or two with us in Tincup. It was the most fun I ever had on vacations—she and I would explore and have the time of our lives.

Our neighbor was a man name Al and his wife, Vi. They lived year-round in Buena Vista but spent most of their summers in Tincup. Al was a retired railroad man and quite a character. He and Vi never had children, so they both were very fond of me and Stacey. He would take us out in his ATV to hunt for mushrooms (and taught us the difference between the poisonous and non-poisonous types), let us ride his motorcycle, and gave us our first beer. We must have been thirteen or fourteen. Vi would go fishing every day and fry up her catch and invite Mom over for some, as she was the only one of us who liked trout. Dad would always help Al with projects around his property. Al was a shorter, stout guy and would always wear one-piece work jumpsuits. Before we actually got to know him, we referred to him as Redman, after one of his fashionable outfits. He also wore blue and green ones. He was always one of the highlights of our stays, and we were happy when we'd pull into town for the first time and we would see his pickup truck sitting next to his cabin.

There were other neighbors in town that we got to know over the years. One was a younger guy named Gene. He had bought an old cabin that was about to collapse and spent many summers bringing it back to life. He had a dog named Demon and loved to take all of us for rides in his pickup truck, especially up to Gold Cup Mine.

I remember one excursion up to the mine where Dad and Mom rode up front with Gene, and Stacey and I rode in the open back with Demon. We got bounced around quite a bit (it was only a dirt path with many rocks), and at one point, Demon had had enough. He jumped right out of that truck bed and decided it was more comfortable to run alongside of us. Smart!

Tincup has been referred to as a ghost town, although technically it isn't because people still live there. One summer, we noticed they would bring in open-air busses with "Ghost Tours" painted on the side. They would drive all over town and show people the town. So Stacey and I had the crazy idea to make a sign and hang it on the small front porch by the road. It said "Ghosts live here" in huge letters. When we saw the bus coming near, we would hide and watch people's reactions, and there was always lots of laughs and picture taking.

Stacey and I used to love to walk all around town to explore and head out of town to see what else was there. There was a lily pond just outside of town. We always tried to reach out and grab a flower off the lily pads, and usually, we would end up getting pretty wet.

There was an empty field on the way to the cemetery road that had one lone cabin still standing, although it wasn't in great shape. Stacey and I decided that was "our" cabin. We loved to play in that one and collect a stray square nail for souvenirs. Amazingly, this cabin was still standing in 2018!

I remember one time Stacey and I wanted to wash our hair but didn't want to take the time to wait for the water to heat up on the stove. We thought it would be a good idea to just use the well pump. It only took about two seconds to realize that it was a bad idea as we got instant brain freeze. However, we had already started, so we had to finish up and get the shampoo out of our hair. Dad almost split his pants laughing at us. Let's just say we never tried that again!

One thing we always looked forward to were Friday nights. Every Friday night, they would hold a square dance at the town hall, and people from all over the area would come in for it. Besides the residents of Tincup, there would be people from the Taylor area and kids from the youth summer camps that were right outside the town.

As teenage girls, we were so excited because we knew there would be teenage boys there! This was the one time Dad would fire up the generator so we could plug in our curling irons and have lights on to make ourselves pretty. The dance was always so fun, and yes, we would always find ourselves some cute young men who would ask us to dance! I would even catch Mom and Dad get on the dance floor as well. There was a group of square dancers from a local club that would always be there in their full dress—the ladies had the ruffled skirts, and they knew all the dance moves. The rest of us didn't, but that didn't stop up from giving it our best try and having the best time.

It's amazing how a tiny town that existed a mere hundred years ago in the middle of nowhere can grab my heart. No one that I talk to has ever heard of it. It was a fluke that we even found out about it. I'd traveled to Colorado since I was four months old, and Mom and Dad had vacationed there since they were kids. Tincup was never our destination.

We took a chance the first time we went there. In an instant, we were hooked and in love with the area and the history. Dad, I thank you for taking me to this special place, and through all our adventures there, a special part of my heart is dedicated to it. More than forty years later, it's still my special spot, and all the memories I have are my special blessings. Whenever a memory pops up, I can't help but smile!

CHAPTER 13
Day 5, Part 2
Thursday, August 9, 2018

Colorado (Tincup)

It is about noon, and about an hour or so ago, I was in Tincup Cemetery, and I found the perfect place to place Dad. I really couldn't have picked a better spot. If you go up on the hill and head over to the right and go along the edge, there's a beautiful pine tree, kind of by itself, and it overlooks the little valley with the pond and the mountain backdrop. Oh my gosh, it just couldn't be more beautiful! So I was able to bury his ashes, and I put out his wire cross and covered it with rocks. It's not too far from an old grave of a woman named Abbie, which, for some reason, Dad always liked that particular grave, so it's very close to her. I thought that would be neat too. So just absolutely beautiful! I know Kevin and I are coming back this weekend, out to Tincup, so I'm going to come back up, just say 'Hi, Dad!' again. Before I put the dirt back over the box, I said a prayer and I also said the Lord's Prayer. And you know, that's really all it needs.

I have to begin this chapter by giving thanks and glory to God. He gave me and Dad the most perfect day to complete this most important part of our journey together!

Once I arrived at the edge of the town of Tincup, I decided that I would go directly to the cemetery. This was mainly because it was around ten thirty in the morning, and I was hoping that there would be less visitors to the cemetery now than in the afternoon. I really hoped that I could do this completely alone. I did not want to share this experience with anyone else. Afterall, this is why I've driven four days and made all the stops on the way. It's been a journey for me and Dad, and I wanted it to be completed with just the two of us. I knew that if others watched or talked with me while I was laying him to rest that it would not be as special.

I drove straight through the tiny town and continued on the dirt road toward the cemetery.

Grande Avenue—leaving town toward cemetery

The Tincup Cemetery is very old, and the majority of the graves are the original resting spots of the men, women, and children who formed this town from the late 1880s / early 1900s. There are newer ones as well, but it's the old ones that intrigue me the most—they were the brave and tough people who lived here back when the gold and silver mining was booming.

ONE LAST TRIP

The cemetery sits outside of town and is very remote and quiet. To get there, you drive on the main street that goes through the heart of Tincup. After a short time, the main road curves to the right, and if you continue on it, it will eventually take you to Cumberland Pass. Just before the curve, there is a small road that exits to the left. A couple more turns through thick pine trees, and you enter into a small flat valley. At the end of this little road is the starting point of the trail that leads to Gold Cup Mine. Near the end of this dirt road, where the occasional hikers park, is a sharp left turn with the sign Tincup Cemetary, with an arrow pointing left. It is a wooden sign with the letters carved into it and each letter painted white. It's rather old—it's been there since I began visiting there in 1976. "Cemetary" is misspelled, and while everyone is aware of that, it has never been changed. It does add to part of the charm of this special area.

Mom, Dad, and me (around 1990)

One more very short drive around a large left curve and you have arrived at the cemetery. There is a tiny area to park your car, then you are ready to explore the interesting history that is Tincup!

The landscape where the cemetery lies is absolutely breathtaking! The mountains surround this small valley, and there is a small pond in the middle. Little creeks run throughout this area, and the sounds of the trickling water is so relaxing and peaceful.

Across the pond, I could see a beaver house and dam and water grass. All the other spaces that are not filled with water are covered with dense pine trees. I cannot begin to explain the smell other than it is the most wonderful scent of pine needles and fresh air. The sounds of the light winds floating through the pines is almost magical. I do believe this is what heaven will look like. God has given me a glimpse of it to enjoy here on earth. I smile knowing that Dad is blessed to be living there now in that absolute peaceful, perfect place!

I have never felt so much peace and joy when spending time here. I remember all the times that Dad and I would walk through the cemetery together, talking about the people who are buried here and what their lives must have been like. We would take photographs and enjoy spending this time together. We would also hunt for the ghost of a little girl who supposedly haunts here. One time, my friend Stacey and I thought it would be fun to walk through the cemetery at night. Around ten or eleven at night, we hiked the dark road to the graveyard and bravely walked the paths. Although we saw no actual ghosts, we heard enough noises to scare the daylights out of us and send us running all the way out and back to our cabin!

Tincup Cemetery was created using the natural hills, or knolls, in the valley. Four of them were earmarked for the burial sites. Each was tagged and named for the faith of each individual. There is the Protestant Knoll, the Catholic Knoll, the Jewish Knoll, and a hill for those who may not have behaved the right way and died a violent death or were considered nondenominational. They were buried on Boot Hill. Each hill is more beautiful than the next, with each having spectacular views of the mountains. The hills are close together and have dirt walking paths and wood board walkways and bridges over the water to connect them. These dirt paths also weave around each knoll, allowing you to walk and visit each grave lovingly placed there.

During the late 1800s, these small towns did not have a funeral home. Nor did they make or use metal caskets. In Tincup, they would make wooden coffins and grave markers. When someone would pass away, their body would be laid out in the parlor of their home, or in the Tincup Town Hall, while preparations could be made for their burial. During the winter, the ground would freeze very deep and it would be impossible to dig through it. If a person passed away during those months, their bodies would be sent to Buena Vista for burial.

The original wooden markers have all but been lost over the years. Some family members of the old pioneers have since placed carved stone markers. Luckily, there have been people who had kept up some of the old markers, either repainting the information in black letters on them or fixing the broken wood boards. Also, over the years, caring people have come in and kept the knolls cleaned up, free of branches and dead pine trees. They have cleared out the paths and around all the grave sites. They built bridges to help cross the water and get to another knoll and built the fences around each one. In 1994, a cemetery committee was formed to survey and record the plots. The community plans to continue repairing deteriorating fences and replace missing or rotten wood markers.

The local cattle ranchers utilize a lot of the land in this area to allow their cows to roam free to graze during the summers. There are structures along the paved roads throughout the area that are called cow guards. These are metal grates placed into and across the road that keep the cattle from crossing. Evidently, they will not walk on them, so it is a way of containment. Some years the cow population is larger than others, and it would not be a surprise to wake up in the morning with several of them grazing around near your windows. You can hear their calls rumble through the valleys, and they seem to not be too afraid of humans. Occasionally, you will see the cowboys come around on horseback or by ATV to take head counts and make sure they haven't wandered where they shouldn't. As the weather gets colder, they will wrangle them up and get them safely placed for the winter. I remember one summer, we were hiking near the cemetery, and we heard and felt a rumbling that got louder and louder. All of a sudden, there was a large group of cows "stampeding" through the valley, and we had to weave back and forth to avoid getting trampled! That is not the norm, however. Usually, they are very docile. Each knoll has a wooden fence surrounding it, with posts in the middle of the openings to keep the cows from climbing into the burial areas.

However, as good as an idea that it is, occasionally, you will see evidence proving that a cow does get in every now and then.

The first hill you come to is the Jewish Knoll...it's straight ahead from the parking area. This is a very small hill, and from doing some research it appears there are only a handful of graves here. It is hard to determine, as I walked around the short path and could only see a couple of clearly defined burial sites. From this knoll, as with the others, you can see the other three knolls nearby.

Once you leave the Jewish Knoll and head toward the larger hills, the first one you encounter is Boot Hill.

Boot Hill is very prominent, although not large. It is on the highest and most centrally located knoll. There are believed to be approximately forty graves on this hill from the old mining era. It is believed that one of the dance hall girls from Tincup is buried here.

View from Boot Hill

There is one grave that is still protected by a wooden fence. The legend states that the original wooden marker read, 'Here lies Black Jack Cameron… He held five aces.' (www.findagrave.com).

One of Taylor Park's most infamous characters, Harry Rivers, is also buried on Boot Hill. When he died on March 7, 1882, he was the town marshal. There are several conflicting stories of exactly how he was killed. According to the Officer Down Memorial Page (www.odmp.org), Rivers arrested a saloon owner the day before for disorderly conduct. The man, Charles LaTourette, had been held overnight and was released from custody. That evening, LaTourette walked out of his saloon holding a revolver to confront Marshal Rivers as he made his rounds then shot Rivers dead. The case was dismissed after his attorney argued he fired in self-defense.

The Catholic Knoll and its graves have not held up very well over the years. I have seen different accounts of how many graves are located there, anywhere from eight to twenty-five. It has not been kept up as well as the Protestant Knoll, and the paths and grave sites have more fallen trees, branches, and shrubs in the way. The fences that one time protected each grave have all fallen down. The cemetery committee that was formed has only surveyed and documented the Protestant Knoll. I hope that eventually it will be as beautiful. This trip, I could not navigate the water crossing to be able to walk around the knoll as the little wood bridge had fallen apart, and I didn't want to risk getting my shoes and feet wet, but I have wandered the remnants of those graves many times over the years.

The Protestant Knoll is the largest and flattest of the four hills in Tincup Cemetery. It is covered by dense pine trees, and the graves seem protected by them. There are around forty original pioneers buried here—the most influential and important people who formed Tincup. Each year, I see more and more newer burials. Considering that I believe this is the most beautiful cemetery, I absolutely understand why people choose to spend eternity here. I would definitely feel blessed to have my ashes placed here.

Protestant Knoll

Protestant Knoll

There is one other area for burials. It is not considered an official knoll. There is one grave that sits by itself in the loveliest setting in the dense pines. Her name was Kate Fisher. There is some controversy if this is her actual burial spot or if she was buried on the Protestant Knoll. She was better known as Aunt Kate. She came to Tincup around 1879 and ran two successful rooming houses and a restaurant. Her first was in a small log house. Her wonderful cooking reputation grew quickly and spread to the nearby mines. She outgrew her business and moved into a larger building, naming her new rooming and boarding house simply Aunt Kate's. She ran it until she passed away in 1902 at the age of seventy.

Kate Fisher was a black woman and a former slave. When she was freed from her master, she headed west to Colorado. She was dearly loved by all the townspeople and the miners. She demanded proper table manners from the miners and guests and always had treats for the children. (Source: *I Remember Tin Cup,* by Eleanor Perry, copyright 1986, p. 19–20.) If she was laid to rest outside of the formal cemetery knolls, I would be very sad.

Mom and me at Kate Fisher's grave (1993)

ONE LAST TRIP

As I pulled my car around the final bend to the parking area, I was praying that I would be alone. I was relieved and happy when I saw no other cars there, but I also knew that visitors could come at any time. I parked and retrieved my backpack and blanket from the back of the car, picked up Dad's ashes, and headed straight for the Protestant Knoll. Dad was a lifelong, headstrong Lutheran, so I knew exactly which hill to go to.

I had an idea of where I would like to place him, but since I had the luxury of time alone, I walked the entire graveyard looking for the perfect spot. I first walked all the way to the end of the "main" path, where the majority of the older graves are. But I knew as I was walking that this was not the right place. I asked Dad to help me find where he would like to spend eternity. I turned around once I got to the last grave and started working my way back. Something was pulling me off the main path to the left. I kept going until I reached the part of the knoll that began the downward slope toward the bottom. I stopped by a lone pine tree and looked up. Instantly, I knew this was it! It was almost like in the movies when you hear a choir sing. The backdrop was breathtaking.

View from Dad's grave

Yes, this is the place! What is funny is that this is the area I had been envisioning all along. I placed my blanket down, opened my backpack, and retrieved my little garden trowel I had brought along. I also unwrapped the wire cross and placed everything out next to the little wooden ashes box.

I started to dig around a bit to find some easy soil to move. Because of Colorado's dry summer, the dirt was hard like concrete. Also, because I was digging under the pine tree and because of all the shrubs in the area, I was running into a lot of roots and rocks. I wasn't going to let that stop me, however, so I just kept chipping away and moving dirt little amounts at a time. My plan was to go down about a foot, but I realized right away that wouldn't happen. I would settle for six to eight inches. That would be just fine.

While I was digging, I could see from my view that a couple was walking their dogs over on Boot Hill. I knew that they would most likely be heading my way next, so I continued to dig but kept tabs on their whereabouts. I had my plan that if someone were visiting this knoll, that I would cover everything up and wait until I was alone again. Once they reached the Protestant Knoll, I slid the blanket over the hole and the box. I stood up and started my own walk around until I met up with them. They were a very nice older couple who had previously visited Tincup, but it had been many years ago. They were out enjoying the beautiful day. We talked for a while, and they told me that they had spoken to someone in town and were informed that the cemetery crew had just been out there the past Saturday to do major cleanup of the entire hill. Wow! Another perfect coincidence! That was only five days ago. It was as if they knew I was coming and preparing the already beautiful spot for Dad!

While they continued their walk through the Protestant Knoll, I strolled around myself and took photographs. I had told them about my history with this place and that it was one of my favorite spots. I love to stop at each grave, marked or not, and imagine the person who is buried there and what they were like while they were alive. I would love to be able to talk to them and hear their stories and get a glimpse of what life in Tincup was like in the late 1800s. I imagine a bustling, noisy place, as it was primarily a mining community. The mines themselves were scattered throughout the area, and I believe that all the machinery and blasting had to echo enormously through the valley. If I could, I would step back in time for one day to experience it all firsthand!

Once I was alone again in the cemetery, I headed back to Dad and finished the digging. I placed Dad carefully in the hole. Before I covered it with the dirt, I laid my hand on the box and we said a prayer together. Then I recited the Lord's Prayer. I replaced all the dirt and packed it down tightly. I dug another hole, but not as deep, right next to where Dad was. This was for the base of the wire cross. I made sure that it was on the side of the grave that would face the fabulous setting.

Once I placed the cross and packed around it with more dirt, I covered both areas with the rocks that I had collected while on my walkabout earlier. I then placed one pine cone on top of the rocks. I personally love pine cones, and every time I travel to Colorado, I collect a bagful to take home with me.

Dad's forever resting spot

The mission was complete. I felt so much happiness and joy! My heart swelled with love and peace. Thanks to God's guidance, I was able to do the only thing I knew to do to honor this special man in the way he deserved. I didn't want to leave him yet, so I just sat with him for a while in the serenity and quiet of that beautiful valley. I watched the beavers play on the rocks, enjoying the sunshine and taking turns diving into the water. I watched two ducks swim by with not a care in the world. I watched the birds fly from tree to tree and even a cow or two nibbling on the grass in the meadow. I sat quietly just listening to the sounds of nature—God's nature. He created every little thing in this valley, from the mighty mountains to the tiniest of bugs. He perfectly designed the majestic pine trees and the trickling streams. He smiles at the wildflowers and the gentle breezes.

There is one more intriguing grave on the Protestant Knoll. Her name was Abbie Weston. She died June 5, 1888, at the age of fifty-five. I wasn't able to find out anything about her, except that her husband was named John. He operated the Pacific Hotel. I assume that it was near the Tincup area. For some unknown reason, Dad and I were always drawn to her grave. She has a stone marker and a fence around the burial spot. It's almost as if she was calling us over to spend a moment or two with her. I have dozens of photos of her headstone. The area where I laid Dad just happens to be near Abbie—there is an unobstructed view of her. She is just a bit above the slope from Dad, as if she can now keep a watchful eye over him. I know that Dad would enjoy being near her!

Abbie Weston's grave

I was finally able to gather my stuff and start heading out. I could have stayed sitting there the entire rest of the day. I heard more vehicles coming around the bend and knew I would be having more visitors soon. It was time to go. I said my goodbyes but assured Dad I would be back in a few days to visit him. I packed up my backpack and made my way back to my car. I was experiencing a feeling I have never had before, and I could not begin to express how it felt. It was overwhelming and special. I felt Dad's approval and could almost hear God saying, "Well done, good and faithful servant."

Dad was not afraid of death. He knew that Jesus was his friend. He knew where his soul would spend eternity. He knew that we would only be separated for a time. I didn't put his name on his grave. I did that for a reason. This journey was not for anyone else. It was for Dad and me. It was for Mom and all who loved him. It was to honor him. He deserves this.

I reached my car and tossed my backpack into the back seat and drove back toward Tincup. My plan was to park and walk the entire town with my camera and capture all the old memories I had here.

I parked next to the Tincup store. I walked into the store to pick up a few gifts for Mom, and I couldn't resist purchasing a mug and T-shirt for myself. I picked up a couple of postcards and a book on the history of Tincup. I spent a few minutes visiting with the lady running the register. I told her how I have been coming here since I was a kid and that I just put Dad's ashes in the cemetery. She was very touched and thought it was just wonderful.

I grabbed my camera and headed straight down the main street toward the town hall. The sky was a perfect shade of blue, another gift from God. I took my time and stopped at all the buildings and landmarks that were so familiar. I had to laugh when I would remember some crazy thing that we did back in the day. I came face-to-face with a cow as it stood in the road right where I was trying to stand to snap the perfect picture.

I photographed the town hall, Grande Street, Washington Street, the Brink's cabin (the one we stayed in every year), Al and Vi's cabin, the Tincup store, Frenchy's Café, the road that leads to Mirror Lake, and even the abandoned iron-wheeled carts that could have been old mining equipment. I captured with my camera the dirt roads, the tiny creek that ran in front of our cabin, and the abandoned cabins barely still standing. I wanted to document every single detail of this small ghost town, every single memory I have of it from the past forty years. I wish I could have captured the smells and the sounds. I will never forget them, even if I cannot express them in words or pictures.

Tincup is my oasis. My heaven on earth. I love it here.

CHAPTER 14

Retirement

Grandkids and travel

In 1988, Dad was listed in *Who's Who in Engineering, Seventh Edition*, with the American Association of Engineering Societies. No one was actually surprised. He was an excellent engineer and deserved it.

He was so good, in fact, that Burns & McDonnell basically had to throw him out when he reached retirement age. We'll get back to that a little later.

I graduated from Kansas State University in December 1988 with a bachelor of science in interior design. The job market for designers was slim at that time, and after three months of searching for a job in the Kansas City area, I was beginning to expand my search area. Although I did not want to move away from KC, there was a bit of excitement for me as I began the Denver area job hunt.

Dad was determined to keep me close, so he talked with some friends at work who were familiar with a competing engineering/architectural company in Prairie Village, Kansas, called Bibb & Associates. They gave me a contact number, and I called them. They brought me right in for an interview and explained that the smaller engineering firm was just about to expand and add a true architectural department. They were thrilled with the idea of hiring an interior designer and offered me the job on the spot. I accepted, and three days later, I was officially a working woman.

Dad was so happy, and we had a lot of fun over the years teasing each other about our competitive companies. His company was much older and bigger, but I liked my one-hundred-or-so-employee firm. Both of our firms worked mainly on power projects, but we also branched out into other areas. It was nice that if I had a question about an engineer's design, I could call Dad and he could explain it to me better than the actual engineers what drew it. Dad worked almost exclusively on HVAC and controls, and I designed a lot of offices and bathrooms for government contracts with local Air Force bases. Not the most exciting work but it paid my bills. Every now and then, we would get what we called "fun" jobs or special projects—Dad spent a lot of time working at a General Motors plant in KC, and I was able to design a gym/spa at a large hotel downtown and a lunchroom for the University of Kansas dormitory system.

I met Kevin in November 1991. A friend of mine had invited me to go with him to a hayride with his church's singles group. I thought it sounded fun but almost didn't go because it was an unusually cold night. There would be a bonfire after the ride, and I thought it would be fun to meet some new people. My friend ended up not being able to go, so I called another friend, and she and I went together. As I pulled into a parking spot at the church, a young man approached my car to introduce himself. He was the leader of the group and didn't recognize us, so he wanted to introduce himself. That man was Kevin. He had me and my friend ride with him in his car to the farm. He continued to stay next to me the rest of the night, even putting his arm around me on the hayride, claiming it was to warm us up. He told me later that on the car ride back to the church, he looked at me and knew immediately that he was going to marry me. A few days later, we had a three-hour phone conversation, and he asked me out on a date. We had a wonderful evening of dinner at an Italian restaurant and a night of jazz at a club called the Tuba in downtown Kansas City. We were inseparable from then on.

We had only been dating a couple of weeks when Dad got a chance to meet him. Not a planned meeting, however. I had been over at the house of Kevin's parent's for dinner and accidentally locked the keys in my car. When I went out to head home, I realized there was no way for me to get in the car. Dad had my spare keys, but they lived on the other side of town, and it was after ten o'clock at night.

I gave him a call and told him Kevin was going to drive me over to grab the spare set. It was dark, and they were already for bed, but both Mom and Dad came out to meet him. They knew instantly that this was going to be their new son-in-law but refused to say anything to me about it for fear of jinxing it. Mom and Dad's driveway was very long and ran along the front of their house. Where it connected to the road (which was the end of the road and had a steep turn-around), there were spots that your tires could drop off, and there was a good chance you would get stuck. Dad warned Kevin to be careful backing up so he wouldn't get stuck. Kevin is a good driver, but that was what precisely happened. With Dad's help, we were able to get the car out without calling a tow truck. What a memorable first meeting with the in-laws!

The first time we all "officially" were together was on Thanksgiving 1991. Dad's firm had a suite at a hotel that overlooked the Country Club Plaza, a shopping and entertainment district near downtown Kansas City. It covers about fifteen blocks and has over one hundred shops and thirty or so restaurants. It's a historic district that began right about the turn of the twentieth century. A man had a vision for this little area along Brush Creek. He and a couple of his friends purchased some land with a vision of building a shopping center near where he had already built residential areas. In 1922, the plans for the area were drawn up, and the Plaza was constructed.

In 1925, someone put up a single strand of Christmas lights, most likely on a whim, and that started the tradition of the Plaza Lights, which has become a world-famous event every year. Every single building in the district is wrapped in thousands of lights, and on Thanksgiving evening, they turn them on with a huge celebration. Thousands of people flock to the Plaza for the lighting ceremony. The lights stay on until the middle of January. It's always been my favorite place for viewing Christmas decorations, and growing up, we fought the crowds many years to attend the lighting ritual.

So in 1991, we were able to view the lighting ceremony from the suite of the hotel with Dad's friends from work. It was amazing, as we were able to stay warm and enjoy the catered food and drinks. Kevin was un-officially part of our family.

In August 1992, he did make it official. During a dinner at his parent's house, with Mom and Dad there, Kevin surprised me with a proposal. I accepted happily, and the wedding planning began. Dad knew he had better just sit back and let Mom and I take over. He was the perfect husband and dad. He would just open the checkbook and say, "Who do I write this to?"

We were married May 7, 1993. Dad walked me down the aisle, of course. I had never seen him look so handsome. He was wearing a tuxedo, and I found out later that it was the only time in his life he wore one. He had worn a simple suit at his own wedding. He was nothing but smiles that day and seemed to have no problem with giving me away to Kevin. He was a very good judge of character, and if he had had any doubts, he would definitely have told me. All his side of the family were there, and it was a wonderful reunion and time to catch up. It was a perfect day!

In October 1993, Kevin and I pulled up our roots and made the move to St. Louis. Actually, St. Charles, Missouri. It was not because we wanted to leave Kansas City, but it was a smart logistical move for

ONE LAST TRIP

Kevin's business. He and his dad, Len, had started Gambill Sales in 1991. They were manufacturer agents for steel companies. Business was finally starting to pick up, and it made sense for Kevin to be farther out east, as his territory was there. It made for less traveling for him during the weeks, so he was home more.

Dad was just as sad as I was for us to be leaving. But he put on a brave face and helped us with the move. He and Mom would make as many trips as they could to see us and to explore our new city.

It wouldn't be long before he had an even better reason to come visit. On April 6, 1995, he became a grandpa. His grandson, Alex, came into the world ready to take it on. Dad was over the moon. He finally had that boy that he could teach all the things that he tried with me. Only this time, that kid would follow exactly in his papa's footsteps. He ate up everything Dad taught him—how a car works, how electricity flows through circuits, how to respect tools, and how to build things out of wood.

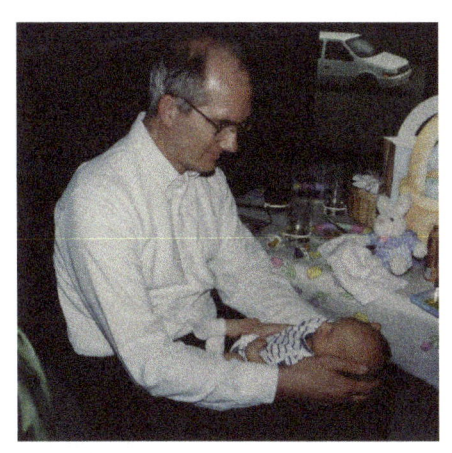

Alex's first Easter (1995)—ten days old

There was a train track just a few miles from Mom and Dad's neighborhood, and Dad would take Alex down there to watch the trains pass by. This began a very long obsession with anything railroad for Alex. He and Dad would build creative track layouts with Alex's wooden train set, and they would play with them for hours on end. Whenever we would visit them in Kansas City, Dad would pull out some of his old train sets, and they would attempt to get them working again. In St. Louis, we have a transportation museum that has an entire rail yard filled with various train engines, cars, and gear that they could climb in and under and learn how they run.

Dad thought his life was pretty good. Then it all changed again. On January 3, 1997, he once again could call himself Grandpa. His granddaughter, Nicole, surprised everyone when she decided to show up three weeks early. Unfortunately, she had a serious infection and had to be emergency transported to our children's hospital downtown. Dad made a straight beeline to go see her. He did pop in my hospital room to say hi then took off, and I didn't see him the rest of the day. That's ok. He was with his new granddaughter, who grabbed his heart from the first moment he saw her.

Nicole's first Halloween (1997)

ONE LAST TRIP

He proved he had plenty of love for both of them. He loved being a grandpa. He made sure that whenever we visited that they had their nightly ice cream (me too!). He loved to babysit them so Mom and I could sneak out to do a little shopping. He would take them out to eat. One of their favorite places was a train-themed restaurant. You would order your food at your table by using a telephone, then when your food was ready, it would be loaded into a train and sent to your table via a track on the ceiling that ran around the entire restaurant. When it reached your table, the tray would drop down so you could get the food.

Dad would take them to parks and museums and to their lake to swim or try their hand at fishing. He and Mom would come to our house, and we would head downtown to go up to the top of the Arch or to a Cardinal's game. He didn't care; he just wanted to spend time with them.

Since Alex loved trains so much, we found a narrow-gauge train ride near Eureka, Missouri. It would run rides on certain weekends each year. We all enjoyed it, but Alex and Dad seemed to be in heaven!

Train ride near Eureka, Missouri (2000)

During one of Mom and Dad's visits, we drove to Springfield, Illinois, to see President Lincoln's home and grave. We also visited an old village that had been restored. Another time, we drove north to Hannibal, Missouri. We took a riverboat cruise and walked through the mines. We even drove bumper cars, and Dad had as much, if not more, fun as the kids.

One summer, Kevin, the kids, and I took a vacation to Colorado, and unintentionally, Mom and Dad had booked a trip there at the same time as well. We were all staying at White Water Resort, so really no surprise about that because we all tried to visit there every year. Our trips overlapped a couple of days, at the end for us and the beginning for them. It was nice that we could all enjoy a couple of days together in the mountains. That was the trip that Nicole lost a tooth and accidentally swallowed it. She was hysterical for the rest of the day thinking that the tooth fairy wouldn't come once we got home because she didn't have the tooth. Dad and Mom talked to her until she calmed down, but they had to take turns because we all thought it was so funny and didn't want to laugh in front of her.

Along the Million Dollar Highway, Colorado (2004)

Each year in March, Hermann, Missouri, holds a festival that is called Wurstfest. It is where local meat companies set up booths and show and sell various types of sausages and snacks. They have live German bands and dancers. We love to go and sample all their varieties of sausage and stock up with enough to eat over the summer. Dad and Mom joined us one year. Since we are German, it's a lot of fun.

Wurstfest in Hermann, Missouri

As the kids got older, Dad and Mom made sure that they wouldn't miss any special event or holiday. They were at the kids baptisms, confirmations, and graduations.

Alex's high school graduation (2013)

Dad was so proud of both of them, but he had an especially proud moment when Alex earned his Eagle Scout and made him a special wooden box as a gift at his ceremony.

In February 1995, Dad was hit with a life-changing diagnosis—Parkinson Disease. He was determined to continue to live his life as he wanted. He would control the disease; it would not control him.

That disease fought with him for over twenty-three years. Ultimately, Dad would win in the end.

In August 1998, we hosted a surprise fortieth wedding anniversary party for Mom and Dad. I had started to plan this party just after Christmas. I sent out save-the-date information to over fifty of their friends and family and told everyone this was to be a surprise. I had a suspicion that they would plan a trip overseas for their anniversary, so I deliberately planned the party for two weeks before their actual anniversary, just to be safe. Over the next few months, all the guests had made travel arrangements and sent me special notes and cards for me to put together a scrapbook. About a month before the party, Mom told me they had booked a trip to Finland (I was not surprised), but for some reason, they decided to go a little early. Turns out they would be in another country during their party!

I had no choice but to pull Dad aside and let him know about the party. I didn't want to give him details but wanted him to see if they could change their flights. He laughed, and they were able to adjust the trip. We were having the party at the house of Kevin's parents, so my mother-in-law and I spent a couple of days before arranging food and decorating. Since they knew we were having some sort of party, we used the excuse that we were going to a restaurant and that my in-laws were going to watch the kids. They assumed that some people would meet us at the restaurant, so when we got to my in-laws' house, they "didn't" answer their front door, which was locked. So we all walked around the back of the house to their beautiful patio where all their friends were waiting. They were quite surprised with the list of loved ones who came. We had the members of the original wedding party (who could make it) line up for a fabulous throwback photo. A beautiful night for a beautiful couple!

Dad and Mom's fortieth anniversary, September 6, 1998

In November 1998, Dad officially retired from Burns & McDonnell. He had been working there since June of 1958, and because of his health reasons and his dedication to the firm, it was time. We traveled to Kansas City to participate in a lovely reception for him. He was very respected and loved by his co-workers. I was so proud of him and his commitment to hard work and loyalty. He wasn't quite done working, however. He became an independent contractor and continued working part-time at Burns & McDonnell and Bibb & Associates (the firm I had worked for) as a consultant for specific projects. He just couldn't give up the workforce, but it allowed him flexibility to spend more time doing the things he truly loved.

Not long after his official retirement, Dad wrote this for our family newsletter: "So far, this retirement deal is great! I should have done it long ago. Of course, Jo thinks I'm not *really* retired because I still go to work so much [3 days a week normally, but I worked 5 days each of the last 2 weeks to help get some work out]. Of course, I don't have to go to work if something more important [or fun] comes up, which really feels great. We are actually making progress on fixing up the house, and I have a couple of small but fun projects cooking. We're going to Colorado late in May. It'll be good to getaway—it's been a long time. Then we'll get serious on finishing up the 'list' of house fixes."

A lot of his "house fixes" were for us and our houses. In our first home, he spent a week with us to build a huge pantry off the laundry room. He even got my kids to "help" by handing them sandpaper blocks to smooth out drywall mud. In our second home, he and Kevin did some tiling and beadboard work in our kitchen and many other small projects for us, including a raised garden area in my backyard and building a workshop-type counter in our garage for Alex. He loved doing it, and it made him feel important and that he had a purpose, especially when his Parkinson's made it difficult to use his hands like he used to for delicate small things.

Dad and Mom spent a lot of time traveling after his retirement. They loved going out to Colorado and especially overseas to visit their exchange "daughters" and "son." He really enjoyed spending time with their children and was so in love with the Finnish culture. They decided to spend Christmas 2000 in Finland. Dad was so enchanted from the trip that he wrote an essay about it.

In January 2002, Kansas City suffered a really big ice storm. Around half of the city lost power, including Mom and Dad. They finally got the power back after being off for exactly one week. They were pretty cold. I tried to talk them into staying with us, but Dad didn't want to leave the house for fear of broken pipes etc. Dad put thermometers all over the house, and by the end of the week, the coldest locations were down to the high thirties. At night, they (plus their four cats) slept on the floor in the family room (their bedroom was too cold) and lit the gas log in the fireplace. Mom actually had jury duty during the week, so she could escape the cold during the day. Besides being cold, they got pretty bored and tried to find things to stay mentally occupied. Dad says, "I just hung around the house and tried to convince myself that I was actually doing something constructive. Mostly, I chipped ice off of cars, the driveway, porch, etc. and kept moving. Got to know the neighbors better."

ONE LAST TRIP

In September of 2002, Dad, Mom, and I traveled to Italy to attend Birgit's wedding. We flew to Switzerland to spend the night with Letizia, and all of us, including her fiancé, drove to Italy together. We spent a wonderful week touring all over Northern Italy. The wedding was in Bologna, which is the capital of the Emilia-Romagna region. The parents of Birgit's new husband owned a lovely estate deep in vineyard country, and they hosted the most beautiful reception. After the wedding, we visited other historic cities, including Venice. It was the trip of a lifetime, and I am so happy that I had the chance to experience it with Dad. It would be the last trip I was able to take with him while he was alive.

Bologna, Italy, September 2002

Shopping in Venice

In 2008, he was faced with another health situation—prostate cancer. Earlier in the year, Mom had had a minor heart attack. They were still living in Kansas City, so I was doing a lot of traveling back and forth across Missouri to take care of things for them. Luckily, her condition was good after they placed a stint. I stayed with Dad while Mom was in the hospital to take care of him. She was fully recovered quite quickly, and that eased my travel. It was difficult for me because my kids were still younger and at home and Kevin traveled for work quite a bit.

Dad's cancer diagnosis came with several options. The doctors were concerned about doing any surgery because of his Parkinson's, so we decided on radiation. The treatment protocol was to be forty doses of radiation every day of the week, except weekends. I went with him for his first appointment. They made a special form shaped to him to use during treatments to keep him in the right position, and he got a tattoo! It was actually dots, or marks, to show the radiologist exactly where to send the radiation. After that, he went daily to get his treatment.

He had very few side effects and was able to drive himself to the center. He did have one incident, however. Mom drove him that day and dropped him off at the main doors to go park. Because of his

Parkinson Disease, he had developed orthostatic hypotension. This is a condition that causes his blood pressure to drop dramatically when he would change positions. This included lying to sitting and sitting to standing. The sudden drop would cause him to briefly pass out and fall. He had ways to prevent problems with it, but sometimes he would just stubbornly keep going. This particular day, he hopped out of the car, and the next thing he remembered was lying on the floor with a bunch of nurses surrounding him, looking down. Turns out his blood pressure plummeted, and he passed out in between the two sets of double doors. The passing out itself isn't dangerous for him, but whatever he hits on the way down is. So he hit his head on something, cut it open, and had to be sent over to the emergency room to get some stitches and a CT scan. Everything was fine. This wasn't the first or the last time this had happened. He evidently had a very hard head!

One spring, Mom traveled with their church to the Holy Land, and since it was the kids spring break, we decided to stay with him for a couple of days. Their friends and neighbors had been keeping their eyes on him and having him over for dinner, but we thought it was a good time to visit. Since Dad was doing ok and the weather was nice, we took a trip to the Kansas City Zoo. He really enjoyed getting out and did great with all the walking.

Kansas City Zoo

In September 2008, Mom and Dad celebrated fifty years of marriage. We definitely wanted to have a big celebration for them, but after the craziness of planning their fortieth party, it would not be a surprise party! We included them in all the planning of this one. My mother-in-law graciously offered her home again. They had moved into a new house, which was large and beautiful and perfect for entertaining. It was a perfect night! We had the food catered (BBQ, of course!), and so many of their family and friends were able to make it. There were a few who had sadly passed away in the last decade, but we still had a wonderful turnout. I had put together a slide show presentation, and guests talked and told stories about them. Their wedding clothes were on display, as were many keepsakes from their wedding and fifty years of life. They both had the time of their life!

This is from the family newsletter, *Rinard Ringers* (written by Julie Rinard Scott): "It's official…an unofficial family reunion for all the right reasons. Saturday, September 6, 2008, will be the 50th wedding anniversary of Sydney Leroy and Joline [Boehner] Rinard. Their daughter Lori [Rinard] Gambill and her extended family will be hosting a gala celebration in Kansas City starting at 6:00 pm. No surprise party this time, so everyone can park closer to the site. We hear that Rinards will be descending from all parts of the country for this festive occasion to reminisce with laughter the way that they always manage to do."

Mom and Dad's fiftieth anniversary, September 6, 2008

Dad was starting to have more trouble with his Parkinson Disease, and he was falling more. This was causing Mom to have more back troubles trying to help him. My travels to KC were becoming more frequent and tiring. Kevin and I had many discussions about what we should do, and we came to the conclusion that they should move to St. Louis and buy a house close to us so we could help them easier. We proposed the idea to them, fully believing they would never leave KC or their beautiful house that Dad built for them. To our surprise, the next day they called and said they were going to do it!

The next few months were a whirlwind. We had to find realtors on both ends. I was so sad to put their home up for sale, as it was where I grew up and I absolutely loved it. We decided that they should find something in St. Louis before they listed their Shawnee house. There was also way too much work to be done there before it could be shown or sold. They both had become "pack rats" over the years, and we had the daunting task of sorting, cleaning, throwing away, and packing up all the stuff they had accumulated. I spent many days and weeks over the next few months taking on this challenge. We ended up with two full dumpsters of throw-aways and several charity pickups from their church. As it got closer to move time, we would simply box up stuff and label them "To be sorted later." I knew that would not happen, but it was a compromise. Dad seemed a little more comfortable getting rid of stuff than Mom, but we still had way too much.

They found a house in Lake St. Louis, an area about fifteen minutes from me in a lake community. The house was similar in design with their other one, and it sat in the woods as well. This made the move easier. Dad loved it. He did not want a typical "cookie cutter" home as were most of the houses in our area. It was built in the 1970s and needed some upgrading and basic face-lifting. Before they moved in, Kevin and I gutted all three bathrooms and rebuilt them, I painted every single room, we had new flooring put in, and we upgraded the kitchen countertops. It had a wonderful screened-in porch that provided absolute privacy due to the surrounding trees. Off the porch was a large, long deck that ran the length of the house.

It was a unique and nice house, although I was worried that since it was a two-story, and Dad was having more trouble getting around. There was a very large room in the finished basement that had been used as a workshop by the previous owner, so all his tools (including the Shopsmith) fit easily into the space. He spent hours each day getting it all set up perfectly, everything in its place. We all knew that he would not be able to actually do any projects, but it was peace of mind for him, and it made him happy. And it kept him busy and occupied. That's all we wanted for him. Years later, every single one of those tools were boxed up and moved to Oklahoma City with Alex. That's what Dad had wanted—for his grandson to have them. His biggest fear was that they would be given or thrown away. Alex was honored and thrilled to have them. He now has them set up in his own garage. He doesn't use most of them, but they are a special gift from his grandpa.

Once we had their new house renovated and ready for move-in, it was time to put their Black Swan house up for sale. We found our realtor, and she did all the pre-work, and the house was to be officially on the market. The night before it went live, their neighbors brought some friends by to take a look at it. They instantly fell in love with it and called our realtor right away with a full-price offer. After some agreed items were fixed, Mom and Dad started their new chapter in life as a Missouri resident.

Dad and Mom in front of their Lake St. Louis home

Moving day was interesting. We had found a mover that was willing to make the trek across Missouri to Lake St. Louis. The morning they showed up, we were still cramming things in boxes. We had about three hours of sleep the night before, but there was still too much stuff. The moving company had sent a couple of nice ladies to help with last-minute packing. Throughout the crazy day, we all bonded and managed to keep everyone laughing. Because of the amount of stuff and that insanely long, steep hill they would have to go up, they decided to use two smaller trucks instead of one large one. Even then, it was extremely difficult for those heavy trucks to get out of Black Swan. I drove back to St. Louis that afternoon, and the trucks headed out that evening and spent the night at a hotel near their new house. Mom and Dad stayed in a hotel in Shawnee that night and drove over the next morning. I met the movers at their new house, and before long, we were neck high in boxes. The new adventure had officially begun!

At this point in their lives, Mom and Dad had more difficulty with carrying boxes and mobility. I spent a lot of time helping them unpack certain boxes and putting things away. One afternoon, Mom and I made another one of our trips to the hardware store, and when we came home, we found Dad stuck in the center of dozens of boxes piled up in the garage. We were never certain how he ended up there, but we had wished there had been some sort of video of it. All three of us laughed so hard we had to sit down, and I had to move away many boxes to get Dad out. He said he was trying to find something and, at one point, realized he had made a bit of a mistake. I inherited that same sense of stubbornness and dedication. When I decide to do something, I give it my all, even if I get stuck in a pile of boxes. Good thing we came home when we did!

There was a front room in their new house that had previously been used as an office, so we got Dad set up there with his desk, computer, and bookshelves. The desk he had was a very large and sturdy one he had built for their old house. It had an L-shaped piece that was the correct height for his computer, and it boasted beautiful walnut-stained drawers with a laminate top. He had built an organizing piece that sat on top of the desk, with lots of little cubby holes and shelves to hold paper and whatnots.

His absolute must-haves were his bookshelves. He had several, and they were all filled to capacity with his books. He loved his books almost as much as his tools. There were some novels, but most of them were his engineering books. There were old textbooks, reference books, binders he had made with practices and procedures that he had written. His engineering mind never shut off, even up to his death. He loved to teach people about anything engineering. He would draw flowcharts and schematics. When we would be somewhere, in his eye, nothing was ever designed correctly—he always had a better solution. His books followed him wherever he was living, even the nursing home. He couldn't see perfectly to read them very well, but he would flip through the pages and re-organize them on the shelves over and over.

He also loved his computer. Of course, he would spend hours drawing spreadsheets and charts, but he also enjoyed sending e-mails to family and friends. The Parkinson Disease took away his fine touch and movements with his fingers, so a simple e-mail would take him quite a while to type. He never learned the fast way to type—he was a one-finger guy. No matter, he enjoyed doing it, and it kept his mind occupied and challenged. On occasion, he would call me and tell me his computer was broken. I would go over to check it out, and it was usually one of his unsteady fingers that had hit a funny button. Of course, with my lack of computer skills, it was more like the blind leading the blind!

Dad inherited his love for writing from his parents. Both of them were writers, and Grandpa had submitted some of his to publishers. I don't believe anything was actually published, but he was very passionate with his thoughts, and Grandpa's use of the English language was beautiful and sophisticated. I have most of his originals and plan to combine them with writings from Dad, myself, Dad's sister Julia, and even a couple that my son wrote into a book so everyone can see inside our family's awesome, crazy, and loving minds. Dad wrote many essays where he expressed his innermost deep thoughts and feelings. Most of these were about God, the Holy Spirit, religion, and his extremely strong faith. They are beautiful and well-thought-out. He knew exactly where he was going after his earthly death, and he felt it was his calling to share the love of God to everyone. A couple days after he died, we all laughed at the idea that he was probably just finishing up asking Jesus all the questions he had been saving!

Dad always had a fascination with the St. Louis Arch. In the 1960s, he had an opportunity to work on a project in Eero Saarinen's office. Saarinen was a Finnish architect and the one who designed the arch. Dad didn't get a chance to meet him personally but was in his actual office. In his office was a mockup of the elevator pod used to take people to the top of the Arch. During his many visits to St.

Louis, Dad had been up the arch several times. Letizia had come to town for a visit, and she wanted to see it herself. Dad was determined to go with us to the top, and the staff was great in helping us get him down the ramps and stairs to the loading area for the tram. It was a lot of work but absolutely worth it as he was so happy to view the sprawling downtown St. Louis.

Because of the Parkinson's, we had been worried about his driving ability for a while, so when he moved to Lake St. Louis, we decided it was the perfect time for him to become a permanent passenger. He knew logically he shouldn't be driving anymore, but because of pride and stubbornness, he continued to try to convince me he could do it. His doctors had said no, and we had said no, and I wasn't going to put him through the embarrassment of being rejected by the Department of Motor Vehicles. I was more than willing to take him anywhere he wanted to go. That was usually to the hardware store, to doctor's appointments, and to go out to eat. The latter was one of our favorite activities, and it usually involved hamburgers. Being a Rinard meant that he enjoyed his food. The funny part is that he was always a slim man. He never plumped up and could eat anything he wanted. But as for his confidence of his driving ability, he was absolutely positive he could do it. Even a month before he died, he wanted me to consider letting him take the driver's test so he could help Mom out.

ONE LAST TRIP

As his disease progressed, he began to have some disturbing side effects. The medication would cause hallucinations, and he had a few bouts of leaving the house because of them. One time, Mom couldn't find him, and the neighbors had called the police because they found him sleeping on their driveway. He wasn't hurt, but for some reason, he left their house, got confused and tired, and lay down to rest. When he started having some delusional thinking that someone had broken into the house in the middle of the night and because his falls were becoming more often and difficult for him or Mom to get him up, we had to make the extremely tough decision to move him to an assisted-living facility. Mom just couldn't take care of him anymore, and neither could I. He agreed it was the right move.

We found a beautiful place very close to my house. It was family-owned and had both assisted-living and skilled nursing facilities. They were in the process of building a brand-new building that would be all assisted-living apartments, and we secured him one of those. He had a wonderful one-bedroom apartment, with a small kitchen and a large bathroom that was all his. His big desk, bookshelves, and electric train sets fit easily, and we made it very homey for him. We bought him a big television so he could watch his favorite shows—the History Channel and old movies. He had big windows that overlooked the front, and it was surrounded by a small park. It was a relief to have extra sets of eyes on him at all times if he needed it. They gave him his medicines every day (with Parkinson's, it is quite a chore), and he got three meals a day down in the beautiful dining room. The food was very good, and he was able to socialize with the other residents. They could help him up if he fell and take care of him if he wasn't feeling well on a particular day. Nobody wanted to have him live there, but since it really was necessary, it was a very nice place.

By this time, he needed to use a walker most of the time. However, in his stubbornness, he would walk around his apartment without it. His legs were always strong. He could get in and out of the car easily and climb the two steps from my garage to my house. He had two main issues with walking because of the Parkinson Disease. The first being that occasionally, his legs would start to shuffle or stutter. The momentum of his body kept going, but his legs couldn't keep up. This would usually lead to a fall. The second issue was a strange phenomenon that Parkinson's people can get—they could be walking along just fine then come to a doorway or change in flooring material, and for some reason, this would trigger something and cause their legs to freeze. They would simply stop at that transition spot for a moment then have difficulty getting their legs to start again. This could also lead to a fall, but usually, they are able to get moving and avoid one.

Because of his Parkinson Disease and past prostate cancer, Dad was very vulnerable to urinary tract infections. They would hit fast and hard. One day he was fine, the next he would be acting almost psychotic. He would talk gibberish, clean up trash on the floor that wasn't there, have vivid hallucinations or delusions, or sometimes become catatonic. These infections almost always ended him up in the hospital for several days to receive IV antibiotics. This was always a problem with getting his PD medications correctly and on time. He would be labeled a "fall risk," as all Parkinson's patients are, so he was not allowed to get out of the bed and move his muscles. This would set back his PD, and he would get worse. It was a vicious cycle.

After he had been at the assisted living for a few months, one of these monster infections took over. He was sent to the hospital as usual, and he didn't make it back to his apartment for five months.

Those five months were a roller coaster of bad and worse, mostly worse. The first infection was so bad that it spread to all his body systems, and he became septic. He was put on a ventilator to help him heal, a feeding tube, and two catheters. The hospital called me and told me that I should get all his papers together and call the family. They didn't think he would make it. I told them that if anyone could survive this, it would be him. He is like a cat—he had nine lives. Plus, he was my Superman and was absolutely bulletproof. They didn't believe me, but a week later, he was almost back to normal and ready to head to a rehabilitation facility to work on regaining his strength. They were all amazed and thrilled!

But things didn't stay that way. While at rehab, he had a relapse of the UTI, which put him back in the hospital. He recovered from the infection then back to rehab. This cycle continued for a full five months. Hospital, rehab, hospital, rehab. He would get so sick, and with each infection, he got weaker and the recovery took longer. After each hospital stay, we would search for a new rehab facility, hoping to put a stop to this.

One rehab facility failed to realize that he was suffering from a urinary tract infection that was so bad that he became unresponsive, even though we kept telling them to have his urine tested. We knew all the signs of a UTI. They didn't do it for three days (it was a weekend, of course, and their weekend crew didn't want to mess with it). They assumed that his comatose state was his "normal." During those three days, they tried to force liquids into his mouth, and they would set his food on the bedside tray. They couldn't get his PD medicines into him because he wouldn't swallow, so they just stopped trying. Without his meds, his Parkinson's would get so bad he practically became a vegetable. We were constantly begging them to get him to a hospital. Finally, the evening of the fourth day, a new nurse came on duty, took one look at him, and immediately called an ambulance, even though she was breaking protocol. The doctor at the ER said Dad was so dehydrated that they weren't sure if he would even survive. By the grace of God, they saved him, but that setback kept him away from home for even longer. We finally found a wonderful rehab place that nursed him back to health and helped him regain his original strength. The day he walked back into his assisted-living apartment after five long months, everyone was cheering and crying.

Everything was ok for the next six months or so. I would continue to receive phone calls from the facility to let me know of another fall that Dad took. Most of them were minor, with no injuries, but occasionally, they would send him out to the hospital for stitches or a CT scan to check for concussions. That spring, we received what is typically known in the assisted-living world as the "eviction letter." They stated that his care had become too much for them and that he would have to move out in thirty days. They felt his fall risk was too high and didn't want the liabilities. We were pretty upset for a couple of reasons. One, we didn't think he was in that bad of a shape for them to not take care of him. Second, we had no idea where he could live or how we were going to pay for it. Assisted living was expensive enough, but skilled nursing was astronomical. Also, most of the good, skilled nursing facilities had long wait lists.

Dad also felt that he was still good enough to live on his own with assistance. They wouldn't budge, however, and we scrambled to find him a new place to live. We originally moved him into a community that was about a twenty-minute drive from me and was highly recommended. However, after a couple of weeks, we were so disappointed in his care that we knew he couldn't stay there. We immediately started the search again. Sometimes in these situations, you can feel God's presence. This was one of those. I called a community also near my house that was less than ten years old and quite beautiful from the outside. Some of the places we had visited in the past or that Dad had stayed in while doing rehab were quite unacceptable and some even appalling.

We wanted Dad to have his own room, not shared with another resident. We also wanted a place with loving nurses and workers who would treat him with the respect that he deserved. Also, we needed medical staff who had a very good understanding of Parkinson Disease, which is extremely complicated. This facility had an available room that had originally been a double-occupancy room, which had recently been converted to a private one. It had plenty of room for his bookshelves, TV, and a smaller desk that we had bought for him. It had sliding doors out to a closed-in garden area. They had a very good physical and occupational therapy departments and speech pathologists to help him with his talking and swallowing. Parkinson Disease affects both of those. PD patients can get pneumonia from aspirating food because of choking. It was the best solution for a problem we never wished we had to deal with. He didn't love the idea but knew it was what had to be done.

He had two nurses whom we absolutely loved. They would call me quite a bit with updates, good or bad, and were wonderful with him. They understood his disease and made the proper adjustments and observations. By this time, he was confined to use a wheelchair. All the residents there were required to use them. He did enjoy his therapy where they continued to work on his walking. His legs were still so strong that he could transfer himself in and out of my car and get himself into my house with a little help. They would catch him walking around inside his room sometimes. He also enjoyed his visits with a lady who brought her trained dog in for therapy. She happened to be a friend of mine, and all the residents loved the pup's warm kisses.

Because his urinary tract infections were getting more frequent and severe, Dad received a surgically placed suprapubic catheter. This type of catheter is inserted through the abdomen and directly into the bladder. This was more comfortable for him and easier for the staff to keep clean and sanitary. It did cut down the number of infections he got but did not eliminate them altogether.

As his disease progressed, he began to suffer from some depression. At one point, he refused to get out of bed and take his medications. They couldn't force either of these, but his nurse spent the day just sitting and talking with him. After a couple of days of us encouraging him, he changed his mind and got up and decided to keep going. This was the first time in twenty-some years that I saw this reaction in him, and it never happened again. He never complained once about having this disease. He never played the victim. He never gave into it. He was stubborn and strong. I admired that about him and still do to this day.

During one of his hospital stays, when he was very much out of it, I was sitting with him. His bed was lowered almost to the floor because of his fall risk. He was awake, and we could talk, but he wasn't making a lot of sense. He wasn't sure exactly what was wrong with him, and I explained that it was another urinary tract infection and that he would be ok after getting all his antibiotics. All of a sudden, he started crying. It was extremely rare for him to cry, and looking back, I really don't remember ever seeing him cry. I'm sure he did, but he kept it mostly private. Funny thing is, I am exactly the same way! I gave him a hug and rubbed his arms and told him he was going to be fine. He started telling me that he couldn't die yet because he hadn't reached enough people. I was confused at his statement but reassured him he wasn't going to die at that time. He kept going on and on about needing to talk to more people. I finally realized that he meant that he knew his job on earth wasn't finished and that he needed to continue sharing God's love with more people. He still had more of God's work to do. He needed to guide them to true salvation. I was so touched, and I couldn't keep my tears from flowing either. What a selfless, humble, loving, and godly man! He was more concerned about saving others' souls than his own life. Later, after he recovered, I asked him if he remembered telling me that. He didn't. That reinforced to me what his true character believed. He was a true servant of God.

Dad loved coming to my house, especially on holidays. He gobbled up large platefuls of food and just enjoyed hanging out watching movies and playing with my cats. One Thanksgiving, I was cleaning up the dishes when I heard music. I peeked around the corner into the front living room and saw Mom sitting at the piano, with Dad in his wheelchair next to her, and they were playing together. Nothing formal or even recognizable, but both of them were having a wonderful time. Such a sweet moment for them to share!

On February 4, 2016, Dad turned eighty years old. His brother Phil had celebrated his own birthday on January 31 but decided he wanted to be with Dad on this milestone birthday. I thought it would be fun to have a party for the birthday boys, so we decorated the living room where he lived, and I made them their favorite cake that Grandma used to make them every year. She always complained that it was a difficult cake to make and had to make two of them because the boys insisted that they each get their own. They were maraschino cherry cakes, and before my Aunt Julie passed away, she sent the recipe to me.

Dad's eightieth birthday, February 4, 2016

Phil and Dad enjoyed their visit together and were talking about things. Phil said, "Well, we all have this disease called life…" Dad finished the thought with "And it's fatal." Not the first time they had thought the same thing, but it turned out to be the last.

After Dad had lived in this skilled nursing facility for about two years, we started noticing a decline in his care. His two favorite nurses had left to work at other facilities, and we noticed the new staff was much smaller and not as knowledgeable of Parkinson Disease. His room was also not very clean, and we were told that most of the cleaning staff had left and that they were having trouble finding new employees. The same was happening for the nurses and techs. Dad wasn't very happy anymore, and because the living conditions were declining, we once again began a search for a new place for him.

I had watched a brand-new community being built nearby that advertised an all-skilled nursing facility. It was very different than anything we had ever seen. It was built around a new theory of cottage living. Each cottage housed ten residents. Everyone had their own room and bathroom, and there was a large shared kitchen, eating area, and living area. It was absolutely beautiful. I liked the idea that there would be one nurse and two techs on duty twenty-four hours a day for the ten residents. That ratio was very comforting.

ONE LAST TRIP

The kitchen was huge and modern, and every single meal was prepared and cooked in each cottage by the staff. They ate those fresh and homemade meals served around a beautiful huge dining table together. The large living space had lots of windows, a nice outdoor patio, a spectacular stone fireplace, and a large television that the residents could watch whatever they wanted, including movies. There was a built-in bookshelf filled with various books and a permanent puzzle table. Each cottage had a salon/spa for haircuts and Jacuzzi baths. We took Dad over for a visit. While we were looking around, he rolled over to the bookshelf and pulled out a book about World War II and started reading it. We asked what he thought of the place, and he said, "When can I move in?" Enough said. A week later, we had him and all his things in his new room at his beautiful cottage.

We all breathed a sigh of relief. He was in an extremely clean, well-cared-for place with friendly and loving staff. They all took to Dad right away. One of his care partners there had quite a little crush on him and kept telling me how handsome he was. Of course, I agreed!

Unfortunately, this beautiful living place came with a very high price tag. He and Mom had been very good throughout their life to carefully save money, smartly set up trusts, etc. We had been paying his ridiculous rent (almost $10,000 per month) out of his IRA. Shortly before we moved him to his new cottage, that money ran out. Our estate lawyer, along with their financial planner, had been giving us advice. In order to protect their money from Medicaid, which was the path Dad was heading once we ran out of money, we had the trust purchase a home for Mom to live in. It did not have Dad or Mom's name on it, so it was safe. This allowed Mom to not have to worry about a place to live, and it could not be taken from us. A few months before the IRA had ran out, Dad's brother Phil had come for a visit. I pulled him aside and told him about the money issue and that once the money was gone from his retirement, he would have to move to a Medicaid bed in a different room, and most likely, he would have a roommate. Phil was not happy about that at all. He loved his big brother so much and was so grateful for all the help Dad had done over the years for their parents and Mom's parents. He told me that when the money from the IRA was gone, he would take over the payments. That was such a godsend because I had been very stressed about what to do.

Dad was very happy in his new home. He told me many times that it was such a better place than the last one and that they were taking good care of him. He also commented on how good the food was compared to the last place. I was constantly racked with guilt over having to "put" him in a skilled nursing place. I know the horror stories from others, and every time I saw him in his room, I almost cried. My mind knew that it was the only solution, but my heart hurt every day. Yet he still never complained. Not once. He is a much better person than I am.

Parkinson Disease can affect handwriting. Because they have trouble with controlling their hands, their handwriting can become very small and illegible. Dad hated that, so he would practice his writing and cartoon drawing. When I would visit him, I would always find pieces of paper around with his doodles. He was determined to get that skill back.

His health declined quickly. Not because of the facility but the Parkinson Disease had pulled out all the stops. He was on the maximum amount of dopamine they could give him without putting him into constant hallucinations and no quality of life. I knew what was coming, but my heart held hope for a miraculous cure.

On Christmas Day 2017, Kevin, the kids, and I went to see Dad. It had become too difficult to take him out and bring him over to our house, so we went to visit him at his place. When I walked in, he was sitting in his wheelchair opening a gift that the cottage had given him. It was the softest blue plaid throw blanket I'd ever seen. I made a comment about how soft it was, and he agreed and just kept running his hands up and down it. We took a couple of gifts and visited him for a while. Mom was having back pain, so we called her on the phone, and she and Dad were able to talk. His voice was in good form. When we had to leave, I gave him a huge hug and kiss and told him I loved him. He hugged me back and said, "I love you!" When I left the room, I turned around one last time, and we gave each other

ONE LAST TRIP

a wave. He was holding on to that blanket so tightly. I had no idea it would be the last time I saw or talked to him.

It was New Year's Eve 2017. Kevin and I were with two other couples for our annual New Year's Eve dinner and party. We had returned from the restaurant and gathered at one of our friends' house to play games before midnight. We had just set up the first board game when my phone rang. I recognized the number as Dad's cottage and immediately knew something wasn't right. It was 9:37 p.m. It was his caregiver who told me Dad was actively dying. It threw me for a loop. I was expecting to hear that he had fallen or was being taken to the hospital for yet another UTI. I asked if they were sure, and she assured me that it was. The doctor had already been there and said it was his time. She said it would likely only be a matter of hours.

They asked me what I wanted to do, and I told them that I would call Mom and that we would most likely come over to be with him. She said they were all surprised too, as he had been having one of his rare good days—he had taken all his medications and eaten every meal, even dinner. About an hour before they called me, he fell into this comatose state. Before I hung up, I asked her if he was aware of anything—his surroundings, people, etc.—or in any pain. She said no. They had tried everything to get him to talk or make a sign that he was at all conscious, and he would not move or make any sound. His breathing was down to eight breaths a minute, and his heart rate was over two hundred. That made me feel a little better that he didn't know that Mom and I weren't with him. I told her I'd call her back in a little bit with our plans.

I dialed Mom, and she answered with "What's wrong?" She knew. I had to tell her the horrible news, and through our tears, we decided to go be with him. I was planning to pick her up, then we would head over to him. I called the nurse back to tell her we'd be right over, and she said he had passed five minutes before. He had several loving people with him and had no pain. We didn't make it. It was 10:27 p.m.

Because it was a holiday, New Year's Day, the funeral home was closed. We had to wait until the next day to meet with them for the arrangements. They told me I had to identify his body because the family wasn't with him when he died or when he was taken to the mortuary. That was very difficult for me, but Mom was too fragile to handle it. They had him laid out in a temporary casket because he was going to be cremated. The first thing I noticed is that he was smiling. He was actually smiling! That must have been his final expression as he left his broken earthly body for his new perfect one. The second thing I noticed is that he was wearing his jeans! How perfect was that? I gave him a kiss and was ready to let him go. Mom spent some time with him, and we left to begin the next phase of our lives without him.

Kevin and I went to his room at the cottage to pack up all his things. I carefully boxed up all the things that he loved so much. I would sort them later. As I was making a trip out to the rental van we had, I came across Ed, who was another resident in Dad's cottage who also had Parkinson Disease. He was younger than Dad, and they had become friends. Besides his Parkinson's, he had a number of other health conditions that required him to be confined to a motorized wheelchair and sometimes needed assistance with simple tasks such as eating. He approached me, and as he got closer, I noticed his eyes were full of tears. He said how sorry he was and that he was going to miss Dad so much because they were friends. I teared up myself and leaned over to give him a big hug. The nurse who was standing there also started crying. I smiled and thanked him and told him that Dad had finally won his battle.

We talked about Dad for a while, and he told me a funny story about a shirt. Somehow, the laundry had a slight mix-up, and one of Ed's shirts had gotten into Dad's closet. Dad was wearing it one day, and at lunch, Ed told Dad that he was wearing his shirt but that he made it look good. Dad smiled and said, "Of course, I do!" They had spent a lot of time together over the months and had great talks. Ed told me about Dad's great faith and the optimism and humor that Dad had even in his weakened condition. I touched Ed's arm and thanked him for being Dad's friend. He said he was the honored one. I do believe that perhaps this was God's final project for Dad.

ONE LAST TRIP

Even though we knew Dad's death was imminent, it was so sudden we were in shock. We had been preparing for this day for quite a while. I had started the grieving process several years prior. I had been through the steps of grief, although there is no set pattern to it—each person has a different path and different stages. But for me, I had already come to the acceptance phase before he died. I took every single day we had with him as an extra gift and blessing.

As sad as I was to know I'd never be able to talk to him or hug him and tell him I love him again, I was so happy for him. He had fought a battle with a relentless, horrible, selfish disease and won. He was finally able to break the chains that Parkinson's tried to wrap around him. He knew exactly where he was going. He was going to live with Jesus. He couldn't wait.

He had finally finished his job here on earth that God had assigned to him. I don't know what that last item was, maybe it was Ed, but God wouldn't have taken him to heaven if he hadn't finished it. Dad always knew his assignment, and he did it well. Everyone loved him and listened to him. He brought a lot of people to Jesus. I know that when Dad stood before God on that first day, God said, "Well done, good and faithful servant!"

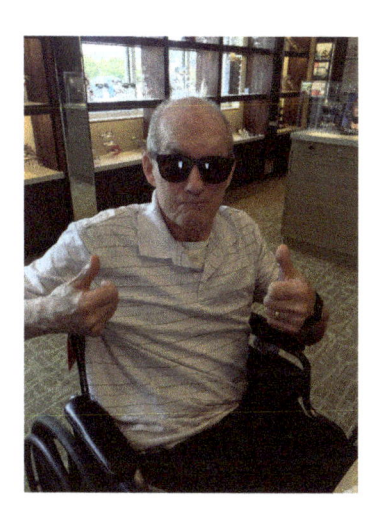

Chapter 15
Studebakers, Chevys, and All Things Automobile

Dad's Car History

Dad was a car guy. Not in the sense that he needed to own the newest or most prestigious automobiles or that he cared about professional racing or participating in auctions or shows. No, he bought cars that he knew would give him hours and hours of work and fun. Some of them were considered cars only in the general consensus. They were made of steel and had various functioning engines in them. He would just show up one day driving down our long driveway with a new toy, usually sputtering and barely making it down to the garage. He would be so proud and excited. We knew what was coming next. In a few days, there would be several hundred little parts spread out over the entire garage floor and his workshop. He had built some sort of contraption that had chains and a huge hook that would lift the engines right out of their carcass. It would swing around and lower to the ground, then the fun would begin. Deconstruction time. He would clean every part, inside and out. He would replace those parts that were worn out or needed too much work. Then the puzzle of rebuilding would commence. I always asked him how he would know how to put it all back together again and what he would do if he had extra parts. He would give me that grin, and to my delight and surprise, the car would soon be one functioning unit again.

ONE LAST TRIP

His love of cars began when he was very young. My grandparents did not even own a car until 1951, when he was fifteen years old, but his engineering mind was already familiar with how they worked. Although years later he appreciated the improved function and performance of the more modern cars, he was frustrated with the fact that he couldn't do as much work on them himself. With all the computers and design, he was forced to take them to a mechanic that had the tools to work on them. He still did as much as he could, including oil changes, spark plugs, brakes, etc.

Dad taught me how to appreciate these powerful machines. Even when I was a young child, he would drag me out to the garage or his workshop all excited to teach me all about engines. I would keep an interest for about five minutes, and that was about it. All those parts just confused me, and I never did get it clear how they all worked. I loved seeing him so excited though! I will say that a few things did stick with me, and I am proud to say that I can successfully jump-start a car, change a tire, fill a radiator, and many other things.

Dad's love for cars and how they run did rub off on his grandson. He would take Alex out to his workshop, and they would tinker together. In that process, Alex learned about engines and how they work. While he was a student at Missouri S&T, he belonged to the Baja Design Team. They would spend each year designing and building these special cars to compete all over the United States. Alex took such a liking to it and spent so much time in the design center working and designing that he was elected to the design/team lead for the last two years he was there. He also was one of the drivers for these races. Even a year after graduation, he was able to attend one of the races not too far from Oklahoma City where he lives. The remaining teammates were thrilled he was there and still asked him to help and for his opinions.

Mom laughs about the fact that when they first started dating, she knew she would expect to see Dad's backside sticking out from the hood of a car. For the next fifty-plus years, that was a very common way to find him. If he wasn't working on the car parts while they were still together inside the car, he was tip-toeing around blankets full of items or standing at his workbench, carefully piecing a part back together. He would come into the house covered in grease and would scrub his hands in the laundry room sink with special soap that had gritty stuff in it. I can still smell the soap and the grease, and I love it. It reminds me of Dad. Besides spending time with me and Mom, he was happiest when he was carefully rebuilding his cars.

After Dad died, I was going through some boxes of his things and came across a booklet of his writings about some of his cars. It was so beautifully written and full of his true love of automobiles. His stories made me smile and laugh. The only problem with it is that he didn't continue on with more of his cars. The following section of this chapter is written by him.

*****

ONE LAST TRIP

Syd's Car Experiences—Events and Adventures with Old Cars
Syd Rinard

A Little Philosophy

They say you can learn a lot about a man by the cars he drives. That statement probably has some truth in it, especially in cases where the car is a powerful, flashy machine with snarling pipes etc. But when I was coming of age in the 1950s, there were many cases where such simplistic cataloging was inadequate. Most youngsters like me had little money to spend on cars, so we couldn't be choosy. We drove whatever we found that we could afford to buy and keep running. For some of us, there was a certain pride in keeping the old car running. The few kids with new cars lacked the sense of achievement we had as we coaxed our old jalopies around town.

In my case, I was fortunate enough to get experience with a rather large number of different cars (one at a time). Most of them are described in this booklet. I started learning about cars and their quirks slowly with my first cars by trial and error. Of course, I made many mistakes. Then as I got more experience, the learning increased, I got cocky, and the failures got more spectacular. But gradually, with a lot of guidance from real experts and some luck, I learned enough to be less dangerous when playing with these machines.

I never owned a "muscle" car with a monster V-8 engine covered with chrome pipes etc. I enjoyed working on cars as a hobby, but I was not looking for trouble. I didn't tear around town with tires squealing (well, not very often) because I knew what it was doing to the vehicle. The price of hard and fast driving was at least a lot of hard repair, work, and money. That's if you were lucky. If you were not so lucky and someone got hurt, a much higher price would have to be paid for such behavior. I wanted to minimize the former and totally avoid the latter.

Anyway, this booklet describes the cars of my youth. They weren't much, and some had only a short time with me. But they probably had as much effect on my personal development as anything else I was involved in. I learned to tackle hard jobs, but I also learned that I couldn't fix everything that broke. I learned about limits while fussing with these machines. They made me appreciate the development and skill of the guys who designed and built them, in many cases, before I was born. I am still amazed at some of the stuff they did with what they had to work with.

The new cars of today are light-years away from my old cars, and they are still developing. Environmental and political concerns are requiring changes in addition to the normal buying tastes of the public. But cars still must carry people around, and they still need occasional repairs, just like the old days. And since there are still many models to choose from, cars may actually reveal a lot about a man's personality. Even though today's cars are too complicated for shade tree mechanics to work on at home, their origins inherited from the old cars are still obvious to someone who is old enough (like me) to have seen both the old and the new. The new cars are better, but my old cars were sure a lot of fun.

Interesting Tidbits

In the middle 1950s, cars were a little different than they are at present. Many people were buying new cars to replace their old 1930s models they had bought before World War II. This resulted in many used cars becoming available. In those days, used cars were simple machines. There were no catalytic converters, air-bags, seat belts, or things made of mysterious plastic. Of course, there were no computers.

Because of wartime restrictions, replacement parts had been hard to get. Junkyards sprang up to collect wrecked cars and trucks. Some of these became very large, and they served as a valuable source of used engines, transmissions, fenders, doors, and other body parts. Customers were allowed to wander through the piles of wrecks and remove desired parts from them. I spent so much times in some junkyards I became familiar with their inventories.

In one case, some friends and I needed to replace the gas tank on a 1935 Plymouth that belonged to my friend Jack. In the junk-

ONE LAST TRIP

yard, we spotted one and reported back to the junkyard owner to make a deal for it. We had noted that the car with the tank was sitting on the ground. The car needed to be lifted to get to the tank. The owner was busy, so he told us to take his crane truck and lift the car ourselves. This truck was an old prewar model with a flat bed and a homemade crane made of welded steel pipe. A hook and cable used a power winch to lift things. We drove the truck through the yard and proceeded to lift the car high enough to allow us to get under it and remove the gas tank. There were no problems, but we were very lucky none of us got hurt. At the time, we considered it to be fun.

Another time we were trying to tune up the engine in the 1935 Plymouth but could not get the spark timing correct. We wanted the distributor to advance the spark as much as possible without causing the engine to knock or "ping" severely when the car was climbing a steep slope. We tried several different positions of the distributor, but the "pinging" was either too loud or too faint when the car was test-driven. Then I got the brilliant idea to adjust the distributor while the car was being driven up the hill. We had the hood off the car, so every part of the engine was exposed. I lay down on the car's huge front fender and found something to hang on to. The idea was to listen to the engine while it was running and under load. I wanted to be able to hear the "pinging" better as I adjusted the timing by rotating the distributor with my free hand. But the noise from the engine, the street noise, and the wind made it impossible to tell when the optimum setting had been achieved. It was a pretty exciting ride on that fender though. Dangerous and fairly stupid, but fun.

At that tender age, we think we are immortal. Actually, the mere act of thinking at all is a work in progress then. These juvenile antics can become valuable experiences for those who survive them.

And those who seriously pursue these kinds of experiences cannot be convinced that these machines are not alive and doing as much mischief as possible to irritate their human "masters."

1935 Chevrolet Coupe
Fall 1952–Spring 1953

Dad's first car

This was an early 1935 model, with the squarish 1934 body style. Later 1935 models had the streamlined 1936 styling.

Features

- This car had the standard Chevrolet engine that was used essentially until 1954. It had 6 cylinders arranged in line, valve-in-head with solid valve lifters. These had to be manually adjusted every so often (with the engine running).
- The car had mechanical brakes. The brake shoes were actuated using steel rods connected to the brake pedal. They would slow the car down a little and eventually stop it.
- The windshield was hinged so it could be cranked open in the summer for ventilation. I never got it unstuck. I doubt if I could have got it closed tightly again if I had succeeded in getting it open.
- The car body was steel but had some wood structural members. The roof had a fabric insert (the later 1935 models had the solid stamped steel roofs that were used from 1936 on).
- The car had real wire wheels, including the spare wheel mounted on the rear of the car.

- The car had a single windshield wiper, mounted above the windshield. It used a flapper-type vacuum operator that used engine intake manifold vacuum to swing the blade back and forth. This was ok except when accelerating or climbing a long hill. At such times, the vacuum would be so low that the blade would slow down or stop altogether.
- The drive train used a "torque tube" with the drive-shaft mounted inside a universal joint at the transmission. Braces kept the rear axle in line and transferred the thrust of the rear wheels to the car's frame.

Notes

This car was a "gift" to my father from Mike Wrigley, a coworker at the Salina Supply Company. Mike tinkered with old cars as a hobby, and he was tired of working on this one. Mike told him the car was a gift for myself and my brother. But my brother was too young to drive, so I took control of the car. It had been parked in the 1951 flood-water. The engine, transmission, and differential gear housing had been full of river water. Before I took over the car, it was checked out by a local mechanic and was put into "serviceable" condition.

The finish was not very good, so I painted the car at home in the driveway. I used the family vacuum cleaner for this, which was a horizontal tubular type that sucked air in one end and blew it out the other. It had a flexible hose that could be connected to either end. The vacuum cleaner had a paint spray "gun" attachment that did a surprisingly good job. Some overspray got on the vacuum cleaner and the adjacent wall of the house. Gloss black industrial paint (from Salina Supply) was used. I doubt if the new paint job would have lasted very long, but it looked great to me during the time I drove it.

The trunk lid was found to be symmetrical, and its frame was wood, so I was able to remove it and rotate the lid 180 degrees, putting the hinges on the bottom, transforming the old trunk lid into a rumble seat that could hold at least two people. A wooden bench seat was added for their "comfort."

The car also had a fabric roof insert that leaked rain badly. They couldn't stamp out a solid steel roof on car bodies until the next model year.

The driveshaft universal joint failed and got noisy. A friend's father (a machinist) offered to fix it for me. He had me get a good one at the junkyard, then he taught me to jack up the car and remove the rear axle so we could replace the bad joint. It took one evening to do this, and it was really my first introduction of the fine art of car repair.

1936 Chevrolet Two-Door Sedan
Spring 1953–Spring 1954

Features

- This car had the standard Chevrolet engine that was used essentially until 1954. It had 6 cylinders arranged in line, with solid valve lifters. These had to be manually adjusted every so often (with the engine running).
- The car had the new hydraulic brakes. The brake shoes were pressed against cast-iron drums by hydraulic cylinders at each wheel. All 4 cylinders were connected to one master cylinder at the brake pedal. This was much better than the 1935. The brakes on the 1936 would actually stop the car.

ONE LAST TRIP

Notes

In the spring of 1953, I traded the 1935 Chevrolet and $15 for a 1936 Chevrolet. It had hydraulic brakes and a solid steel top. Both features were much better than the 1935.

The finish was not very good on this car either, so I painted it in the driveway using the same paint-spraying attachment on the family vacuum cleaner. Two-toned green industrial paint was used. The body was light green, and the fenders were dark green. New paint didn't help much.

A friend and I did drive this car from Salina to Abilene (about 20 miles or so). We were trying to meet some girl friends we thought were over there. We never found the girls, but we got caught in a thunderstorm. The wind blew so hard it forced rain into the car at the bottom of the driver's side door and up to hit the ceiling upholstery until it was wet. The storm passed, and we made it to Abilene. We had gasoline, but the engine was low on oil. We only had 25 cents with us, and that was enough to get a quart of reprocessed oil. We drove back to Salina without incident (or girls).

I don't remember the fate of this car, but I got rid of it after a short time.

1938 Plymouth Coupe
Spring 1954–Winter 1954

Features

- This car had the standard Plymouth engine, a flathead type. It had 6 cylinders arranged in line, with solid valve lifters. These had to be manually adjusted every so often (with the engine running), which required removing a sheet metal cover screwed to the side of the engine block. Not easy to do.
- This car had some unknown damage in the transmission. The low gear made a clanking noise, like a gear tooth had broken off. It always worked, however, so I never attempted to repair it.
- A true salesman's car, it had a huge trunk with a partition just behind the driver's seat. This partition had several shelves on the driver's side for storing stuff, plus an access panel into the rear trunk space.

Notes

I bought this car for $40 from Mike Wrigley (the same guy that gave my father the 1935 Chevrolet).

The finish was not very good on this car either, so I painted it in the driveway using the same paint-spraying attachment on the family vacuum cleaner. Dark-green industrial paint was used. Before painting the car, I removed the chrome strip on the hood and the hood ornament (a ship). I filled the holes with solder, using an electric soldering iron. (This was popular to do at the time. Clean hoods were "in" and were cool.)

I was working at an automobile upholstery shop in downtown Salina, from which I brought a huge sack of scrap material. Using that material, I upholstered the door panels in brown and white material. I glued some tiger skin stuff on the dashboard. Very sharp.

I learned some things working on this car. After hours of struggling with something under the dashboard, I came out of the car very angry. I slammed the driver's door shut very violently. That felt so good I walked around the car and slammed the passenger door even harder. The next day, it started to rain, so I rolled up the window on the driver's door. Its glass was completely smashed. So was the glass in the other door.

ONE LAST TRIP

Lesson Learned

The machine (i.e., the car) doesn't care a bit for your troubles when working on it. If you stupidly try to take out your frustrations on it, all that you will gain is more work to do. The machine always wins that struggle.

When I left Salina to go to K-State in Manhattan, I left the car at home. I put it up on blocks in the backyard with the wheels off the ground. Whenever I came home to visit, I would start the car (on the blocks) and run it for a while to charge the battery.

I never really drove the car again until I bought the 1939 Dodge. I then gave the Plymouth to my friend Jack Gebhart. He took the body off and drove the car around his farm as a "rail job." He eventually bought another car, a 1935 Plymouth, and used my old 1938 for parts.

Side Note

Jack's 1935 Plymouth led an interesting life. He acquired it for $10 from the farmer across the road. It was a huge 4-door sedan, a "gangster's car" as we called it. Jack and I worked on it all summer, and one evening, it started and ran. It had one headlight that glowed brightly enough, so to celebrate, we drove it to the drive-in movie theater just down the street. After the movie, the car wouldn't start, so we pushed it home. The carburetor was clogged with dirt and debris from the fuel tank. We cleaned the tank and put new fuel line tubing, but the car would always only run just long enough to get across town before stranding us. We eventually replaced the fuel tank with the one we removed from the wreck in the junkyard. We cut the exhaust manifold in two and ran two exhaust pipes under the passenger side running board. With the small loud mufflers we put on, those two pipes could really roar. Jack took the car with him to Manhattan, where he rebuilt the engine as a class project. It looked sharp when finished, freshly painted and sparkling, but in the car, it still leaked oil. We had a lot of good times in that old car.

LORI RINARD GAMBILL

1939 Dodge Coupe
Spring 1955–Spring 1955

Features

- This car had the standard Dodge engine, a flathead type similar to the Plymouth engine but slightly more powerful. It had 6 cylinders arranged in line, with solid valve lifters. These had to be manually adjusted every so often (with the engine running), which required removing a sheet metal cover screwed to the side of the engine block. Not easy to do.
- The car had highly streamlined styling, with lots of chrome on the front and sides.
- The speedometer had a feature common to Chrysler Corp. cars in those days. At night, the speedometer illumination light would change color as the speed increased. At vehicle speeds below 30 mph, it was normal. Between 30 and 50 mph, the speedometer turned yellow, and at speeds over 50 mph, it was red.

Notes

I was at home one weekend, and my father asked me if I was interested in looking at an old car to buy. It belonged to his secretary's father, who had died several months before, and she wanted to get rid of it. We looked at it in her garage, and I bought it for $50.

ONE LAST TRIP

I drove it back to Manhattan that same weekend. It ran ok, but it was pretty stiff, and the exhaust pipe laid down a smoke screen behind the car. About half-way to Manhattan, the smoking stopped and the engine began to run much better. I used it successfully for several months there.

Then one Saturday morning, I was driving back to Salina to work at Salina Supply with two girls who wanted to visit at home that weekend. The trip was uneventful, and the girls were sleeping (it was about 7:00 a.m.) when the engine began making loud, clattering noises. I immediately shut it down and stopped on the shoulder, waking up the girls.

We were discussing what to do when a farmer came along and took us to Salina. I got rid of the girls and got to work on time. I called Jack, and after work, he took me to the car. We towed it to my house, where I took off the oil pan and looked at the piston connecting rods. The rod bearings had broken loose and were spinning freely on the crankshaft, cutting off the oil. I decided to scrap the car, so I put the engine back together with some cardboard behind the bearings to keep them from rattling too badly. I drove it to the junkyard with Jack following me in his truck. At the junkyard, they paid me $12.50 for the car.

1946 Studebacker Two-Door Sedan
Spring 1955–Winter 1960

Features

- This car was a Studebaker Champion built after World War II using prewar design featuring separate fenders.
- This car had the standard flathead-type engine. It had 6 cylinders arranged in line. The transmission included an overdrive gear that could automatically engage at highway speed.
- The car had turn signals, with the turn direction arrows built into the speedometer (not commonly done in those days).

Notes

After the 1939 Dodge was gone, my father saw a nice-looking car for sale on the used car lot of the Studebaker dealer across the street from Salina Supply. He told me about it, and we took a look at it. The price was $245, and the dealer had taken it in trade for a new car. The previous owner was a professional photographer. After the trade, the dealer had installed new piston connecting rods, and the engine ran smoothly. It was 9 years old, but it seemed like a new car to me after driving all those old worn-out cars. I talked to the dealer's mechanic who worked on the engine. He said the car was in good condition and would probably last about a year with a young fellow like me driving it.

ONE LAST TRIP

I needed a car, and I liked this one. Its styling was similar to contemporary Fords and Chevrolets, but it had its own unique overall look. It wasn't the most powerful performer, but it was peppy, and it had personality. I bought it on the spot.

The only significant visible flaw was a broken piece of chrome on the front grille. I got a new one from the junkyard. As I drove the car, I became more familiar with it. It still had its owner's manual, which was an excellent guide for most operation and maintenance procedures. I fixed many small problems as they came up, mostly routine stuff. On the highway, I usually drove the car about 50 mph with the overdrive engaged, which resulted in very low engine speed. I wanted it to last a long time. (The high-speed Kansas Turnpike was under construction at that time, and 50 mph was reasonable on the existing 2-lane highways then.)

I wanted to have the exhaust make some sound. I liked the particular sound of a 6-cylinder engine with two exhaust pipes. It's not the ear-splitting blast of a V-8 engine. It is more like a soft purring, very pleasant. I took the cast-iron exhaust engine manifold off the car and cut it in two. Then I reinstalled both halves back on the engine and added a second pipe and muffler. The muffler was small and was fairly noisy. The other exhaust pipe still used the original stock muffler. Once installed, this combination of pipes and dissimilar mufflers produced the soft purring sound I wanted. The noise was not unpleasantly loud during normal driving, but at high engine speeds at full throttle, the sound became an ear-splitting roar. A gasoline filling station attendant gave me the ultimate compliment by telling me that I had the best-sounding pipes in town. It made my day.

In the spring of 1956, I bought 4 new white sidewall tires, which really improved the ride and handling. I removed the chrome strip on the hood and a big medallion on the front of the hood. I found a Chevrolet truck hood strip that fit my hood perfectly. I had it painted to match the car. The overall effect was a very clean, uncluttered look.

In the summer of 1957, I made two trips to Coffeyville to visit Jo in her home. The first trip was routine with no problems with the car. I drove it slow in overdrive as usual. It was hot weather, and I had put water in the radiator instead of antifreeze to help the car run cooler. The engine temperature was still high, and the oil pressure was low, as usual. The second trip to Coffeyville was a disaster for the car. The weather was still hot, and about half-way there, I began to hear connecting rods bearing clatter. I found that by slightly accelerating the engine and then coasting back on the gas kept the rods quiet. I couldn't work on the car during my visit, so on my way back to Salina, I used the same driving technique, which worked until I was approaching Eldorado. Just outside of town, the overdrive broke, and the car rolled to a stop in front of a farmhouse. It was still 100 miles to Salina.

I saw a junkyard nearby, and for a fleeting second, I had thoughts of just letting them buy the car from me. Then I remembered those nifty white sidewall tires, the purring dual exhaust pipes, etc. and decided to rebuild this car. The town of Eldorado was in sight, so I walked until I came to a pay phone. I called home and told my parents my situation and location and asked them to call Jack to come and tow me to Salina.

While I was walking back to the car, I decided to disconnect the drive-shaft from the rear axle so the damaged engine and transmission would not be turning while I was being towed. I had the tools with me to do that, but I needed some wire to support the shaft after it was disconnected. I asked at the farmhouse for wire. The farm girl got me some wire, and I got the drive-shaft secured. I was watched closely through all this by the girl and a friend of hers, and they sat on the porch and made comments on how lonely it was out there in the country. I hoped Jack would come quickly. But it was my parents who showed up because they couldn't find Jack. I attached a 12-foot chain to their car, and they towed me home (a 2-hour drive at night).

The next day, Jack and I towed the car to the home of an old mechanic friend of Jack's. He took over the project of rebuilding my car. I bought an engine at the junkyard for $50 and a transmission for $25. The mechanic rebuilt the new engine, so it was as good as new. I paid him $40 for his trouble. He gave me a formula for estimating how long a repair job would take. You estimate how long you think the project will take. Then you double that and add one day. I have found this formula to be pretty accurate.

When all this work was done, the car ran better than ever. The cause of the old engine failure was low oil pressure due to worn crankshaft main bearings. When the Studebaker dealer replaced the rods, he had not replaced the main crankshaft bearings. These control oil pressure, and these were worn so badly the oil pressure was about half of normal. He used rods that had soft metal bearing material (called Babbitt) that failed under the heat and stress. The Studebaker mechanic's prediction of one year of service had come true. My slow driving habit didn't circulate the oil and cooling water adequately, so from then on, I drove 70 mph instead of 50 mph. The junkyard engine we had put in the car had strong bronze bearings instead of the soft Babbitt bearings.

Jo and I were married in September 1958. Before the wedding, I was afraid that some of my "friends" would steal the Studebaker as a prank. So I changed the starter wiring so that a couple of things had to be operated at the same time to start the car. Very clever. But in the process of doing that, I caused a nasty short circuit and burned a lot of wiring. The system eventually worked, but it was a waste of time. They didn't even try to steal the car.

Jo and I moved to Kansas City with the Studebaker. The Studebaker was showing signs of wear. Finally, in the winter of 1960, I was driving through some snow and the steering wheel felt funny. The front wheels were pointed in a *V*. One of the steering tie rods had come loose from its wheel. I put it back on and got home. Jack had asked me to let him have the car when I wanted to get rid of it, so he came and towed it back to his stable of drag racers in Salina.

In Salina, Jack put a large Chevrolet V-8 engine in the Studebaker and made a dragster out of it. He sold the car to someone and later bought it back. I never did understand all that business. Jack now keeps it in a shed with several other vehicles that were undergoing restoration and/or "souping up" with large engines. Later, during high school reunions, he and I took the old Studebaker out for a spin. It's extremely hard to drive now. The steering is flaky, and the monster engine is hard to hold down. Jack painted the car red, but otherwise, the body is the same when I had it.

For an inanimate object, the old 1946 Studebaker has led quite a life, and it's still going as far as I know, defying the Studebaker mechanic's prediction of one-year survival. It will probably go out in a ball of fire someday. That would be more fitting than being neglected and slowly rusting into dust.

Dad gave me photos of other cars he owned. A lot of them I don't have any memories of because they were before me. I don't really know a lot of details about some of them, but the ones I do remember, I am including here.

1962 Chevrolet Corvair (Mom's car)

This is the first car I do remember. This was Mom's car that she drove until I was well into elementary school. I loved riding in it, and once I turned sixteen, she would let me take it out myself every now and then. There were a few hiccups with it, however. First, there were no seat belts. That wasn't illegal when it was built and even when I would drive it as a teenager in the early 1980s. Second, there was no air-conditioning. That made it uncomfortable to drive around much when it was really hot outside. Third, it had a gremlin leak that Dad could never quite find, so you didn't want to drive it when it was raining, or your feet would get wet. Other than that, it was so fun to drive. I would get a lot of turning heads on the road, and even though I knew that they were looking at the car and not me, it made me smile!

The first model year for the Corvair was 1960. That year it was named *Motor Trend* magazine's Car of the Year. Mom's 1962 model was classified as first generation (1960–1964). It was an American designed and assembled car. This two-door coupe had a rear-mounted, air-cooled engine, with automatic transmission.

The name Corvair was a combination of Corvette and Bel Air. There was some controversy about how it handled in a book by Ralph Nader in 1965, but a report for the National Highway Traffic Safety Administration in 1972 found that the 1960–1963 Corvair had no greater potential for loss of control in extreme situation than its counterparts.

Eventually, Mom got a new everyday car, and the Corvair spent most of its days tucked safely in the garage. Dad finally decided it was time to sell it and found a buyer from a Corvair Club in Kansas City. It was sad to see it go, but we knew it was going to someone who would appreciate it and take good care of it.

*****

Like most families, we had a variety of other cars over the years. We always had a station wagon, which was the family car and was great for taking vacations. I loved traveling in them because Dad had built me a little desk-type thing that he put in the back of the wagon.

Mom would fill it with paper, crayons, and other fun supplies to keep me busy while on the road. It even had a little cupholder. I would sit cross-legged by it, surrounded by suitcases, coolers, etc. It sure made the travel go by quicker. I could just hop over the back of the seat to get to my little oasis. Today, there is no way that would be acceptable, and probably for good reason. But back then, it was great. Everyone would move all around the car when it was going—climbing over the seats, sliding back and forth from window to window, and playing "squish," which was a game we would play when the driver would turn a corner and the goal was to completely crush the unfortunate soul on the wrong side of the car.

In those days, there were no seat belt laws, and not many cars were even built with belts installed. They could always be installed aftermarket, but most people didn't bother, and until I took driver's ed in high school, I didn't care either. I did start to wear them when I was driving and tried to get Dad and Mom to wear them as well. I remember the controversy when the seat belt laws were first introduced. People really didn't like the law telling them they had to wear them. It has been proven to be good, and many lives have been saved because of them. I'm so used to wearing it that I have trouble just driving to the other side of the neighborhood without it on. Dad was never fond of them, and once I took over all the driving for him, he knew he had to put it on, or I wouldn't go.

The following are three more of Dad's cars that I remember and even drove two of them. These were junkers that he found and drove home for major surgery. He would drive them for a year or two, then would somehow find a buyer, then turn around and purchase another one. Mom didn't mind for a couple of reasons—it saved us a lot of money, and it kept him busy.

ONE LAST TRIP

1960s Volkswagen

I don't know the year or model of this Volkswagen, although this was one that Mom and I really disliked. It had to be from the 1960s. This photo was taken in August 1977. It was a really ugly shade of gray, so we called it the Mouse. We don't know what Dad's reason was for buying this one, as he was an American-made car man up to now. It was his first and last journey into the German automobile spectrum. If I remember right, this car was falling apart daily. It didn't have much good going for it, and it had a funny smell. I don't remember how long he owned this one, but I'm pretty sure it was a short duration.

1973 Mazda RX-3

This was my first car. Dad had bought it a year or so before I got my driver's license and drove it himself after its deconstruction and rebuild. I believe he paid around $400 for it. I turned sixteen in May 1983 and had dreams of that beautiful sports car or convertible sitting in the driveway with a big bow on it. Silly me. Dad handed me the keys to this Mazda and said, "Here you go!"

I had many hesitations about this automobile. First, it wasn't exactly "cool." I was going to be driving this to school, out with friends, etc. At least it had room for a bunch of us, and there were times I had it crammed full of brave souls willing to take the chance that we would get to our destination safely.

Second, it was a four-speed manual transmission. I had done all my learning and practicing in automatic transmission cars—our station wagon and the cars at my school driver's education class. Dad would take me to empty parking lots for me to learn how to drive it, using the clutch and shifting gears. Well, those sessions never ended well, as I constantly killed the engine and never got anywhere except frustrated and mad. Dad just laughed at me—he knew I would eventually figure it out. One evening, Dad and I went out to pick up some pizzas, and on the way home, he got in the passenger seat and told me to drive. I pretty much had a panic attack because I had never tried it on actual roads, and I still could never get the clutch to catch the gear. I did ok at the beginning. There was a hill at a stoplight on the way home, and I prayed that it would stay green, but alas, it turned red just in time for me to have to stop. A woman pulled up behind me pretty close, which did nothing to help with my anxiety attack. Sure enough, I couldn't engage first gear and kept rolling back and tapping her front bumper. She started yelling at me through her window, something about if I can't drive etc. It got a bit ugly, and after I yelled something back to her, I got the gears suddenly connected, and that Mazda took off like a rocket. Dad was pretty embarrassed about the whole situation (mainly what I was yelling back to her), and once we finally got home, I don't think I talked to him for quite a while. Ultimately, however, if I wanted to have a car to drive, I had to learn how to drive it, and I did. Once it clicked how to get those gears, I never killed it again.

Third, it was pretty obvious that this car was on borrowed time. I called the color of it rust held together with red paint. Now I did love red cars, and still do, and it was many steps above the Mouse. There was a hole in the floorboard in front of the driver's seat that was a good one to two inches in diameter. I could actually watch the road as I drove. It had leather seats, but all of them had various lengths of tears in them. I had wrapped the steering wheel with new leather because the original was getting very worn. The radio did work ok, and the engine had surprising power, so much so that I did get a speeding ticket one evening on some back roads. I was taking a friend home, and that police officer was not sitting along that road when we drove along it the first time! I was honestly surprised it could even go that fast without falling apart! But it did, and one court appearance later, I learned to keep it under control. That's how I got my nickname Lead Foot from Dad.

The gas gauge stopped working sometime during the two years I drove it. I never had much extra money for gas, so I tried to keep track of how many miles I had driven and guess how much there was left in the tank. I only ran out of gas one time while driving to a friend's house. Luckily, I was only a couple of blocks away from her house, and this was way before cell phones. I walked to her house and called Dad, who met me where I left the car with a gas can. He tinkered with the gauge but could never figure out why it wouldn't work.

The driver's side mirror was ripped off one time when I got sandwiched between two other cars. A car in the right-turn lane at a light changed his mind and decided to go straight instead, but no matter how hard you try, three cars cannot fit into two lanes. That was fun.

One day after school, I came out to the car to head home when I noticed something didn't look right. As I walked around the car to check it out, I realized that my license plate was missing. I went back into the school, talked to the school officer, and we called the police. They told me that it was most likely taken off my car to use on a different car that was stolen. Nice.

I wanted to take it to college with me so I could have a car, but Dad said it would never make it. He ended up selling it to some poor soul for about $400. Same price he bought it for. I can't say I ever missed that car, although it did have some sentimentality as it was my first.

Ford Pinto

The Ford Pinto was the car that Dad bought for himself when he passed along the Mazda RX-3 to me. I think he was glad to get back to an American car, but we thought it was an odd choice. First of all, it was bright orange. It was in much better shape than my Mazda, and he was able to keep it running and looking nice for a while.

The best part about it was that it was perfect for us to drive in our senior homecoming parade. My high school colors were orange and black, so we decorated it and had fun participating. He didn't seem to mind all the balloons and crepe paper. He got coolest dad of year, at least from us!

Dad kept this car until sometime during my college years. He then bought his much anticipated, most desired car—the sports car of his dreams.

Mazda RX-7

Dad had been wanting a Mazda RX-7 for many years. After much encouraging from us, he finally bit the bullet and purchased one. I've never seen anyone so excited to buy a car. It wasn't new. It was an 1983 or 1984 but it didn't need to be taken completely apart and rebuilt. He spent so much time taking care of that car, cleaning it, putting new brakes and parts on it. It was his pride and joy.

It had a sunroof on it, and the glass sections could be taken off. It didn't make it a convertible, but it was our first experience with an open top that we thought it was perfect. Every now and then, I was allowed to drive it, which, of course, was a thrill for me. I learned how to take the top glass off, and what a rush I would get driving it around that way. One summer after I graduated from college, Dad and Mom went to Finland for a couple of weeks, and he told me I could drive it while he was gone. I thought I was in heaven! I drove it the entire time. All my friends at work (all men) would come out at lunch and fawn over it. One evening, on my way home from work, I got bumped in the back by another car at a red light. I jumped out ready to take down whoever wrecked Dad's car. Turns out there wasn't even a scratch on it, but I would have defended her till the end. I never told Dad about the incident until many years later. He just laughed!

Dad drove that car for many years. He was so proud of it and had so much fun taking it on drives. We were all sad to see it go, but eventually, it started needing too much work. Dad's Parkinson Disease was progressing, and although it was a slow decline and he was still doing really well, he decided it was time to trade it in for a new car. It was getting harder for him to do major work on cars, and a new car wouldn't need all the work. But I'm so happy that he was able to own his dream car after all those years driving junkers!

Subaru Outback

Dad's last car was this Subaru Outback. It turns out he was really proud of this one too, almost as much as the RX-7. He bought it brand-new, right off the lot. It was a great car and perfect for all the things that he needed it for. It could haul wood and materials from the hardware store, furniture and treasured things from antique stores, and suitcases for a vacation to Colorado or Branson. It made many trips to St. Louis after I moved there, and he would even take Alex out for driving lessons in it way before he was of driving age.

The Subaru was perfect for driving in Kansas City winters. The neighborhood we lived in was a wooded community surrounding a lake with very long, steep hills. Our house was at the bottom of what was called Suicide Hill. No one ever actually died on it, but it was the steepest hill in the county. The snow could make it very difficult to get out, and this car handled great in it.

When Alex turned sixteen, Dad and Mom had just moved to St. Louis to be closer to us. Dad's Parkinson's had made it dangerous for him to continue driving, so he sold the Subaru to Alex for $1. Alex was so excited to have a car and especially to have his papa's car. It was so hard for Dad to have to give up driving, but knowing that Alex would have his Subaru made it easier on him. Over the years, Dad had taught Alex how to do a lot of the maintenance on cars—oil changes, brakes, etc. Alex loved being able to take care of his own car, and those grandpa/grandson moments will be memories he will have forever.

Chapter 16

Day 13
Friday, August 17, 2018

Kansas (Salina), Home

Tonight I will be sleeping in my own bed. Generally, when someone travels for close to two weeks, they are ready to be home. Kevin and I were able to enjoy some well-deserved time away together. For some reason, I am not ready to go home. I actually do know why. This entire journey has been so special and God-led, and my heart is not ready for it to be over. I will always have these memories, and every time I reflect back on them, a smile crosses my face.

But before I get home, I have one last important day today. I am in Salina, Kansas, where Dad was born and grew up.

Salina is located in Central Kansas along Interstate 70 and is the county seat for Saline County. It is a regional trade center for this area of the state as it is located in one of the world's largest wheat-producing areas. Before it was founded in 1858, the Kansa, or Kaw Nation, lived there. Early on, Salina established itself as a trading post for immigrants heading west, as well as prospectors and area American Indian tribes. During the Civil War, most of the men living there left to join the Army, so the town growth stopped. After the war, agriculture became the main economy, building mills to produce flour from the wheat farms around. An airfield was established just outside of the town, which was used during World War II, and when the US

Department of Defense closed it as a military base, it was converted to Salina Municipal Airport and industrial park.

Interesting fact about Salina: it was the location of the first garment factory of Lee Jeans in 1889.

Salina is in the Smoky Hills area of the Great Plains. Two rivers run through it—the Saline River and the Smoky Hill River. The city itself is only twenty-five square miles. It does lie within Tornado Alley and is prone to severe thunderstorms. In the 2010 census, the population was around forty-eight thousand.

It has been many years since I have visited Salina. I felt that it was an important stop and the most appropriate way to end this trip. My family has a reserved area in the Gypsum Hill Cemetery in Salina. It was purchased by my great-great-grandfather Martin Lebert. He purchased a large area in the cemetery with approximately fifteen to twenty grave sites. Martin's daughter Anna married Alonzo Rinard, and their youngest child was Leroy, who is my grandfather. The graves that are here include Martin Lebert and his wife Maria, Alonzo and Anna Rinard, Leroy Rinard, Julia Rinard Scott (my aunt), and several of my cousins.

I want Dad to be included with his family. Although I had buried some of his ashes in Colorado and the rest of them are still at my house, I thought I could at least get him a stone marker. My grandpa Leroy wasn't actually buried here either. After he died, my grandma Mary scattered his ashes along the four-mile walk he took every single day, rain or shine. Dad had purchased a memorial stone for him, and I wanted to do the same for Dad. We have since decided that we will be burying the rest of his ashes in this cemetery. Mom would like to be buried with Dad, and I would also like to have my remains put there in the site next to Dad and Mom.

My first stop of the morning was to actually visit the cemetery. My uncle had given me some great maps and directions, and I had no problems finding our family plot. It is located in a beautiful, peaceful section of the cemetery, with a large tree anchoring the corner, giving perfect shade on the headstones on this very warm summer day. I walked among the stones, remembering those who I had known and thankful for the rest of them for our family history.

I went to the main office, and they were so helpful in making arrangements for Dad. He told me a little about when my great-great-grandfather purchased it and that all the sites within our plot were already completely paid for. There were still a number of empty or unreserved sites here, so we chose the plot that was directly behind Leroy (his dad) and next to Julia (his sister). He gave me the name of the stone company they normally do business with and told me to run by there today to order the marker. I planned to do that but had to make one very important visit first.

Jack was one of Dad's best friends. They were friends in high school but became very close when they were roommates in college. Jack was Dad's best man at his wedding. At Dad's funeral, Jack was there, and we had a nice visit, although he was very emotional. He was having a very hard time dealing with Dad's death. I told him that I was planning a trip over the summer and that I would love to stop by when I was in Salina to see him and his wife, Martha. He was overjoyed with the idea, and a couple of months later, I mailed him my itinerary and invited them to lunch. And that's what we're going to do today.

But there is one thing we have to do first. In late high school / early college, Dad owned a 1946 Studebaker. It had been a dream of his to get one, and he was so excited to buy it. He would spend hours working on that car, babying it, fixing every problem. Some of the stories were legendary. Jack told me about a time that it broke down on the highway between Salina and Coffeyville (where Mom was from). Dad and Mom were dating at the time, and he was going to visit her during the summer between semesters at K-State. That Studebaker quit working along the way down, and Dad called Jack to come get him and tow the car back home, which he did. Eventually, Dad was ready to move on to a different car, and Jack offered to buy it from Dad. Dad gave him that Studebaker, and Jack has spent the last sixty years restoring it, replacing the engine with a huge V-8, and entering it in local car shows. Once a month, the community car club has a parade in Salina, and Jack and Martha proudly drive it with the other prized automobiles.

ONE LAST TRIP

Jack knew I wanted to see it. I've told him in the past that when he's ready to sell it, to call me first. We would love to have that car back in the family. My son would just be thrilled to have it to tinker with, but mostly because it was his papa's. It's a classic, for sure. But really, it's sentimental. He would love for me to have it eventually, but he has a couple of step-sons who might also like it. We'll see what happens. Just so it stays within our family, and Jack is definitely a part of it.

So as I pulled into Jack's driveway, there she was in all her glory, her red paint shining so bright in the sunshine of this cloudless day. My heart actually jumped! I can't explain the feelings I had seeing it, knowing that this is Syd Rinard history right in front of me! As soon as I touched it, I could feel Dad bursting with happiness.

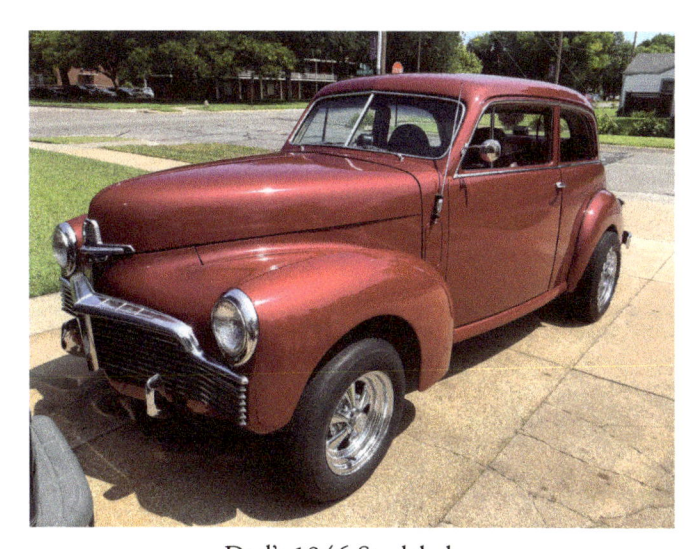

Dad's 1946 Studebaker

Jack and Martha met me outside, and after admiring the car for a few minutes, we went inside to visit. Jack was very excited to show me something, and as soon as we entered the house through the door leading in from the garage, he pointed to a framed picture on the wall. It was a large frame, with four individual pencil drawings of cars. Jack told me how Dad used to draw all the time and that he would watch him in wonder at his talent. They were both car guys and loved to work on cars together at home and at school. Jack's family used to own a large part of this end of town, using the land to farm. Jack's dad had built a huge garage/workshop on the property, and this was where Jack and Dad spent many, many hours together working on their automobiles. One of the cars in these drawings was Jack's, and he has treasured these sketches since college. He told me that Dad didn't even know that he had them until about ten or fifteen years ago. He and Mom drove out to Salina for a visit and, of course, to see the famous car. Jack had just added the monster engine, and he and Dad went for quite a ride together. Dad was extremely touched that Jack had these drawings and that he had framed them and put them right next to the door so he would see them every single day. Then Jack took the frame down and handed it to me. He really wanted me to have them. I was moved and thrilled but didn't want to take them away from Jack since I knew the attachment he had to them. He was insistent, so I gladly put it in my car to come home with me. Now it's a permanent part of our family treasures.

We all got in Jack's car, and he drove me around this area of town, showing me where their family farm used to be and how it's since been sold and divided into neighborhoods. We went to lunch, and afterward, he drove me by the stone memorial company that I would be going to after I left their house. The owner was actually an acquaintance of Jack's. It's funny that in these smaller towns, more people know each other than where I live.

When we got back to his house and I was ready to leave, Jack asked me if I happened to have any more of Dad's ashes with me. Normally, that would seem like a strange question, but as I wrote about in the day 1 chapter, I actually had another jar of them with me. Before I had left home, for some reason unknown to me at the time, I had filled a small jar with extra ashes at the same time I was filling the box. I had also printed off a photo of Dad and glued it to the bottle. I tucked it safely into my backpack for this journey. Something at the time was telling me to do this, and now suddenly I knew why. God was instructing me to prepare a gift for Dad's best friend who was struggling emotionally with Dad's passing. When I told him I did and pulled it from the car and placed it in his hands, it was as if I had just given him a million dollars. His smile went from ear to ear, and he clutched that jar to his body so tightly. He couldn't thank me enough. He was inside his house when I retrieved them from my car, so I took the opportunity to place them in the Studebaker and take a photo. I was so happy to let Dad sit in his Studebaker one last time!

We finally said our goodbyes, and I was off to the stone maker. I showed them photos I had taken of the other markers in our plot and told them which stone I knew he would like best. Some of the markers there are brass, but the ones marking the graves of Dad's grandparents were beautiful, simple stone with simple carving. This was perfect for Dad—he was a simple yet beautiful man. We got it ordered, and I once again drove to the cemetery to give them all the information. The stone company would set it for me as soon as it was ready, and they would send me a photo of it in place.

When I was done at the office, I again went to our family plot. Now it had more meaning for me than earlier that day. I could envision where Dad's forever marker would be, and I was so happy. I know he approves. This is a good day.

It was time. I had to get back on the highway and get home. On the way out of town, I had one more thing I wanted to do. My uncle had also given me a highlighted map of Salina with each of their houses they grew up in. I've talked about these homes in a previous chapter, but it was fun to drive by both of them and actually see a large part of Dad's history. I could envision Dad as a child coming out of those front doors and playing on the porches. I could see them running down the sidewalks or strapping their roller skates on. I could imagine them hitting baseballs and chasing girls in the yard. It was such a simpler time. More trusting, more innocent. There were no televisions, computers, or cell phones. They used their imaginations and made their own games. They rode their bikes and built crazy inventions. They knew when it was time to come home, just from the angle of the sun or the streetlights coming on. There were lots of laughter and love.

I turned my car onto Interstate 70 and began the final six hours of my trip. My only stop on the way home was in Kansas City so I could gobble up some of my favorite BBQ, which I miss tremendously living in St. Louis. The last few hours alone in the car was filled with reminiscing about the last two weeks. I smiled a lot and even laughed out loud a couple of times. I also lost a tear or two.

Pulling into my driveway, I was feeling so exhilarated and satisfied. I knew this journey was perfectly designed by God. He called me to take Dad on this trip—to visit his brother, to be in some of his favorite locations, and to be placed to rest in peace eternally in our little heaven on earth.

Thirteen days…3,755 miles.

My journey with Dad came to an end last night. Such an unbelievable trip—going down memory lane and creating so many new ones!

I am praising God for keeping me safe and allowing such a beautiful and special journey! And special thank you to Dad—I felt you every step, every mile… I love you!

CHAPTER 17
Celebrations of Life

January 13, 2018
March 24, 2018

O'Fallon, Missouri
Shawnee Mission, Kansas

I've never liked the idea of a "funeral"—mourning, sadness, even despair at a loss. Even though these things are happening, I prefer to think of that service as a "Celebration of Life." It is a time for everyone who loved the lost one, or had a special connection with them, to gather and remember the wonderful life that person lived. It's a time for stories, laughter, family connection, and yes, a few tears. I want to remember them for the amazing person they were here on earth instead of only the sadness of their passing. I know Dad felt the same way, and I wanted to honor him just as he would want. In New Orleans, they do it right—start with solemn respect then end with a fabulous celebration. At my own celebration, I hope my family throws the biggest party the town has ever seen!

We had some decisions to make and some planning to do. Since we were going to have Dad cremated, we had the luxury of more time. We knew we were going to have a service at my church in St. Louis but also knew it could be difficult for some family and out-of-town friends to make it because of the distance and possible bad weather, since it was January. It was for these reasons we decided to have two services—one in St. Louis and a second one in Kansas City in March. Dad had affected so many lives that we had no hesitation to plan the second one to allow more people to share their stories and celebrate with us.

That turned out to be a very good decision. Dad's first Celebration of Life was on Saturday, January 13, 2018, at my church, Joy Community Church in St. Charles, Missouri. That weekend, a nasty winter storm was moving through the Midwest, and Kansas was going to be hit with a lot of snow and ice. Most of our out-of-town guests live in Kansas, so a lot of them didn't want to take the chance of battling the storm.

I put together photo boards chronicling his life, and we set out a lot of objects that represented Dad perfectly. This included a large shadow box with a pair of his blue jeans and white T-shirt. At a lot of funerals for military people, their uniforms will be proudly displayed, with all their medals, bars, and awards. This was Dad's uniform. More often than not, you would find him in his favorite jeans and a white T-shirt. I found it quite fitting to display that, as that's how most people would remember him.

We also displayed his Burns & McDonnell hard hat. He would wear that when he would visit certain work sites. He loved goofing around with it at home and would sometimes walk into the room wearing it for no reason. Maybe he was afraid he was going to be in trouble with Mom or me and was protecting himself.

We put out his various awards and certifications from engineering, which he was very proud of. I set out some of his drafting instruments and his favorite slide rules. I also found some of his old car manuals, which took their rightful place on his memory tables. Some of his wood carvings were displayed as well, with his plant stands holding beautiful flowers and his candle stand cradling a lit candle.

The altar was laid out simply and beautifully. Mom and I had chosen a perfect container to hold his ashes. It was a simple wooden box made from walnut, which was his favorite wood to work with. We had it engraved with his name and dates. He definitely would have picked the same one himself. He was not a fancy guy, and I bet he would have made it for himself. Sitting on either side of it was a heart-shaped flower arrangement from me and a single red rose from Mom.

We carefully chose the right reading and songs. Dad's favorite hymn was always "A Mighty Fortress" written by none other than Mr. Martin Luther himself. The readings were 1 Peter 1:3–12 and Psalm 23, which is Mom's favorite. I decided to sing at both of the services. I chose "Amazing Grace," which is one of my favorites. People couldn't believe I could actually make it through the song, but I relied on God and couldn't imagine a better tribute of the most amazing man I knew.

My pastor conducted the service, and Kevin did the eulogy. A few years ago, Dad and I were talking one day, and he was excited to have me read something he had written. It turns out it was his own eulogy. It was so beautiful, and as my tears rolled down my face, I asked him if he would like it read at his funeral someday. In his usual humble manor, he replied, "If you want to." I wanted to, and Kevin actually included it and read it in his own eulogy.

Dad's Celebration of Life

Kevin's message

I want to thank you all for coming out today to celebrate Syd's life.

I just got an e-mail two days ago from Phil, Syd's brother. I love this e-mail. This is how Phil started it: "If it fits your scheme of things to read some or all of this note at your father's service, feel free to do so. If not, don't worry about it." That's Phil. So I'm going to read it, because I like what it had to say. And Phil could not be here. Phil is having some health issues of his own right now. Here is what he wanted to share:

> *Although I cannot be with you in person at this service, I have some special thoughts at this very hour about Syd and how my big brother impacted my life so positively.*

Being 3 years older than me, I started learning about life from Syd almost immediately. More friends his age lived nearby than of my age, so I also learned from all of them as a very junior playmate. Rather than hire a babysitter, I was a hanger-on of the Cub Scouts group our mother ran, giving me even more fun times with Syd and this older bunch.

Then the family moved to a larger house far away from the gang. Syd in Junior High was getting attracted to engineering pursuits (mostly about cars) and I began to find my own interests too (like atoms). So for a decade we went our own ways while sharing a large bedroom.

When I started college Syd returned to my life, took me in as a roommate and introduced me to college ways. I didn't even realize then that this feeling of family obligations as the big brother would become even more dominate later in life. He was rarely around on weekends when he would drive to Kansas City and spend time with a special gal known as Jo. But this school year sharing a room took us back to the earliest years when we had so much in common all the time.

Time moved on, Syd graduated, got an engineering job, and married Jo. I followed my path and a decade later had a similar result, although in physics, and my wife was named Carole. We lived in cities in Kansas not so far apart and frequent visits were always fun, especially when a little girl named Lori came along. Home-made ice cream was a staple of every gathering, following a tradition we learned from our father and using a great recipe Jo contributed. Times were good.

A trait of Syd's that became more obvious with age was his feeling of responsibility to others in the family as the oldest son. He was a great help to Jo's parents and then our mother as age and infirmary took its toll. Syd went to great lengths in helping them while Parkinson's was increasingly taking away his own capabilities. I added this sense of responsibility towards others onto my list of admirable traits of his.

Then the disease relentlessly overtook Syd who had long been so active in engineering, cars, woodworking, and especially grandkids. Painful as it was for the rest of us to watch, he's the one who had to endure it daily. He resisted as much as anyone could, but it wasn't a fair battle and he had to lose it—which he did.

This now leaves us with memories of Syd. Today I've put down only a tiny number of mine in abbreviated fashion. The rest are still with me and I know he did much to shape my life. It's my big brother's lasting gift to me.

Phil Rinard

*****

Rinard, Sydney L., of Lake St. Louis, Missouri, passed away Sunday, December 31, 2017, at the age of 81. Loving husband of 59 years to Joline B. Rinard, beloved son of the late Leroy Martin and Mary Alda Rinard, devoted father of Lori Gambill, cherished grandfather of Alexander Gambill and Nicole Gambill, dearest brother of Phil Rinard. He is preceded in his death by his sister, Julia Scott.

Syd loved working with his hands. He enjoyed woodworking and tinkering with cars. Sydney was dearly loved and will be greatly by all who knew him.

That was Syd's obituary in the newspaper. There are some great facts there, some nice little tidbits, some names. And for a lot of people, that is maybe the last thing anyone ever hears about that person. So what I want to do today is celebrate Syd's life. I want to tell you a little bit more about the man that changed *my* life.

He gave me one of the greatest gifts I ever had in my life when he and Joline gave me Lori to be my wife. And twenty-five years later, here we are. Now I told them, when we got married, we're moving to St. Louis because I have to work out there. I'm opening a new office out of St. Louis. I don't know if they really believed me, but six months after we got married, we moved. I'm not sure if they've ever forgiven me for that yet.

But there's so many great things about Syd. Syd was such a caring, loving man. Now Syd was not a hugging guy. He wasn't the kind of guy that when you met each other, he gave you a hug. He would maybe shake your hand. But he really showed his love through his actions. I never saw Syd get mad. I knew he was mad sometimes, but you would never really know it. But he left no doubt with his actions that he did care for you. He was a loving husband for fifty-nine years. When he got to the point that he couldn't do things for himself anymore, he would call Lori and I and say, "Hey, make sure that you get Jo some flowers for Valentine's Day for me. Make sure you get this gift for her," because he wanted to make sure.

We met for hours, and he was so concerned that he hadn't financially planned enough in his life to carry on and let Jo have everything she does. And guess what? He did a great job! And she is without need.

He was a loving father to Lori, as an only child. He took Lori, and he tried to teach her how to change the oil in the car, tried to teach her how to build things. And I know that Lori learned a lot, because she's still very good at those type of things right now. But she still liked dresses and dolls, so he would build her a dollhouse. And he would build those things and interact with her in ways that she needed him to. And Lori, to this day, just adores her father.

He was a great brother to Phil and Julie. Julie was kind of the black sheep of the family, and Dad made sure that she was ok. If she needed money, and sometimes I think Mom didn't even know, Julie got some money from Dad. She needed to be taken care of, and Dad was that person.

He was a very influential grandfather to our son Alex and our daughter Nicole. From the time that Alex was this big, he had him out in the shop, teaching how engines work. Alex loved it tremendously. He listened and absorbed it. Syd would make a circuit board and show Alex to put a battery here, connect this wire here, do this, push this button, and this light comes on. By the time Alex was six years old, Syd would say, "I want you to build a circuit board that does, this, this and this." And Alex would have it done in twenty minutes. And he went on to become a mechanical engineer also.

And Nicole. It was so fun watching Syd interact with Nicole. I've seen many pictures of Syd with Lori when they were younger. He would do the same things. He would pull out the old dollhouse that he built for Lori and play with it with Nicole. He would teach her how to ride a bike. He would try to show her how a car works, but she wasn't interested.

And his friends. He cared for his friends. The one thing he had to contribute was he could fix things. So he would go over to people's houses when things were broken and fix them for them.

Another thing is that he and Joline, both very caring, loving people, hosted foreign exchange students every year. That made a huge impact on Syd and Joline, but they also had a huge impact on their foreign exchange students. So much so that Letizia is here today. She came from Bern, Switzerland, to celebrate Dad's life today. Letizia wants to say a word.

Syd Rinard, my American dad

When I first came to Shawnee Mission in August 1985 as an exchange student (over 32 years ago), the Rinards, my host family, picked me up at the airport rather late at night. While waiting for my suitcase to appear on the conveyor belt, Syd tried to make some small talk to me. At that time, I could not understand one single word...but his eyes were kind and his voice was soft, which in that moment was everything I needed to make me feel confident about this upcoming "American adventure."

Before leaving Switzerland, I had been told that I would soon call my host-parents Mom and Dad. That seemed really strange to me, and I thought, "No way, they are strangers after all." Boy, was I wrong! In a matter of weeks, that first impression of being entrusted in the care of people with soft voices and kind eyes changed into a solid certainty: this was my family, my American family. Not only did I start calling them Mom and Dad and referring to Lori as my sister but I soon felt really, really comfortable with all of them. I grew to love them as much as my family back home.

In fact, I felt so comfortable that we could talk about anything and everything. I've always loved sharing and exchanging ideas on ways to look at the world, but discussing things with Dad was definitely something special. Even if he was not known to be very talkative, we would debate and talk for hours on environmental issues, on politics, on religion, on socio-economical topics, on education, and our exchange of ideas was, thanks to Dad's calm, patient, and reflected manners, always constructive and respectful...in spite of my lively temperament. My real father back home had passed away due to cancer only a few years before I came to the United States...and Dad, Dad managed, with no intention and just being himself, to become the father-figure I still needed.

After my year in KC as an exchange student, I came back a few times to visit. They came to see me in Switzerland, and we shared some trips and always kept in touch. Dad learned to use the com-

puter, and he and I often exchanged e-mails, where we continued sharing our common love for all those matters and mysteries of life that affect human kind; it was always profound and enriching.

When my father died when I was 15, it was the first time I realized (together with my mother, my brother, and sister) that even if this life on earth ends, love never does…it lasts, persists through the many memories of incidents and experiences shared with those who pass to better life.

Not only when I think of my biological father but very much when I think of Dad, my American dad, I not only have those memories and souvenirs, I also have my own personality and insight that daily reminds me of Dad as one of the most important people who strongly contributed to my mental and spiritual development.

I love you, Dad, and I will always cherish the memories I have of what we shared.

Letizia Ciardelli

*****

Dad was such a loving and caring man, and people thought the same way about him. He was a dedicated man. Fifty-nine years of marriage. He worked forty-five years at the same company, at Burns & McDonnell. Engineering was his passion. I remember when he had an opportunity to get promoted into management, which most people would think, "It's great, I'll make more money, and I get to be manager." He did it for a while, but then he said, "I want to quit this. I want to be an engineer." And that's what he did.

He was a life-long Lutheran, who was very dedicated to the Bible and the teachings of Christ.

He was dedicated to one other thing—fashion. If you had a chance to look in the back, there's a pair of blue jeans and a white

T-shirt in a frame. If Dad wasn't in anything else, if he wasn't at work, he was wearing a pair of blue jeans and a T-shirt, that's it. He was dedicated to that look.

He loved to work with his hands. He built the first two houses they lived in by himself. The second home, they bought the land in 1973. It was a beautiful piece of land. It was in the woods. The house was designed perfectly. The girls were excited to move from their house on Beverly over to the new house in Black Swan. And I think they prayed a lot—hey, Syd, why don't you get some help on this? Three years later, he finally completed the house, and they lived in it until they moved to St. Louis.

He had a passion for cars, fixing up old junk cars. I see we have a couple of his buddies that he used to work with cars together, and I have heard stories about these guys the whole time I've known Syd.

He was a great woodworker. He built many beautiful pieces of furniture. What the flowers are on, he made that. And he did the Alpha and Omega signs out there. He made a lot of different things for the church. He liked to work with walnut. That's why his ashes are in a beautiful walnut box. He later became interested in clocks and fixing old clocks.

He loved to write. We heard one of his writings. He's still going to have the last word during the ceremony today. He showed me a textbook he wrote about how power plants work. It could have been used in universities. I didn't understand any of it, but it looked great.

Syd was also a strong Christian man. Like Letizia said, they would talk hours at night. When Syd would come to St. Louis, we would be up until one o'clock at night, talking about Christianity, the Holy Spirit, about what does it all mean, how does it all work? As an engineer, Syd wanted to know the hows and the whys. He had more questions than answers, and it seemed to frustrate him a lot. But it never weakened his faith in Christ. People always say they wish they had more Holy Spirit in them. We all have the same amount of the Holy Spirit. Syd just let the Holy Spirit use him more than I've seen most people in my life allow.

Syd was diagnosed with Parkinson's in 1995, and his Parkinson's was a very slow-progressing case. But as the years went by, slowly he started to lose abilities to do things that he loved to do. He lost his ability to drive and to work on clocks and cars, to do woodworking, and ultimately, to even write. In all the time, his mind was as clear as a tack. He thought he could do these things because he tried. We'd have to say, "Dad, you cannot do that." He'd say, "Yes, I can." And he kept trying. But he couldn't.

This Parkinson's is a terrible disease. He slowly lost his ability to communicate. Even though his thoughts were clear, his brain would not make his voice or mouth work. But the amazing thing is that through the twenty-four years Syd went through this, he never once wanted any pity. He never blamed God or yelled at God. I actually think this whole thing brought Syd and God closer together.

The one thing that Syd did have control over was to stay alive and to fight. There have been many times in the last five years that we actually thought Syd was going to die. He was septic in the hospital, and they called us and said we might get up there immediately. So Lori and I would get up and go as quickly as we could. Two days later, Syd was walking out of the hospital fine. He was in a coma for three days, and they said the same thing. We might want to prepare. And we looked at him and said, "Well, I don't think so." And guess what? Four days later, Syd walked out of the hospital. Fall after fall he took, getting out of bed and walking around. His head would be cracked open, and he always ended up fine.

You know, Syd had nine lives like a cat, and he used every single one of them. But something changed this last December when he saw the doctor. He told the doctor that he was finally ready to go. Whatever he had been holding onto that kept him alive was complete. I don't know what that was, because he couldn't tell me or even write it down, but it was done. And he passed away quickly, painlessly, on his own terms. That is one question I can't wait to ask him when I meet him again. What was that thing?

Syd always wanted to do things himself—build his own houses and furniture, fix everything. Even at death, he wanted to make sure that everything was exactly as he wanted.

We were going through Syd's papers many years ago, and we found this. It says, "At My Funeral." Syd wrote his own eulogy. I want to read these beautiful words to you.

*****

At My Funeral

Funerals are hard work. Not for the person who has died, of course. But for those the person has left behind, it's a tough time. Not only is there a sense of loss but there are all those details to work out. Insurance policies, disposal of stuff, etc.

I can't stop any of that from going on when I am gone, but I hope I can ease your minds a little by reminding you that what we call "death" is not the end of anything but our earthly existence. This earthly body is just a temporary container, like a paper bag, for our real self, which we call our soul. Death frees the soul from the container, which is then no longer needed and is discarded.

And my soul is now free. Since I was obviously still "alive" as I wrote this, I couldn't then know what it really means to be "free," but I know now. But now I can't tell you what it means. But I am now free for the first time in my memory.

So please, please listen to me now—*do not feel sad for me.*

Instead, rejoice with me at the wonderful gift of true life that God has given us. I have no idea why he has done this for us, but we are his children. As we love our own children and forgive their "sins," so does God forgive us our weaknesses. I gave up trying to figure that all out long ago. It just made me tired to try. I just accepted it, without conditions, and a great weight was removed from me.

Now I understand the true meaning of God's love for us all. That is why I urge you to rejoice in my death. It is the best thing that could possibly happen to me. My only regret is that I spent so little of my earthly time with all of you. I squandered it trying to figure these things out when all I had to do was wait. Now we are separated, but it is only a temporary situation. You will all join me one day, and we will know what real happiness is.

ONE LAST TRIP

So one more time, *this is a wonderful, happy time! Be glad!* Go and love each other as brothers and sisters in God's family.

*****

Will you join me in prayer? Dear Lord God, our Heavenly Father, I want to give you thanks for every person who is here today to celebrate Syd's life. We are better people by knowing Syd and having him a part of our lives. We rejoice today that Syd is in your loving arms, he is getting the answers to all the questions he had about you, his soul is free, and Parkinson's is no longer a part of who he is. Give peace to Syd's family and loved ones as we go forward in his absence and help us all realize the peace that only comes from a resurrected Savior, Jesus Christ. Help us all live our lives, as Syd stated so eloquently, in love for each other as brothers and sisters in God's family. Today we do not say goodbye to Syd but, rather, "Until we meet again."

If you could please join us in the prayer that the Lord taught us: Our Father, who art in Heaven, hallowed be thy name. Thy kingdom come, thy will be done, on earth as it is in Heaven. Give us this day our daily bread, and forgive us our trespasses, as we forgive those who trespass against us. Lead us not into temptation but deliver us from evil. For thine is the kingdom and the power and the glory, forever and ever. Amen.

*****

One of my other foreign sisters, Minna, was not able to join us for the celebration. She and her husband, Ari, and children, Emmi and Aleksi, live in Finland. She did send me a written memory to be included in honoring Dad.

In the memory of Syd Rinard

Syd Rinard, Dad, was so much loved. We will always remember him as kind and helpful father and grandfather. He taught us how to make fish face, carve pumpkins, and have our daily vitamin CH (chocolate). He gave us advice and time, love and comfort over thirty-five years that we were honored to know him. His memory will stay in the fields and forests in Hameenkyro, Finland.

I met dad for the first time at KCI airport in August 1983. He was that kind of a man that seventeen years old girl from Finland, Europe was able to trust at the first sight. I came to stay with the Rinards for a year as an exchange student. One of the first memories is how we went to clean up a car for Lori to drive to school. Red Mazda "Al" became our daily "friend." We girls fixed and cleaned it under Dad's supervision. Dad got himself a car too—an orange Pinto that was fun. We took a long trip to Los Alamos with a huge Pontiac station wagon. On the way we got "snowed in" to a small town, Clayton, Kansas. I had the hottest chili con carne of my life, that we all remembered for many years.

When Dad came over to Finland five times, he always had his own "projects." He fixed our wall clocks, drove lawnmower and visited different building sites. He also fixed Finnish Christmas lights to fit American electric system.

Dad was testing some new Parkinson Disease medicine and during the visit to us he realized that he did not have enough pills with him. Soon we realized that little print on the pill box said "Made in Finland." Next morning we found out that one of the doctors of the developing team lived in our village. So Dad ended up meeting this doctor and got to refill his pill box. It seemed like a fairytale!

ONE LAST TRIP

Thank you Dad so much for everything. We love you so much and remember you always.

Minna, Ari, Emmi and Aleksi Kulmala from Hameenkyro, Finland

*****

How do you honor such a man? A man who was so humble, so loving, so spiritual? We did the best we could at his celebrations, but no matter what, we could never give him the full respect that he deserved. I will never exist at his level, although I strive to. He never let the day-to-day junk bother him. I have been guilty of that.

He wasn't perfect. No one is. We are all sinners by nature, but God made sure that we are made clean through his son. Dad knew that, and he aspired to share that with the entire world.

The lessons that he taught me throughout my life are priceless to me. He taught me to respect people and things. To take good care of myself. To appreciate the beauty of nature. To drive a stick-shift car. To not put a wet glass on a wood table. How to change a flat tire and jump-start a dead battery. He taught me to love Jesus and all people.

He was proud of me no matter what. He loved me every single second of my life, even when I didn't deserve it. So how do I honor him? I wrote a book to share him with the rest of the world. I want everyone to know him and to be able to call him a friend. That's what he would have wanted.

I love you, Dad. Until we meet again.

Chapter 18

Epilogue
July 2019

Tincup, Colorado

July 13, 2019

It has been nearly one year since I traveled that one last trip with Dad to Colorado.

All year I have thought about that trip every day.

I felt an overwhelming tug to revisit Tincup and his grave in the cemetery. My friend Stacey, who used to travel with us to Tincup each summer growing up, and I had been trying to plan a girl's getaway to reconnect and catch up. When our calendars wouldn't sync up during the winter for a tropical trip, we decided that our only option was to travel in Colorado and revisit our childhood. And that's exactly what we did.

We spent months finalizing our plans, and I headed out west with plans to pick her up at her home in Boulder, and then we would go back to our old stomping ground.

I decided to travel out early so I could spend a few days in the higher altitude to help my body adjust to make it easier while we were together for hiking and exploring. I also wanted to have one day in Tincup by myself to spend with Dad alone.

The day I finally arrived in Tincup was cloudy, and because of some road construction, I had to make a detour over the Continental

Divide, which pushed back my arrival time to closer to two o'clock in the afternoon. The mountains have a fairly good chance of afternoon rain, and I could see the dark clouds forming over the mountain where Tincup sits.

I wasn't going to let that stop me. I wanted to spend some time alone with Dad and make sure his grave was still intact. I drove straight through the town to the cemetery, determined to get there before any rain started. As I turned the corner to the cemetery parking lot, I felt an overwhelming calm and happiness spread through my body and soul. I was alone in the cemetery, so I grabbed my camera, the lunch I had packed, and a blanket. I walked right to where I had buried him the year before, holding my breath that I would see his small metal cross still in place. As I walked to the downhill where he rested, I was beyond thrilled to see that cross still there under the tall pine tree, standing tall and proud.

A tear of happiness rolled down my cheek as I spread out the blanket and pulled out my lunch so I could eat with Dad. I said hi to Dad, and as I ate my sandwich, I talked to him about life. As I sat there, I realized that God has had his armor of protection around this cemetery and Dad, making sure that his special spot under that pine tree stayed safe from the weather and the animals. I know that he is forever safe in that serene, beautiful place.

While I sat there, I could hear muffled voices. I assumed there were a couple of people in the cemetery somewhere having a conversation. Occasionally, I would hear a little light music. I got up and walked all over to see who was here, but no one was around. The parking area was empty, except for my car. If people had been riding ATVs, I would have heard the loud vehicles. I was definitely alone in the cemetery and the surrounding area.

I was still on the Protestant Knoll and walked through the entire graveyard searching for the source of the talking. I could feel an energy around me and was sure that I was surrounded by the spirits of past living beings. I desperately wanted to communicate with them and told them they could talk with me. The voices faded away, but something was knocking on a tree right next to me when I told them they could make a noise for me. I looked up through the tree and saw no birds or animals in it. As strange as it sounded, I was feeling so peaceful to share this area with them and that they felt comfortable enough to reach out to me.

I sat back down by Dad and pulled out my computer to do some writing on this book. At this time, I started feeling the raindrops hitting my face and knew I didn't have much time until the rain took over. I told Dad I really wanted and needed to hear his voice. When I only sat in silence, I decided that I would shift my plans around for the next day and return to Tincup for a few hours. The weather forecast was for sun the next day, so it really wasn't a difficult decision for me.

The rain hit just as I got into my car, and I pulled out of the parking area. I was feeling happy and excited that I knew I would be back again in the morning.

July 14, 2019

I awoke early so I could get to Tincup as soon as possible. My resort was about a thirty-minute drive, and I made a few stops along the way to take some pictures as it was a beautiful, sunny morning.

I arrived in Tincup about nine thirty and stopped at the Tincup Town Hall building to take some photos. A man was unlocking the front door, so we visited for a few minutes. He was getting the hall ready for the weekly Sunday morning church service that began at ten thirty. I told him I was planning to attend, as I had seen the signs the day before. I explained that we used to come here every summer when I was a kid and that we would always attend the worship service. I told him I was heading to the cemetery first but would be back, and he said to make sure I get here early as it fills up quickly.

I arrived back at the cemetery parking area, parked my car, and once again spread my blanket by Dad. I decided that since the sky was the most perfect shade of blue that I would walk the entire cemetery, all four knolls, and get some better photos than the day before. Once that was done, I returned to Dad.

I again told him that I really wanted to hear his voice. After a moment, I told him to please touch me or play with my hair so I would know that he was with me. Instantly, I felt a poke or a slight push on the outside of my right arm—the one that was closest to his grave. I smiled and said, "I felt that!" I wanted to make sure that I wasn't having an involuntary muscle twitch, so I said, "Dad, if that was you, please touch me again." And again I felt the same poke on my arm. Determined to find out if it was just a spasm in my arm, I waited. I knew that if I were having a physiological issue with my muscle that it would continue to twitch or spasm. After waiting for what seemed like minutes, I was thrilled to see that it never did it again. I knew exactly that it was Dad. I said, "Thank you, Dad. I felt you and know that you are sitting right next to me." I couldn't stop the tears of happiness.

My dad just touched me. What more could a daughter want or need? I felt his presence, and his playful poking was the perfect gesture. I laughed and cried at the same time. My heart was bursting with love for him, and I felt his love for me as we sat together under the pine tree on the side of a hill, looking at the most beautiful backdrop of mountains, trees, and ponds.

It was time to head back to town for the worship service. As I entered the hall, all memories of being here with Dad came flooding into my mind. I found an empty wooden pew and sat down. I could see all the scratches and marks on the wood plank floor and remembered the square dancing we did as kids here and wondered if any of those scratches were made by me. The pews faced the front of the hall, and the big windows exposed the most stunning scenery of mountains. There was no doubt that God was in the building!

While we waited for the service to start, I was having trouble keeping the tears away. I was still overcome with emotion after my experience in the cemetery and with the memories of the past. Just as I was feeling that I had it all together, a lady sat down at the old piano and played the most wonderful version of "The Old Rugged Cross" I had ever heard. It was so lovely and beautiful, and it was one of Dad's favorite songs. I could feel the water-works trying to start up again.

As we sang songs from the hymnal, I could channel Dad's traditional Lutheran beliefs and favorites. As I listened to the retired naval pastor give the message, I could feel Dad's presence in that town hall turned worship chapel. As I looked at the magnificent view of the mountains from my seat, I knew that Dad's spirit was soaring like a bird, free from the pain and disease that had taken over his earthly body.

    I love you, Dad!

> But those who hope in the Lord will renew their strength. They will soar on wings like eagles; they will run and not grow weary, they will walk and not be faint. (Isaiah 40:31)

About the Author

Lori Rinard Gambill has a passion for sharing stories that will touch hearts and produce smiles. With her undergraduate degree in design and graduate degree in Christian counseling, she uses her many various life experiences to reach, inspire, and motivate people. Raised on love, faith, compassion, and belly-busting laughing, she writes about family, inspirations, and everyday things. With a twist of humor.

She calls O'Fallon, Missouri, home, along with her husband and grown kids (and miscellaneous cats). You can connect with her on her website, www.inspiredhopealive.com, and her blog, www.inspirationswithatwist.wordpress.com.